PARADISE LUST

Two bewitching teenage girls shimmered up beside me, both with rather coy smiles, quite an achievement for ones so worldly. We drank, smiled, uncertainly placed hands on knees, with beguiling Thai modesty, for Thais frown on public displays of emotion, especially the obnoxious slobbering, kissing and groping so beloved of hairy-backs. For all the world like kids on a blind date, they were playing a well-rehearsed part, though I wasn't. They were both the standard centrefold: long, shiny dark hair, slim, quite big-breasted, with nicely rounded bottoms and smooth, svelte bare legs, under black miniskirts, agreeably skin-hugging, and the soft maternal curves of bare shoulder and breast beckoning to delights within.

Mentally, I licked my lips, delighted at the youth and freshness of it all. No sleaze, no bedraggled, lipstick-smudged, cigarette-dangling hustlers, no large minders called Vinnie. Just fresh, organic country girls, giving a dutiful impression that they were reasonably pleased to see me.

PARADISE LUST

Kit McCann

This paperback edition first published in
Great Britain in 2007 by
Virgin Books Ltd
Thames Wharf Studios
Rainville Road
London
W6 9HA

A catalogue record for this book is available from the British
Library.

ISBN 978 0 7535 1266 1

The paper used in this book is a natural, recyclable
product made from wood grown in sustainable forests. The
manufacturing process conforms to the regulations of the
country of origin.

Typeset by Phoenix Photosetting, Chatham, Kent

Printed in the UK by CPI Bookmarque, Croydon, CR0 4TD

1 3 5 7 9 10 8 6 4 2

CONTENTS

1. PROLOGUE

There is a just man that perished in his righteousness, and there is a wicked man that prolongeth his life in his wickedness. Be not righteous overmuch; neither make thyself overwise; why shouldst thou destroy thyself?

Frankly, like most single males, I went to Thailand in a quest for sex. No, wait a minute: the ultimate sexual experience. Sounds almost spiritual. That's what Thailand is famous for, and foreign tourism (i.e. sex) is its biggest industry, although there is a wealth of culture: the gold and red Buddhist temples, the mysterious, charming festivals involving flowers and floats, which materialise without warning. Then there is the fabulous food – when not sleeping, Thais are usually eating. As well as the mountains of pineapples, mangos, papaya, and other fruit, some of which we occasionally recognise, there are the sublime dishes and soups with basil, garlic, ginger, and coriander, lemon grass, coconut milk, and lots of chillis and nam-pla ('fish water'), the stinky sauce of fermented anchovies. From street stalls you can buy duck or fish soup, succulent barbecued chicken or pork, spring rolls, freshly grilled fish, yellow ants or ants' eggs in lime and chillies, deep-fried maggots and baby frogs in batter (yum!), king scorpion, crickets, spiders, grass-hoppers, locusts ...

You have the mountains, the islands, the rain forest, all bathed in this miraculous pearly light under a baking sun. (Orwell wrote that all novels set in the Far East are really about the landscape.) But most of the millions of visitors a year come for sex, if not to do it, then to look, and bask in the naughty ambience. And a lot of it, indeed most of it, is naughty. Many travel writers avoid mentioning any night-time activities of the lubricious class, I suspect because they know that the wife will one day read their script. Unhampered by any such inhibitions, I can present this place as it really is. I tell you things I do, and things other people do.

It is possible to tell you about Thailand without writing about sex at all. You can talk about Buddhist monks in saffron robes, paper lanterns, spicy food, and happy, smiling water buffaloes, and the colourful cuisine. Or you can describe drug barons, gang warfare, the golden triangle, jail horrors. However, most visitors pay scant attention to these things. They see free-wheeling, dusky love goddesses, and that is why the tourists come here: to have their hearts broken, and their jollies jollied, in an unending pursuit of pleasures either unavailable at home, or available only sordidly, or with difficulty.

It is wrongly averred that the tourist resorts Patong and Pattaya (official motto 'The Extreme City') are 'not Thailand', just as New York is 'not America', and London is 'not England'. They are Thailand, seen through a prism. Those tourist Meccas are what every Thai village dreams of becoming, honey traps awash with lustful foreigners ready to pour the cash from their pockets on to the fingers of Thai ladies. Thailand is a living demonstration of the desire and heartbreak inspired by an entire population of ravishing girls, who cheerfully have sex with anybody, all day and night, for what they need most, money, and then have more sex with anybody else.

A grown man, weeping into his beer over a fickle and absent Thai girl half his age, just before his plane leaves, is a strange and forbidding sight. Thai women deserve respect, as funny and enchanting sex goddesses, and inexhaustible sources of those vital fossil fuels, grief and ecstasy. In defiance of purists who insist there is a difference between 'ladies', 'women' and 'bar girls', I use these terms as appropriate, often preferring the highly accurate demi-mondaine, or midinette. Like most things in Thailand, these terms are at the same time perfectly clear yet indistinct.

The way to stay sane, if stuck here, is: if in doubt, don't ask. Thailand is a dream come true, or the death of dreams, Disneyland run by Machine Gun Kelly. Of course, it's hot and cheap, but that applies to any number of countries where, however, teenage girls are oddly averse to falling in love with complete strangers in the time it takes to guzzle a beer. Whatever foreigners tell you about beaches, shopping and the ubiquitous scuba-diving, most of them are in Thailand for its unique mixture of charm, innocence, and sleaze, with golf, gormandising, and drinking, to pass the time between sex, or even during it. There was a golfer in Pattaya who used to hire glamorous girls as caddies, so that he could ... oh, well, why not read the book? It spans the course of some years, but, Thailand being Thailand, it could as well be some minutes. Everything in it is true.

NOTE. Currency amounts are generally stated in Thai baht, or US dollars, which most of us understand. Rough equivalents at the time of writing were:
£1 sterling = 70 baht
1 euro = 50 baht
$1 = 40 baht

2. THE GARDEN OF EDEN

The southwestern island Phuket is the richest province in Thailand, and made its fortune with tin mines. They switched to planting rubber, when it was discovered this material made a more agreeable condom. Now its biggest industry is sex tourism, its airport is the country's second largest, and the most expensive town in Phuket, and in all Thailand, is glittering Patong Beach, across the green-girt mountain from Phuket City. Recently, there was tragic loss of life in a tsunami, engulfing the place somewhat, but business picked smartly up, and carries on with the usual urgency. Sex business.

The first sign you see, as you wind down the hairpins through the tropical greenery towards the turquoise Andaman Sea, is:

WELCOME TO PATONG BEACH
REMEMBER TO DRIVE ON THE LEFT
PLEASE USE A CONDOM

This is a puzzle. Suppose you have rented a car and driven

the 45 minutes from the airport, have you already forgotten to drive on the left? Surely it is a little late, after the hair-raising dash, or crawl, through the drenched green hills, the magical flowers and trees and the militaristic rubber plantations of Phuket island, past wheezing buses, cars, trucks, heedless mopeds with three loose-limbed beauties straddling the pillion, and all seeming to drive everywhere but on the left?

It takes about a week in Thailand to realise that there is a rule about which side of the road you are supposed to drive on. Mainly, you drive on whatever side seems 'lucky', and Thais figure they are always left of somewhere – Burma, say, or Indonesia. You do not rely on silly traffic lights – which are indistinguishable, in the glitter of neon – but on luck. Say you wish to turn right.

What is the point of wearing out your engine by lengthening your journey to make the turn at the road junction itself, like some neurotic westerner? Far more sensible to streamline your approach, and start your turn on the other side of the road, a good six or seven kilometres before the actual manoeuvre.

You might imagine that wearing a condom is mysteriously connected with this strange ritual of driving on the left. Are you supposed to wear a condom while driving? Or at all times? Most puzzling of all, this notice is only in English. Has this something to do with the accident statistics? Six hundred thousand motorcyclists a year hospitalised after road accidents, a third of them while using cell phones, half without obligatory safety helmets, and motorcycle fatalities (possibly sans condom) the largest share of road deaths, with one motorcyclist dying on the road every hour of every year.

It is assumed that all cash-stuffed farangs are mysteriously able to speak English. Perhaps Thais themselves are not required to drive on the left, wear condoms, and are not partic- ularly welcome in Patong Beach, as there are quite enough of them already, mining the pot of gold. The smiles of smiling Thailand are biggest for those endowed with a pale skin, and a wad of currency, as evidence of their spiritual goodness in past lives. Thais are remarkably tolerant of sexual outrageousness, as long as the plastic cards shine, and the paper stuff crinkles satisfactorily as it leaves your pocket for theirs.

And you, the middle-aged foreigner – farang (from 'Frank', which is what the Saracens called the French crusaders) – with the pink visible scalp, pale skin, beer paunch and wad of real money, with the ex-wife and ungrateful children back in freezing Birmingham, Bremen or Buffalo, are delighted to let them extract the fruits of your lifetime's labours in the dungeons of the western economy, because look what you get in return: Thai ladies. They are the reward of your thankless toil, your endurance of cold weather, nerves and heart attacks and boredom and ugliness. The moment a Thai lady smiles at you, you know that there is a heaven and it is here in Thailand; the turquoise sea, the bougainvillea flowering everywhere, the pineapple and banana plants, the smells of duck and fried chilli and dried squid and lemon grass soup – you know that everything else, all the western money and cars and houses and things with fatuous brand names are worth nothing compared to a Thai lady's smile, and the promise of more.

And they all smile at you. Right from the moment you get off the plane: the immigration girl smiles at you, the customs girl smiles at you, the lady aimlessly sweeping dust from point A to point B and back again smiles at you, as if your arrival here, alone amongst the arrival of the million (or billion) farangs who arrive each minute, is somehow the culmination of their lifetime's dreams, the juiciest, most tempting thing that has happened to them all day – or at least since the arrival of the last planeload of sexually frustrated, cash-flush, predatory paleskins. Oddly, the Japanese and Korean tourists, who outnumber the Europeans, are not called farangs, they are nippoon, and they travel in boxes – the bus, the hotel, the shopping centre, the Japanese-only karaoke – protected and directed by tour guides with whistles.

You wipe your brow, as the heat instantly flattens you, and you start to pour with sweat; Thai ladies giggle, as if you have provided them with the most marvellous fun. You are directed to a taxi – the most expensive, least air-conditioned, most roundabout taxi in all Asia – and they smile in genuine delight because it is all such fun, and you, as you part with huge piles of banknotes, smile back, because it is. You order an iced coffee and the lady, whose sole job is selling iced coffee, beams at you as though you have just enchanted her with a startling novelty. Why? Because, as you sink into Thailand, the sultry heat makes all your worries melt, as your shirt and socks stick to you in a swamp of sweat. Because the air is full of flowers and perfume, and the musk of women; the smells of fried chicken gizzards, locusts and squid waft temptingly from a million street vendors. And there is no female too old, wizened, crippled or broke to smile at you.

You feel, suddenly, that this is real life, far from the grey world of work and money-making, where the only way out of the grisly dump you are stuck in is to put in an eighteen-hour day, to make more and more money to spend on things, to help you forget the squalor of your toiling existence, whose sole purpose is to enable you to afford things, possession of which justifies the squalor of your toiling existence. You breathe Thailand and, perhaps for the first time, you breathe real life. It never gets cold; nobody starves; there is always rice in the paddies and mangos on the trees and prawns in the ocean. And if you fancy a plate of spaghetti alle vongole, why, you just go and dig a bucket of clams from the beach. If you need an injection of culture, why, you go to Bangkok, where there will undoubtedly be an Elton John concert. There is no Christianity to make you sinful, no psychiatrists to make you uneasy, only the Buddha, smiling at everyone whether they are rich or poor, chaste or unchaste. And Thai ladies...

Everywhere you look, for heaven's sake, there are ladies. Never mind for heaven's sake, this is heaven. It is the Garden of Eden, where you are allowed to eat all the apples you want. The air itself is sexy. A Thai lady is firm, compact, brown, silky, funny, welcoming. Every flash of her eye, or shift of her haunches, every flicker of her tongue-tip, every crunch of a deep-fried chicken intestine between her sultry lips, says 'enjoy me'. Never mind the Michelin guide, with its meanderings on hill tribes and Buddhist temple architecture; never mind the inane backpackers' guides which burble about meditation and mantras, and issue dire warnings about 'prostitutes' and 'the sex industry'.

There are no prostitutes in Thailand, for prostitution is illegal, and there is no Thai 'sex industry'. Yet there are regulations governing sex workers, who officially do not exist. In adjacent countries there may very well be (most of the bar girls in Singapore are Thai); in Hamburg's Reeperbahn or Amsterdam's Oude Zijds Achterburgwaal, in Old Compton Street, or the Rue St Denis, in Sydney's King's Cross and in Las Vegas, there are hints of a 'sex industry', but not in Thailand. There is sex, like air, everywhere; air is not an industry. Thailand has so many beautiful and willing ladies that a sex industry is a contradiction in terms.

And that is why you have come here. Not for temples or meditation, or even recreational drugs. You are a man with ample leisure time (your cement factory in Trondheim will look after itself in your absence), with money in your pocket, and you have come for the ladies. Because they do it.

We have been obliged to avoid a common yet curiously distasteful Anglo-Saxon word which, alas, is the best thing the English language has to offer, to describe the gymnastic exchange of money and body fluids (but please use a condom), which is Thailand's main activity. Thai ladies do it all the time, every day, without qualm or hiccup or a whisper of the dread words 'commitment', 'relationship', 'I thought we were just good friends', 'I need time to think', and other western mantras. Thai ladies do not need time to think. Unkind souls suggest they do not have much to think with. They have sex, the way they eat noodles, brush their teeth or iron their panties: it is what a good girl does to stay happy and healthy, to get money to lose at cards, buy fake designer dresses, or water buffaloes, and donate for tambun – 'merit' – so that celibate, vowed-to-poverty monks can buy Marlboros and Benzes. After satisfying these needs, they can get down to their most pleasurable activities, eating and sleeping. Sex comes an honourable third. This is not the oriental paradise of free love that some romantics imagine, and nothing is free, because food and cars aren't free. You pay for what you get, and you get what you pay for.

Languages reveal their differences most when describing l'acte sexuel. English is po-faced, crude, vaguely coy, and often taking refuge in the glacial modesty of Latin: pudenda, cunnilungus; German, grotesque; Italian, absurd; Spanish, homicidal; French, elegant. (The word 'jazz' comes from the brothels of old New Orleans, where musicians accompanied the flirtations. *Jaser* is French for 'chat' and was the euphemism employed by ladies, who would invite gents upstairs 'for a chat'. So jazz music is really doing-it-music.) Happily, the simplified vocabulary of Thai creates a blend of pidgin English, known as Thaispeak.

There are various Thai euphemisms for sex, like the robust 'boom-boom', accompanied by appropriate gestures, and the more refined 'bouncing', pronounced boon-sing, which sounds like an oriental art of flower arrangement. There is also the basic 'You want short time?' and the equally vivid greeting 'I go with you?' Thus has English euphemism been incorporated into Thaispeak. (When we say a couple are 'going out together' we mean that they are staying in together. When we say they are sleeping together, it means that sleeping is coincidental.) These are not the only things a Thai lady will say to you. Many have an extended vocabulary, mostly involving sums of money, but no matter what the topic of conversation – soap opera, game show, or the cost of silicone enlargement of nose, breast and bottom – bouncing, and its expected financial reward, is never far away.

Foolish farangs cannot understand the equation between sex and reward, and imagine love is on a loftier plane than money. They do not understand how a girl can adore sex, but also expect to be paid for it. Love should be its own reward …!

Now, sailors generally like sailing, and soldiers like soldiering. But if the captain suddenly announced that, since they were all having such fun, they would in future get no pay, there would be a mutiny. Thai ladies like sex, but try keeping your bankroll in your pocket, and find out what a mutiny feels like.

A Thai lady – and one always calls them Thai ladies, because that is what they superbly, stunningly, and deliciously are – knows the score. She knows what she wants, and what you want, and it is usually the same thing. She knows what her body is for, and what yours is for, too. She knows that for some strange farang reason you adore her lovely brown skin. (Thai ladies do not like being dragged to the beach, for they do not want to turn 'black'.) Unlike western women, she does what she wants, not what others persuade her she ought to do. There is no agony aunt looking over her shoulder. She is not confused. If she accepts an invitation to dinner, it is not in order to have a headache after you have paid the bill. If she does not fancy you, she will say politely 'I have boyfriend.'

Of course, if bouncing does ensue, it does not mean she has no boyfriend, or even several, but rather that he is drinking Thai rice whiskey with his mates, or other girlfriend, wondering how much cash can be extracted from you. She, for her part, will give you the impression that meeting you has made her see the sun shine for the first time, and that it emerges solely from your cash-crammed fundament. After a few weeks, you may glimpse your photo, jostling in an album with all her other fatuously grinning true loves, and room for plenty more, as the jets roar in from London and Stockholm and Frankfurt, laden with dreams and loot. Then, you will either weep, and return to the cold canyons of Mammon, to make even more money for your next heartbreak in paradise – or else, after a while in the Kingdom of Smiles, you will learn to shrug, like all wised-up farangs, and say 'T.I.T.' This is Thailand. Please remember to use a condom.

3. ET TU BRUTE

The reason I came to Thailand was simple: a woman told me. It was when I was living in Turkey. She was English, and worked for a travel company. When I enthused about the cheapness and charm of Turkey, she said that she had just come back from Thailand, and it was even cheaper and more charming. Moreover, unlike Turkey, it never got cold. There were red light areas such as Patpong, Patong Beach, and Pattaya, but you could easily avoid them. I made a mental note of all the places to avoid. She said that Thailand had no downside. That, of course, was wishful thinking. So I got on the next plane to Thailand.

Thailand and Turkey are opposite poles. The Turks do not ogle their luscious women, as they are unavailable; the Thais do not ogle theirs, as they are totally available. The Turks are broke, because they keep their money under the mattress, peasant-style. Most Turkish women never even get to handle cash. That is why they are broke. Most Thai women do little but handle cash. That is why they are broke.

Ninety per cent of purchasing in western economies is done by, or for, women, which is why we are rich. Our money moves round the economy like lifeblood, because women spend it on things they don't need. Thai women spend money all the time, when not asleep, and when they have no money, which is most of the time, they borrow. They cram supermarket baskets with skin-whitening cream, things for their nails, innards, hair, or skin; creams to make their bottoms tighter or their breasts bigger ('Bust-firming Mud, with Extract of Horse Tail'), creams for bright brown eyes and red lips, creams for good luck ... then they buy dresses and shoes exactly the same as the million dresses and shoes they already possess. They buy tablets and potions 'for good body'; they buy statues of the Buddha, or fluffy toys, or ... anything. They buy each other gifts, and they are really buying friendship, for they are terrified of being friendless. Thailand has a thriving economy, because the money flows like blood. And sometimes vice versa.

The modest English lady admitted that she had briefly, nose-up, toured the red light district of Phuket Island. However distasteful, it did seem such ... jolly good fun. She did not add that the red lights occupy not a district, but the whole town of Patong. So, after eleven hours in a tin can in the sky, I disembarked at Bangkok's Don Muang Airport. My fellow passengers seemed mostly hairy-backs intent on adult pleasures (et tu, brute), and I decided that they were not here for the temples and hill-trekking. The beauty of cheap long-haul travel! John Ruskin, complaining about railways, remarked: 'Now, every fool in Buxton can be in Bakewell in half an hour, and every fool in Bakewell in Buxton.' There was no inspection; there was a sign saying 'Welcome to the Land of Smiles'. The air was hot, sticky, perfumed with lust. The women, especially in uniform, were ravishing. Their brown uniforms clung to their brown bodies. I sensed serenity. I decided Thailand was probably a Good Thing.

'T.I.T.', the phrase we farangs use, is the verbal equivalent of a shrug, often accompanied by a roll of the eyeballs: 'This is

Thailand. (What can you do?) …' My first taste of T.I.T. was trying to find the airport rail station, which offers the quickest and cheapest way into Bangkok. Outside, traffic jams the smog-shrouded freeways. Obviously, a rail link was a logical part of the airport planning. Avoiding the (mere) tourists arguing with taxi touts, I went in search of the rail link. Now, in most first world airports, everything is admirably signposted, so that it is practically impossible to avoid getting a train of some kind. In Bangkok Airport, there were no signs, and it took a dozen enquiries before I found anyone who knew there was a train station. At last, I learned that you headed to the airport hotel, on a walkway over the hurtling freeway, where a derisive sign invited the deranged or poverty-stricken to go down the steps to the rail halt, rather than mess up the glamorous hotel.

When you got to ground level, you had to walk over the tracks to the platform – which sleeping Thais shared with their chickens, etc., just as in some village upcountry – sandwiched between the glittering airport hotel and the roaring motor traffic. I was enchanted. Thailand felt homely. It was so … weird! Of course, it is not the airport rail halt. It has nothing to do with the airport, which is embarrassed, and deprived of revenue, by this relic. If you take the train, you are not spending money on taxis or coaches, and nobody at the airport gets a cut. The railway is out of the money loop, which Thais just hate. I woke up the ticketseller and bought a ticket for the forty-minute journey to Bangkok. It cost 10 baht, a fiftieth of a taxi ride. I stumbled over the tracks – again – and the pleasant, fan-cooled Bangkok train sped me past the taxis stuck on the clogged freeway alongside. I felt smug. T.I.T!

4. SPEAK YOUR WEIGHT

Bangkok is a huge, skyscraperish place, as big as London, or perhaps Texas, yet, viewed from a train, as opposed to a traffic jam, it looks almost sleepy. I had been prepared for a hell of car fumes, which it is, but saw lush greenery everywhere, the skyscrapers like brontosauruses raising their necks in search of a mate: an urban jungle, not a concrete wilderness. The skyscrapers had shanty towns, palm trees, flowers and cabbage patches tacked on beneath them, with people sleeping, as though, after the skyscrapers had sprouted, the lifeware had been programmed in. Things will not stop growing in Thailand. They call Bangkok 'The Big Mango' in emulation of 'The Big Apple'. (Why is New York associated with apples?) Thais call it 'Krung Thep' or 'City of Angels', Bangkok being a small, ancient district – like calling New York 'Manhattan'. I had been careful to telephone, to book a hotel beside the railway station. I arrived, pouring with sweat, in a 40-degree heatwave, at midday; they remembered my call with hilarity, and told me to come back at six o'clock, when, with luck, there might be a room available. Or not. How should they know?

I eventually settled at the River View, in Chinatown. From the eighth-floor restaurant, the stunning vista of the Chao Praya river in an orange sunset is alone worth the visit. I was happy to spend a week in Bangkok doing almost nothing. I visited temples a bit, took riverbus rides, and learned that even on the river, in a long boat crammed with a hundred passengers, Thai drivers are just as reckless as if on a moped crammed with three. (Bus drivers routinely fail alcohol breath tests.) Many a little old lady was saved by a kindly arm from being catapulted into the filthy water, as the boat roared off. Nobody seemed to care much, except to giggle. *Mai pen rai!* This, along with *mai mi a rai*, and, in English, 'Up to you' and 'No problem', are the key Thai phrases, used at all times, and meaning 'who cares?': the verbal equivalent of a shrug. I learned to use it.

I even got to shrug about the sexual delights of the much-touted Patpong 'red light' district, naturally my first port of call, before the temples. There are not many red lights, simply go-go bars and girly bars, packed alongside the vendors of deep-fried locusts and fake watches, and the four tiny streets which comprise it are a mere sliver of Bangkok. Yet that is what farangs know Bangkok for. There are many others, like Soi Cowboy, and Nana Plaza, but it was too hot to explore them, and Patpong was enough. I figured the merchandise elsewhere would be similar.

The place is potholed and grimy, but the bars are impeccably well mannered, and relatively honest. I entered one more or less at random. It was just a normal bar, only with an American porn film heaving discreetly on the TV, and girls, clad, or less clad, with their warpaint on. You are presented with a sort of sex menu, from which you select. Dizzied by novelty, I selected two girls for a 'two-girl massage', and was told by the mama-san that the price for a two-girl massage was – obviously – twice the price of a one-girl massage. A three-girl massage was three times the price, and so on. She addressed me as though I were an idiot. I had expected such naughtiness to be ten times the price. But this was just business ...

Two bewitching teenage girls shimmered up beside me, both with rather coy smiles, quite an achievement for ones so worldly. We drank, smiled, uncertainly placed hands on knees, with beguiling Thai modesty, for Thais frown on public displays of emotion, especially the obnoxious slobbering, kissing and groping so beloved of hairy-backs. For all the world like kids on a blind date, they were playing a well-rehearsed part, though I wasn't. They were both the standard centrefold: long, shiny dark hair, slim, quite big-breasted, with nicely rounded bottoms and smooth, svelte bare legs under black miniskirts, agreeably skin-hugging, and the soft maternal curves of bare shoulder and breast beckoning to delights within.

I mentally licked my lips, delighted at the youth and freshness of it all. No sleaze, no bedraggled, lipstick-smudged, cigarette-dangling hustlers, no large minders called Vinnie. Just fresh, organic country girls, giving a dutiful impression that they were reasonably pleased to see me. Erectile, for sure – so if I had any problems in that arena, things would not bode well in paradise. When the back room was free, the two charming ladies and I stripped off in something slightly larger than a shoe box, with a bed. A clean sheet! This was posh. Their bodies were young, and superb, with no evidence of motherhood, or at least immoderate motherhood. Lovely creamy breasts, flat bellies, sleek trimmed bushes, thighs like lollipops, and those cute, firm bottoms. The whole package just the right delicious shade of caffè latte, apart from toenails, painted, I rather inanely recall, peach and cerise respectively. I can happily report that my infernal regions reacted con brio.

As was befitting, this was a nameless fuck – it seemed corny and rather infra dig to make introductions – and also my introduction to the mysteries of fruit-flavoured condoms, which they allowed me to select from a recycled chocolate box. Banana? Strawberry? It may well have been lychee. It was a straight wham, bam, thank you, ma'am, apart from preliminary stroking and kissing and kneading (etc.) those delicious bottoms. I was dipping my toes into Asian waters, getting the lie of the land, and other mixed metaphors, and didn't wish to commit some dreadful Buddhist faux pas. Later, I learned that a Thai girl will indulge almost any weird sexual tomfoolery if it makes her an honest dollar.

I got a proper massage, with oil and powder and everything, and then they took turns marching up and down my spine. While I did it with one, the other continued to tread on my back, and kick me here and there. It was a pleasant experience, and I appreciated the fact that the girl whom I left undone still felt obliged to earn her money. She did not remain idle, while her colleague feigned pleasure under my bouncing, but massaged to the end. I tipped them well, and got smiles and bows. A pleasant, if cramped, experience. Of course, once tipped, they fled before I had time to fall in love with them.

I should add that the reader may assume all couplings I describe below took place under the protection of the Rubber God. Using a condom is not as tiresome as tiresome people claim and, after all, it is the 'won't-take-a-bath-with-my-boots-on' brigade who are always exploding in warts, boils and pustules. In fact, if the event is sufficiently passionate, ecstatic, earth-moving etc., and your mighty power is making her grunt, squeal, writhe, and similar female-type activities, you don't even notice the thing. There is a sardonic or possibly heartless satisfaction in knowing the business is tidy, over, done and dusted, and you aren't going to be disturbed in a year's time by surprise paternity demands; nor, if she gets, or already is, clapped up, can she accuse you of being the clapper-upper.

However, love avec condom, in a tiny room, with an obliging but overworked bar girl, after which you emerge into din, chaos, and carbon monoxide, is not the same as love by moonlight, under the whispering palms; just as champagne, slurped from a plastic cup, does not taste the same as when sipped from crystal at the Ritz. I was bemused by the friendly and businesslike ease of it all, and liked Bangkok, especially, um, the girls; I had to tear myself away from the delights of Patpong. It was so nice! So ... corny!

Being introduced to Thai sex in Patpong has an advantage. The bars are so uncomfortable, and so obviously places of business aiming for a rapid turnover, that you have neither time nor inclination to 'fall in love' with your half-hour honey. There is no beach to frolic on, no desire for walkabout in Bangkok's grey traffic fumes, no windsurfing, or going to see the elephants. Patpong is mass production. She has so many clients every day – every hour – that you feel less inclined to make her your 'girlfriend' for a week, than in romantic Patong Beach, or Pattaya. Nevertheless, in every bar I saw geezers – regulars, buying drinks for their honeys and her few dozen friends – obviously enamoured. Some poor souls are stuck in Bangkok. They have to make fools of themselves somewhere.

I learned the appeal of Thailand over other, not dissimilar, temple-beach-jungle tourist spots. Sex here permeated the air. It was part of daily business: visible, palpable, and sweet-smelling, like duck soup. I spent much time gorging on the omnipresent food: mangos, melons, grapefruit, lemon grass soup, mountainous plates of giant prawns ... but I had promised myself to see the country. Multi-templed Chiang Mai in the north is a 'must', and an air-conditioned first-class train whisks you there overnight in twelve hours. Or there is a daytime train leaving at 8 a.m. But it was scarcely possible for me, seriously nocturnal, to rise in time for the sightseeing train. Another air-con train left for Sungai Kolok in the deep south, on the Malaysian border. That went at 2 p.m., a gentlemanly hour. Furthermore, the guide book dismissed Sungai as a 'seedy brothel town', so there was no contest. After a comfortable twenty hours by myself in a two-berth air-conditioned cabin, with bathroom, and for pennies, I arrived in Sungai.

Anyway, as I learned later, tourists were avoiding Chiang Mai, which literally stank – the refuse collection was inadequate, and neighbouring provinces refused to accept Chiang Mai garbage, even for money. Tourists also shunned the deep south, because of the ongoing insurgency by Malay-speaking Muslim separatists, who resent the Thai conquest of their country a century ago.

Sungai Kolok is a delightful country village, which just happens to contain a lot of rather sleepy girly bars. It is – or was then – quiet as a churchyard, in the stifling southern heat, and nothing like the raucous venery of Patong or Pattaya. In Sungai, girls loll in front of drowsy bars, or in hotel lobbies, and smile pleasantly, but without making too much effort, though they perk up on seeing a farang who, exotically, is not Malaysian. Most people are Muslims, and many women (not the girls, at least not on duty) wear the black headscarf, but all smile shyly and beautifully. For such a small village, the omnipresent bars were obviously for the legions of Malaysians, who get laid in freewheeling Thailand. But why should such a small town have so many hairdressing salons? There seemed to be two kinds: 'Hairdresser' and 'Family Barber', the latter being more numerous.

Obviously, a 'hairdresser' was swank and expensive, so I chose a family barber. The door and windows were draped in red velvet; I imagined southern Thais were shy of being seen having a haircut. (Something to do with Samson and Delilah?) There were half a dozen lovely girls, seated on red banquettes, and painting their nails, chewing gum etc., which activities they broke off on my entrance, to preen and cross their legs several times, giving me big come-on smiles. Quick as a flash – nothing gets past me! – I realised that 'family barber' was a quaint euphemism for maison close, and any relation to personal grooming was purely tangential. A haircut? (delighted giggles) – you go to hairdresser! (more giggles).

They all spoke fractured English, presumably to communicate with their Malaysian clientele. Five out of five for the British Empire, I thought. The door was not opened for me to exit, nor did I move towards it. A haircut began to seem like a decadent and absurd western affectation. Instead, I took the offered seat beside a brown-eyed girl, called Nok, which means bird, as she had the biggest, though unbirdlike bottom, and the nicest smile. Thai ladies usually have monosyllabic names – Porn, Om, Nok – of some flower, animal, food, or natural disaster, or else shortened forms of real names which are too long for them to remember.

When Nok took me into a comfortable air-conditioned bedroom, I was amazed at the playful grace with which she undressed, as though her clothing somehow melted from her body, and then deftly undressed me, sparing my trembling fingers the embarrassment. She was in no hurry, yet all of a sudden we were naked. Here in sleepy Sungai, we seemed to have all the time in the world, and I regretted having dawdled in the smoky hubbub of Bangkok.

Her figure was simply gorgeous, all naughty bits perfectly sized and in harmonious proportion. Long straight hair (of course), delicately brushing her nipples – so big and brown and chewable! – thighs firm as marrows, a coyly swelling, downy mons veneris, and ... that ... bottom! Shyly, she asked if I had a condom. I repressed a laugh – a barber shop without condoms! – and admitted I was condomless. This was speedily rectified, after I had produced the relevant banknote.

Thereafter, it was all awfully nice. Emboldened by my Patpong experience, I set to some serious bottom-worship, and, having been persuaded to squat on my face, she accepted my enthusiastic nosings and mouthings with sweet little giggles. There is nothing like the coolness of a woman's bare bottom! How do they keep them so cool? Yet another female mystery. I thought of planets, celestial bodies, and so on. Weight being a factor in our operations, I asked how much she weighed, as it felt about two hundred kilos.

'Only 46!' she protested; you must not joke about a Thai lady's weight.

Big rump, big smile. Boy, was there a lot of her! I took her from behind, rather gently, to show how fascinatingly sophisticated I was, and the sight of those bare brown globes delicately dewed with sweat ... heavens, I thought, how can anybody fail to get it up? Who needs sex aids when you have a Thai girl's silky bottom shivering before you? Although most people don't, I suppose.

Already, I was light years from the ghastly mechanised contrivance of western 'sexuality' ... 101 new sex positions to find the G spot, or the F spot, or the Z spot ... Dr Hag's sex tips for the over-90s ... squirt your knob with ozone-friendly pheromone goo ... perfect that killer smile ... get your abs or lats into shape ... achieve your best orgasm ... What turns him on? What turns her on? Human bodies, like cars in a showroom. But in Thailand, you do what comes naturally. Even me, young enough to wake up with a hard-on but old enough to be blasé about it: just your standard *homme moyen sensuel*.

With Nok, time did not exactly stop, but it did seem to take up a healthy chunk of the afternoon, as did similar operations the next two afternoons. I never got a haircut all the time I was in Sungai Kolok. The girls called me 'weigh machine', and were great smilers, though I only ever weighed Nok. I refrained from pointing out that the person weighed was supposed to put money into the weighing machine, not the other way round. *Mai pen rai!*

5. BIG BEACH BALL

Hat Yai is a scruffy, bouncy depot town in the middle of the southern snake-tongue of Thailand, but its name means 'Big Beach' and the nearest beach is 80 km away. It is a sort of Tijuana for the Malaysians, who come across the border to buy T-shirts, and get laid. I had a wonderful meal at an open-air restaurant, mountains of duck, rice and veggies, done to perfection; such places thoughtfully do not add chilli in the cooking process, but leave an array of spice jars on your table. When the boy said 300 baht, I thought it well worth it, and handed over a 500 baht note. After a long wait for my change, I was about to remind him, when he came back with 470 baht. He apologised for the delay, having gone to the bank to change my large note. The meal was not 300, but 30 baht.

On that first visit, all the merchants sold zingy American pop art T-shirts: I figured Malaysian shoppers must be pretty cool. On my next visit, six months later, avid for these sophisticated T-shirts, I rushed to buy. Now, the T-shirts were all Walt Disney characters, every shop selling exactly the same ones.

Roy Lichtenstein or Donald Duck? It is just what the truck of fate brings.

Where Sungai has family barbers, Hat Yai has 'Ancient Thai Massage' parlours, which are exactly the same thing, only bigger, and more showy, with the windows displaying casting-couch photos of the numbered, unancient girls to be found inside. The Ancient Thai Massage parlours had slick-haired touts to beckon you in. Hat Yai is crammed with girls, so I remained unpersuaded. At the hotel, the boy said, 'You want lady?' It seemed quite natural to save a walk by saying yes, and handing him the small sum demanded. Pot luck! A blind date in steamy Thailand! I had never been on a blind date before. I had visions of a crone, a doper, a psycho; it was a cheap experiment.

The lady duly arrived. She was a beautiful teenage monosyllable, who spoke two or three words of English, consisting of her age, name, and home town (nearby Narathiwat, where a girl had just been imprisoned after stewing her new baby for her boyfriend's dinner). It was like name, rank and serial number. Things would be easier if bar girls did have ranks and serial numbers, so that you could remember which ones you had had before, like the squiggles little old ladies make on murder mysteries from the library.

This one, happily, though shy, had unusually large breasts, a lovely mane of hair, and was pleasing in every department. A real centrefold, I smuttily suspected, from her curves underneath the tight jeans and T-shirt, which gave her number in a fictitious American basketball team. She accepted a soda pop, and we sat on the tiny sofa and awkwardly watched TV, with the equal awkwardness of mimed small talk. We established the facts of the case over and over: yes, she was eighteen, had three sisters and a water buffalo to support, and Narathiwat was in Thailand. Just when I thought the rituals of courtship were satisfactorily complete, there was a knock on the door, and two further girls came in, bowing politely. Now, they were old-timers, a good 21 or 22 and, while elfin, were hard as nails: serious workers.

'My friends,' was the introduction.

They plonked themselves on the floor and gazed at the TV while I served them sodas. Wild fantasies surged in my brain. Had I misunderstood – had I paid for three girls, and a mad orgy of southern depravity? Or was this going to be a good old-fashioned clip? Happily, it didn't matter – I could afford to waste my small investment. We all sat without speaking, until I ventured to ask what the new monosyllables actually wanted. In a mixture of pidgin English and sign language, I learned that they were also working girls, surprise, and had customers 'in other hotel' in an hour.

Evidently I was to serve as waiting room. I wanted to get the business done; not from urgency, but because it was business, and I had paid for it, and, with my unreconstructed western mentality, wanted to accomplish something else with my precious time, like reading a book. In Thailand, time is not precious; it scarcely exists. Space doesn't really exist either. If there is a chair, you sit in it; if there is a couch, you lie down. It doesn't really matter whose house they happen to be in, for, sooner or later, other Thais, perhaps vaguely related, will drop in to occupy your chairs and couches. Accommodation arrangements are casual. Not understanding this, I began to indicate bouncing, with a shower together as a hygienic preamble. I confess to my fantasy of two other beauties eagerly getting naked for a 'four-in-a-bed-session' (whee!), or at least joining us in the shower for wet bazongas fun, and then cheering from the touchline while we bounced. But I vaguely realised that whatever I imagined I wanted, would be provided only after further cash offering. Stingily, I felt one would suffice for the moment. If they wanted to watch for free, of course, that was fine ...

The two girls helped my girl move the sofa, so that it was directly between the bed and the TV. They sat down again and continued viewing, with their backs to the bed and bathroom. Now, I witnessed for the first time the extraordinary ritual of a Thai girl modestly stripping naked. Nok had not been modest in that way – the Patpong girls had not been modest in any way – but she wore a loose, delicately shed, dress, and we had showered separately; not that she made it a big deal, or locked the bathroom door, like some.

This girl wrapped herself in a towel and, under it, began the most amazing gyrations to rid herself of her clinging jeans, bra and panties. The T-shirt somehow slithered over the top of the towel without dislodging it. It was like watching Houdini get out of a strait jacket. My own stripping took about two seconds, but I obediently donned a towel, feeling foolish, as at some alien religious rite. No one peeked. The repositioned sofa created privacy for us, as the two extras were, technically speaking, in a different room. So, unwatched, we went to the bathroom to shower. Unused to such intimacy, she allowed me to soap her breasts and bottom and things, her hair bundled in a plastic cap (Thai girls will wear them even when not in the shower). I wobbled her soapily about, but when I got more basic, she politely gyrated away from my eager fingers. Hurry, hurry, she mouthed. She was a bit embarrassed by her wonderful hour-glass figure, and an absolutely massive pubic forest, now unfortunately soaked, which would require the effort of drying.

We rewrapped ourselves, and I went alone to the bed, while she laboriously dried her bush. The TV babbled, with tinkly music. At long last she slipped into bed, where she allowed me to prise the towel from her body, leaving us both, amazingly, naked. The eyes of my self-invited guests did not stray from the TV. I hoped they might snatch a naughty peek, but no. They were in a different room! Thai ladies usually trim down there, but not this one. It is impossible not to be a fan of primaeval jungle, such as now rose towards me, like a giant sea anemone. She was lovely about it, and blushed, and – at last! – made a little shy giggle which had my heart all aflutter, and our eyes met – (etc., etc.). She was not unhappy!

I understood that she knew the appeal of this Matto Grosso, so left it untrimmed, although it embarrassed, even frightened her; some raw beast of sensuality, and ur-fertility, set to engulf her. Or maybe she was just lazy. I had the eerie feeling of being in some German fetish movie, made in Marbella: *Jugs und Jungle* or similar. I made appropriate noises of bush appreciation. Well-endowed ladies expect you to be laddish about them; poetry is unbecoming. I dutifully teased and curled it, and smelled the aroma of it; I did everything except put it on hot buttered toast. The stuff was massive! Like crab grass on speed. I expected to see a miniature Tarzan swinging from a creeper.

The Bangkok assembly-line girls didn't count, but Nok, I was sure, genuinely liked me ... this one was too consciously a centrefold, maybe preferring some whiskey-glugging Thai thug, somebody who didn't like her. Already I had begun to fall into the Thai trap of 'she's-different-ism'. How many geezers have I joked with about the dangerous charm of the Thai lady, and how many of us she has reduced to tears, only to be introduced to his own lip-glossed, sultry money box, with the words: 'But my Ook is different ...'

It was all quite nice, but I didn't want it to take forever and, of course, it didn't. Once or twice during my plungings I looked back to see if we were being watched, to aphrodisiac effect, by the other two girls. But no; one soap opera had weepily ended, and another was starting. No eye was unglued. As soon as it was finished, she leapt up, quick as a frog. I wanted her to go – the night was young for her – and take her chums along. Then I could settle down with my book, and enjoy the strange bliss of being alone. All three sat primly on the sofa, one swived, the others unswived, but as though bouncing was something that took place on another planet.

'My friends want money,' said Miss Narathiwat, to which I feigned surprise.

I had visions of a violent scrimmage, cops called, brutal foreign rapist led away in chains, sobbing Thai virgins violated by lustful stranger, etc. Only later did I find out that the tourist police in Thailand are there to protect farangs from girls, not the other way around.

'How much money do they want?' I drawled, as Bogartishly as possible.

I persuaded myself that I didn't care, as it was funny money, anyway.

'They want 20 baht for taxi,' said Miss Narathiwat.

I widened my eyes in an attempt to stop laughing. The *Bangkok Post* cost 20 baht.

'Each?' she added, uncertainly: making a whole dollar!

Gravely, I reached for my wallet, and handed a 20-baht note to each girl, as if I was entrusting them with the Holy Grail, and they all departed, bowing in thanks.

I thought, where else would a girl shake you down for the price of a newspaper? I just loved Thailand! And despite everything, I still do. I read my book, and laughed sporadically until trusty old Dickens sent me to sleep. In Hat Yai, *The Pickwick Papers* seems far funnier than it really is.

6.   SWEET HOME PATONG

From Hat Yai I got a bus to Trang, home of an erstwhile prime minister (who had given a box of fish to the leader of the opposition, advising him that they would make him more intelligent, like people in Trang, while the opposition responded with the gift of a box of eggs, to make the PM less feeble; such is the sophistication of Thai political debate), and a lovely, sleepy Thai town where nobody in the four-star hotel, or anywhere else, spoke a word of English. I remained chaste, as I did in further palm-fronded paradises, because, though there were smiles everywhere, I was uneasy about dipping into sexual waters reserved for Thais. Frankly, I was embarrassed to ask the nice girls at the reception to recommend a suitable establishment, although they would have been precisely the most helpful, had they spoken any English. But, such is the allure of Thailand, that I wasn't there purely to get laid, like other guys ... I was looking for a place to settle. Every town in this lush southern landscape beckoned; but nobody spoke English, and there were no farangs. Even loners sometimes want conversation. I got another bus, to Phuket.

It was about this time that I started to have a strange dream, which returned a couple of times, in Patong and Pattaya. It was strange, only because I rarely have dreams, and never remember them, but this one I did. Nothing much happened, and, being dully unparanormal, I avoided ascribing any meaning to it. I certainly never mentioned it to any Thai, because they would at once panic, thinking I was haunted, and start feeding me noxious ghost-busting foodstuffs. It wasn't a particularly erotic dream, though it featured a slim woman with long dark hair, and I assumed she was Thai, although I couldn't see her face, which was in shadow, or a blur, like the way the government censor fuzzes out the TV screen whenever a movie shows a bare nipple, gun or cigarette (sometimes there are so many offensive images that the whole screen is prude-blurred, save for a spurting jugular). She didn't do anything, I mean there was no plot, she just hovered around me for a bit, then hovered away again, which made me inexplicably wistful. Thais would have taken this as a visitation from a long-dead princess (good), or murderess (not), about to be reincarnated. I was quite happy to have this dream, when it recurred, but I didn't think about it much. It was too banal to be spooky.

The buses are efficient and air-conditioned, and whisk you around on good highways. Bus and truck drivers take illegal methamphetamines – ya-ba, or crazy medicine – to stay awake, and there was only one accident en route, where the bus crashed into a motorcycle on the way to Phuket, delaying us for an hour while uniforms did their stuff. There was mild, but not extraordinary, interest from the hut-dwellers along the highway; if anything, it cheered them up, as we bought snacks and drinks. Road crashes were obviously costed into their business day. The only problem is that the seats, even in the poshest air-con buses, are made of vinyl. After a while, your soaked and itchy buttocks are screaming for air, while you are sneezing and snuffling from the enthusiastically frigid air-con.

Ya-ba, by the way, is now somewhat passé, superseded by the even deadlier crystal meth.

I consulted the map, and figured I could get back on the rail network a few hundred kilometres north, then back to Bangkok, and the temples of Chiang Mai, a city which, I noted purely en passant, also contained service girls. The island of Phuket did seem worth a visit, since I was near, and all the buses seemed to go there. It was Thailand's number one tourist destination, after all, and Patong Beach was depicted by the guide books as the glitzhole from hell. Mindful of my English advisor in Turkey, I imagined a concrete Torremolinos-style horror, pullulating and scuzzy, but felt it my duty just to glance, if only that. The scenery of southern Thailand is indeed as pleasant as promised. It is hilly, green and lush, and Phuket proved a paradise of gorgeous gentle hills. The King of Sweden is a regular visitor, in his capacity as top dude of the World Boy Scout Federation, as he is to Pattaya, where the Woodlands Hotel displays photos of His Swedish Majesty cavorting in *Lederhosen* with the scouters, and Thai girls could not believe this proletarian figure was a king.

Thais do not share our western Romantic obsession with scenery, nor distinguish much between city vs country. Bangkok is jungly, and the jungles are villagey. In Thailand, your home village remains home. Spectacular beauties do not interest; they enthuse over comfortable, humane ones: rivers, orchards, meadows, waterfalls, flowers, especially as a source of food or money. If people persist in eating exotic endangered species and deforesting forests, the ecologists are down on them, so – no problem! – now they have lucrative eco-tourism.

Thailand, like England, is an independent monarchy, stand-offish from its neighbours, whose rural beauties are more valued than its urban ones. Bangkok is just a smog-choked village of eight (ten? twelve?) million people, and, like Londoners, many residents know only their small corner of the city. I expected Patong to be a similar concrete nightmare, and after a night in placid, old-colonial Phuket town – where I detected few signs of lust, though in fact it seethes, like everywhere else – I travelled the 15 km over the mountain to Patong Beach, early the next afternoon, expecting to be appalled, and able to retreat north, back to the real Thailand. The tuk-tuk taxi whirled down corkscrew bends, and there was this stunning vista of sea and beach, enfolded by green hills, with signs of human habitation parked cosily at the bottom. I noted the advice that I should wear a condom, presumably at all times, and resolved to remedy my condomless situation.

Deposited at the beach end of pseudo-glitzy main street Soi Bangla, I stood bemused in the sweltering heat. Everything seemed asleep. Was this it? The cauldron of lust and depravity, the concrete paradise from hell? It looked like any Thai village. In the hazy distance towered a very few high-rise hotels, peeping, from the lush verdure, as though embarrassed by their bulk, just like the ones in Bangkok. But the rest of it was two-storey shacks, a jumble of bars, shops and restaurants and shady nooks for Thais to sleep in (which is what they were doing), and I wondered where this tourist jungle actually was. I began the long trek up Soi Bangla, to my guidebook-chosen hotel. As I write, I remember so vividly that lengthy hike up the baked empty street, the twitter of birds, the lushness of the shading trees, the roll of the ocean behind. 'Garden of Eden' sprung to mind. But after a while here, the furnace-like heat gets to you, and you lust for air-conditioning. My deliciously Maughamesque hotel had that blissful amenity. Thank you, Americans! How did those tropical travellers manage in the days of Empire?

The best introduction to Thai girls in fact is Bangkok, where the discomfort of heat, smog, distances, and lack of privacy conspire against impulsive folly; the best introduction to the weirdness of Patong is a sleepy afternoon, not the pulsating night, when the lights, women and music are loudest and most inviting. Patong is so easy! It is sub-compact, bite-sized, a depraved Legoland ...

Like the Las Vegas strip in daylight, it looked unglamorous. I stopped at Alice's Bar, where Alice (this was just after she allegedly had her boyfriend murdered, and she had not yet been arrested) served me an ice-cold drink with a smile. I inspected the main street bars, all with a few ladies scruffily dozing. It looked as though it might become glamorous, given the additives of sin and darkness, but now … just a lot of Thai girls, asleep, or dreaming of sleep. I plodded on, past the supermarket and the side streets of deserted girl bars – which I sought, and recognised, because the guide book disapproved of them. The strains of 'Sweet Home Alabama' floated in the distance, competing vaguely with those of 'Hotel California': the two semi-official anthems of tourist Thailand.

I thought, I have been here before.

A Mexican border town, a Greek or Caribbean island, a fun-in-the-sun dump in the Canaries, the Costa del Crime – anywhere that dopes are parted from their money, and where the 'fun' actually starts when the sun goes away, and the locals wake up, put on their smiles and open their cash registers. I know these people. I can deal with them. It was an uncanny feeling of immense familiarity; partly because most signs were in traditional Smutglish, with various unsubtle plays on the words 'pussy', 'wet', 'hard', etc. At the deserted crossroads where Soi Bangla is flanked by the Rock Hard Disco and the Shark Disco, standing guard like Rottweilers of lust, with the condom-rich 7–Eleven across the road, all asleep at this hour, a smiling traffic cop waited for a car to come, then stopped it, for me to cross.

I entered the restful, shady cul-de-sac of Soi Saen Sabai (Healthy Street!), naturally known as Soi Mai Sabai (Sick Street), and noted the bars, with the British flag, the German flag, the French flag, the Scottish (!) flag, the Swiss flag. I had a cabana in a leafy garden. The hotel was German-run, by Bavarian Rolf and his henpecking Thai wife, and there was a little open-air bar, propped up by Rolf, and a wrought-iron gate, to which residents had a key. The room was a dream, air-conditioned, mini-barred, TV'ed and fluffy-towelled to perfection. A regular passion palace, I thought, grubbily, and a tenth the price of Florida or some Costa. This month, May, the rainy season officially started, and the tourist season officially ended. I worried that, like other beach resorts, notably the Greek islands, Patong might shut up shop for the low season, and the girly bars might be padlocked. No! If there is one solitary American tugboat on the horizon, if there is one farang geriatric in town, every girly bar in Patong will be in full squawk.

After ablutions, TV play, and bed-testing, all with sighs of satisfaction, I began to think that maybe Chiang Mai could wait. I had two weeks before flying back to London, and a few days' rest from the rigours of tourism, so they might as well be spent in Patong as anywhere. So I paid for three days, and said I might want to stay longer.

'No problem,' said Rolf.

I asked when the, er, 'bar scene' opened up.

'After dark,' was the prompt reply. 'About eight o'clock, the bars are swinging. But if you're in a hurry, Kristin Massage is open from one till midnight.'

He sounded rather wistful, for, so tight was the leash on which his wife kept him, that he was not allowed to drive his own car and, often, not allowed to go out at all. I had seen hundreds of signs offering 'Traditional (rather than 'Ancient') Thai Massage' but Kristin was obviously where you went for the whole nine yards. I was still enthralled by the naughtiness of depravity, and had yet to learn that in Patong depravity is as naughty as whole wheat toast. If I was in a hurry for a quick lube-job, why, Kristin Massage was there to oblige. I thought this charmingly efficient. After you spend a while as a resident of Patong, sex is just the air you breathe, as refreshing, or noxious, as it is unremarkable. Part of sexual excitation is its unexpectedness. A single wink from a sloe-eyed Muslim lady, wearing a tent, would, I imagine, be spine-tingling, like a nude in the *Christian Science Monitor*. A whole bucketful of smiles from a demi-mondaine, wearing practically nothing, unfortunately isn't. Context is everything. In Patong and Pattaya, sex is the context.

'You go with me?'

'No problem!'

'You have short time room?'

'No problem!'

'I want you to stand on your head, with a banana in your ear.'

'Up to you!'

'Hello, sexy man! I go with you?'

'Yes, but I not have money.'

'No money, no honey!'

They say that a lot. Sometimes, the farang gets to yearn for some continuity in his bedazzled social life, perhaps some peaceful concubinage, or the shadowy lady of one's dream.

7. BAR HENRY

On that first afternoon, I stepped out of the hotel again and ventured into Henry's Bar, which had just opened for the day. Henry bade me a rumpled good day, as though I had been coming there for years. There were women in here, but they did not seem to be bar girls. They did not have the 'hardcore' look, where the face muscles are tightened by constant smiling, and rearranging expressions. I sipped and contemplated the arrival of darkness, which at these latitudes falls in a dramatic rush. Henry's Bar is an institution central to the whole fabric of Patong farang society, for even the most ardent farang cannot have sex 24/7, try as he may, and sometimes wishes to relax in the undemanding company of other farangs. Henry's Bar is where gents go to talk to other gents, and get away from mind-numbing music and gonad-shivering female lusciousness, though the latter is omnipresent, even in 'Bar Henry' as Patong girls call it.

Henry even has a stack of tabloid newspaper clippings, detailing the depravities of various errant British aristos, which, damningly, include 'frequenting Henry's Bar'. This is one of the few bars in the world where geezers gather, and do not talk about football. In Thailand, macho guys talk about women.

The bar is plain, austere, stark, sort of Bauhaus/outhouse. There is an inaudible TV, which flickers with the incessantly repeated movies on the cable channel, and a sound system on which the benign Henry will very occasionally play the Bee Gees at deafening volume as his expression of a bad mood, ignoring his customers' screams of 'turn that fucking shit off'.

There are various young female hangers-on, or clingons, who use the place to sit, gossip, intrigue and eat, in return for which they act as unpaid barmaids. They will, um, date the customers, if offered money, but they are not specifically there for that purpose. Actually, they are a tiny bit long in the tooth, or deviant from the centrefold norm, to sit comfortably as bar girls; but, in full warpaint, they pass muster in the Heart of Darkness, the chamber of horrors bar complex adjacent, where they go after midnight.

Henry used to run two girly bars, but gave up, as the girls and their problems became too nerve-wracking: faithless Swedes, drugs, slashed wrists (usually, non-fatally, Henry assured me, across, instead of up and down, and some girls wear a forearm full of knife or needle scars, like medals), and sick water buffaloes needing immediate cash handouts. So he has a geezer bar instead. On paper, it is owned by his fiery missus, Porn, thirtyish, an ex-bar girl (the 'ex' a courtesy title), who has her ups and downs, in every sense. Henry has been through it all before; he was legally married to a seventeen-year-old bar girl, and then bitterly divorced. Yet, like all farangs here, he seems quite happy to go through the Thai loop again ... and again. This time it's different ...

When Porn has 'disappeared', or been seen canoodling with some Thaiboy, the normally placid Henry gets drunk, and snarls at the TV, for he is too polite to snarl at actual people.

'They're all the same! I know the score, I've been here thirteen years! I'm having nothing more to do with her or any of them! I picked her out of a bar and she can go back to it!'

That's a common lament amongst farangs, who see themselves as Sir Galahad, rescuing their cuties from lives of woe, doing them a big favour when, most of the time, the cuties actually prefer woe. When Porn comes back, pretending to be chastened, then Henry gets drunk and maudlin, and puts on ghastly records from the 1960s to remind himself of his youth, when he was a rocker in wildest Buckinghamshire.

'I knew she'd come back ... she's a one-man woman, same as I'm a one-woman man. She knows I don't mess around, and I know she doesn't. It's all jealous minds and yap yap. That's the trouble with Thai women, they won't listen to a farang, only to another Thai, no matter how rotten ...' etc., etc.

The last part is certainly true. Nothing a foreigner says has any effect on a Thai. If you show a Thai lady how to peel an apple, she will watch politely, then go and ask another Thai how to peel an apple. If you assure her that New York is in America, she will go and ask a Thai where New York is. And so on.

Despite having been here thirteen years, life-battered Henry is no less susceptible to 'she's-differentism' than the rest of us. When not joining in the laughter at tales of pussy-whipping, he is living it himself. The funny thing is, Henry could fool around, if he wanted to. Many of the girls 'fancy' him, as he looks younger than he is (opposite of the Patong norm), and is awesomely reputed to 'have good heart'.

Across the road you see a pseudo-German bar full of drunk girls, a pseudo-French bar full of squawking girls, a pseudo-Austrian bar full of enormous girls, and Fiddy's Guest House, announced by the cross of St Andrew, and full of Scots soccer fans, well-bevvied. Nearby is the short-time 24-hour hotel. Bar Henry's style is that it has no style at all, which is why everybody sooner or later drifts in, and lingers loserishly at the round table, open to the street at the front of the premises, and called the 'round table of doom'. Apart from Fiddy, that is; on the occasions when he has celebrated some Caledonian triumph, and embraced various geezers, assuring them 'you're my best pal, so you are', he thunders 'I'm no' sittin' doon there! It's the table of death!' You learn most things about Patong from sitting at this table with an open ear, but you only believe half of what you hear. The trouble lies in knowing which half. Of course, Patong, or its surrounding, is not just bars. There are the usual glitzy seaside pleasures, big hotels in secluded bays, restaurants and more restaurants, water sports ad nauseam. Some farangs come to open the bar of their dreams, others to open the diving-school of their dreams. But the core business of the town centre is bars, i.e. sex.

The Anglo symposians at the round table are oil-riggers, hotel-keepers, NVMs (no visible means of support), regular transients, transient regulars: in a word, expats. In any country in the world, you always recognise that expat look: the same mingling of despair with forced jollity. There is Magical Mervyn from Bedford, an NVM in a blue blazer. He is also called 'Sir Mervyn of Beds', and excuses his fondness for girls a twentieth of his age by saying he is 'scared of sleeping alone'. There is Lord Harry of Bethnal Green, thought to be the missing Great Train Robber, Kray brother, etc., who will sing ancient Broadway tunes, interrupted with: 'Do you remember Soapy Sid from Walthamstow? Found him in his cell with his throat cut. Maximum security. What a joke. Noo Yawk, Noo Yawk, tum tee tum tum ...'

There is Chris the Cybernaut from Seattle, who knows everything about computers and has a demonic lair full of flickering screens, where he spends the night double-clicking through the stock markets of Asia.

'I made a whole bundle of Vietnamese dongs today,' he says.

There is athletic Chester from Nevada, who owns the Sea View hotel across the road, which has no sea view. Chester is about nine feet tall, a swashbuckling type who, given a swash, will at once buckle it. He explains his dismay as a teenager when, leaving brothel-crammed Nevada for the first time, he found that prostitution was illegal elsewhere in the USA.

'I feel right at home in Patong,' he says, earnestly.

He can never remember the names of his various girlfriends, and explains that they all look the same, as their heads mostly reach as far as his waist, and that is pretty much as far as he wants them to reach.

There is Two-Ton Tony from Sydney, who keeps a succession of restaurants, and a succession of ever younger, and ever more criminally insane, Thai mistresses, usually with a policeman or taxi driver 'brother' who, as is customary, turns out to be her husband. At each visit he shows off some new scar, from meat cleaver or carving knife wielded by his latest honey, and quietly boasts he has shown her who is boss.

'I told her straight – the next time you stab me, you can pack your bags.'

Tony seems to spend so much time in police stations and hospitals, avoiding being murdered, or threatening to have other people murdered, or complaining about being murdered, that you wonder how he has any time left over to serve food, and indeed, where your steak actually comes from.

'Thailand is home,' says Tony proudly. 'Who'd wanna be any place else? I'm happy as a pig in shit.' – Fine, if you're a pig, and like ... oh, let it pass.

There is Gorgeous George, a fortyish Australian car salesman, who has abandoned his wife for a live-in harlot, notorious and dangerous, even by Patong standards. But to George, she is ... not like the others.

'I've had 'em all, believe you me, but this one (– yes! –) ... she's different.'

People who are about to say the most outrageous, stupid, or unbelievable thing in the world invariably preface it with that 'believe you me'.

There is Fackin Douglas, another Australian, who keeps his own girly bar off Soi Bangla. Most of his girls are ladymen, 'but you can't tell the fackin difference. They got dicks no bigger than fackin clits.' Fackin Douglas drops in at 4 a.m., full of his own bar vodka, which he replenishes, before moving on to the Blue Mood bar, scuzziest of the scuzzy, in the Heart of Darkness next door.

'The fackin girls there like it up the ass, see, just like fackin poms!'

At dawn, Fackin Douglas proceeds home to his Thai missus and Australo-Thai kids.

There are various Canadians, called Dale or Mike; various Scandinavians, called, collectively, 'Burnt'. All are permanently drunk, and all emit superior sneers about other parts of Canada/Scandinavia, to which they have not been. One of the Mikes flies from his oil rig in Alberta for two weeks of sex and beer.

'You must like it here,' I say.

'I don't.'

'Why not?'

'Too many Americans.'

'What's wrong with Americans?'

'They don't know how to drink.'

Harry, a drinking American oil-rigger from Houston, works in Mongolia and takes four-day breaks in Patong. To get here, he must spend five hours in a truck to take him to Ulan Bator; a flight to Beijing; another flight to Bangkok, and another flight to Phuket. It takes him three days to get here, for four days of fun. Another Canadian Mike affirms his three-point mastery of Thai girls: once in the bedroom, it's air-conditioning on (Thai girls don't like air-con, as it gives them a headache), gum out, and TV off. A third Mike says he doesn't like Patong much, either: 'If losers could fly, the sky'd be black.'

There is Fred. Fred is from Yorkshire, and is a self-made man, and is not afraid to tell you, again and again. Sometimes, someone asks what materials he used. Fred's favourite subject is the greatness of Yorkshire, and, by implication, Fred, since they are roughly the same age. Fred has been ripped off by

Thai honeypots – cars, houses, cash – more times than he has had tripe and onions for dinner. This does not stop him from knowing everything. A builder by trade, he will provide a running commentary on any construction going on, which is all the time: in Yorkshire, we'd use a wodger groppett, with a fifty-fifty slurry and sawdust mixture, on an upspangled cavity, oh dearie me, that house won't stay up for long. Fred will sing songs popular in the reign of Queen Victoria. Fred assures you that Yorkshiremen, even over a hundred years old, have no need of Viagra. He remembers his Second World War identity card number, and those of his brother, sister, and parents, too, and will recite them for you. When Fred comes in, people remember that they have urgent appointments.

Everybody speaks that special expat language which is the same everywhere, and incomprehensible to homebodies: about airlines, bribery, visas, girls, murder, fraud, sexually trans-mitted diseases, bankruptcies, jail, mindless adultery, alcoholic poisoning; drawling of daily crimes and depravities on every continent, and agreeing only on how weird Thailand is, how awful everywhere adjacent is, and how back home is the most awful place imaginable. This theme is ubiquitous amongst farangs in Thailand, and serves as an enabler to start conver-sation with any stranger, much as the weather, or a nice cup of tea, serve the otherwise reserved English. There is a tone of apology, and desperate mutual reassurance. We know we're jerks, choosing this easy, mindless life, but we're much better off here, aren't we? Aren't we? Some of Bar Henry's denizens are in their 20s, some in their 50s, some apparently in their 150s. But the round table is a democracy. Watch the lustful, or wryly knowing, leers of the middle-aged as young juicy girls slither past. Then watch the bleary ogle of the twentyish hunk, shakily draining his beer as he actually rises on shattered thighs, and launches his palsied body after her. The oldies grin: been there, done that, but their grins are tolerant. In Patong, whatever his birth certificate says, every farang is automati-cally fifty years old.

A decrepit English guest at Chester's hotel woke up to find twelve thousand baht, about three hundred US dollars, missing from his wallet, which he had placed on his bedside table. His girlfriend, 22, was fast asleep beside him. Awakened, she said she had heard nothing during the night. The money must have been taken by a sneak thief, or the night porter, or, most likely, a ghost. The night porter protested his innocence, insisting that he had been asleep in his chair all night. The cops were called. A neighbour said she had seen the girl sneak out the back door at 4 a.m. to a bar down the street, where she stayed for five minutes, before sneaking back into the hotel. Questioned at the police station, she was found to have 7,000 baht in her purse. (A larcenous Thai girl will rarely clean you out, but take an odd sum, which she needs for a specific purpose, usually paying off gambling debts. She's not a thief! She doesn't want your money, she wants her money.) With her heart broken into a million pieces, she burst into tears, and confessed: yes, gambling debts, water buffalo, bail money for errant bro, and so on. The Englishman refused to press charges. His wife and daughter had tragically been killed in a car accident five years before (car crash bereavement is surprisingly common with farangs), so understood the pressures on his honeypot, and knew what stress was. She stayed in his room for the next week, and they walked around Patong hand in hand. It had all been a misunderstanding. She was not like the others. She was different.

Or, as Chester put it, 'Hell, he hasn't fucked a 22-year-old since he was 22.'

8. PUSSY FOOT

For several nights, new to Patong, I had a different girl every night. That simple. My three nights turned into 'indefinite'.

'No problem,' said Rolf, with a helpful, rather envious smile, while his scowling wife, at the stove, did alarming things to hamburger patties.

They were all centrefolds like Miss Narathiwat, all nice as pie. Exotic practices were out of the question, but it was good to have a body sharing the bed: even though communication was nil, due to the universal lack of English. I was sleeping with strangers, who were doubly strangers, since a teenage girl lives in a world of her own, its language spoken only by other teenage girls. I didn't get much sleep, partly because it was like sleeping with a wrestler. Just as I dozed off, I would be crushed in a neck hold, chest lock, leg scissors, or whatever: immobilised by this sound-asleep girl who wanted to cling to her teddy bear. It made no difference if I retreated to the furthest corner of the bed; she would follow me there, stalking me like a crab.

Thais are afraid of the dark, of being alone, of ghosts. 'You sleep alone!' is a dreadful insult.

Nok, at the ripe old age of 23, began to seem like a mature and highly desirable property down there in Sungai Kolok, enthusiastically barbering. She knew things, had been round the block. Mind you, I had never spent an actual night with her. Now, I made a Patong fool of myself with the best of them, playing the stupid games in the box bars, buying drinks for various 'my friends', until the time came to whisk my chosen beloved back to the splendour of my hotel room. They were compliant and dutiful, but not too impressed by luxury. One fondly imagines it is a grand experience for a country girl to get a night in comfort, away from her dirt floor; but she spends most nights in the same sort of hotel room, and would actually prefer the dirt floor, with her chums.

To get some sleep, I would expel them at 6 a.m., lying that the owner's wife disapproved. Rolf's good lady, like most Thai hoteliers, expected the guests to bring girls in, and didn't care – it was her hard-drinking husband she had her eye on. The poor henpeckee had to travel by moped, if allowed to travel at all, and submit detailed route plans, with ETA, for the smallest journey. The family car (his) was kept locked in the garage, as Mrs Pussywhip could not herself drive. Now, she was different. Or perhaps just a typical, wildly possessive Thai wife.

Nevertheless, it was a relief to get rid of the teenage wrestler and grab some sleep, for in Thailand, as dawn approaches, you do not want to be asleep; with birdsong and flowers and bright sunlight, time seems precious, and you do not want to lose any of it. Later, you get into Thai habits, and realise it is the other way round: sleep is precious, and you don't want to waste any of it with real time. Moreover, you realise that rutting need not be hurried; you can take your time, as they are all lovely, and you are not going to miss any bargains by arriving late. After a few days, one could stroll of an evening (having woken at 2 p.m.), and observe the young studs in their erotic haste, with some condescension.

I also observed them bargaining the price of lust, and smugly congratulated myself on being a generous tipper. Actually, it still annoys me when farangs underpay, when the whole thing costs small change anyway. Make the girl happy by giving her what she wants – which, if not the pleasure of your fetid embrace, is certainly money. That way, the sensible farang avoids guilt: he knows the family will get its new water buffalo. But there is a tinge of guilt, that must strike even the most degenerate stumble-wreck occasionally. Many of the girls are real party animals, who escape from the village to seek the bright lights, drink, drugs and razzle. But many are shy and reluctant, forced into bar work by poverty, and the need to look after family. You see a love doll, but you get a human being.

In a short time, I imagined myself a veteran. I hung around Henry's Bar, and my hours got later and later; Thailand seemed to fit some nighthawk biological clock: or else, I never changed from European time, so that midnight was really 6 p.m. and I was full of vim. But – horror – it gets boring, bouncing with a fantasy, when, despite all her adorable shyness, she is really a warm, animated doll. Docility thrills the male ego for a while, but the thrill wears off. I began to see the charm that held Rolf under the thumb of Mrs Pussywhip.

All these teenage Thai girls were so ... sweet. It didn't seem right to invite them into exotic perversions – surely cunnilingus and toe-sucking don't really count? – so I didn't. I found I got tired of the incessant thump of overloud disco music in the rows of competing box bars, the contrived 'fun', the tourist bloats showing off. I started to take it easy, realising that in tourist Thailand every night was Saturday night, and every day was Sunday. There are no fixed hours; you can have anything, anytime.

Mai Lee, the Laotian chambermaid, was happy to sit with me upon my awakening, at 2 p.m., and chat over a beer from my mini-bar. She spoke a mixture of English and French, having been at a French convent school in Vientiane. She was from Laos proper, and had no ID card, thus an illegal immigrant.

Mai Lee was fortyish, good-looking in a bony sort of way, and kept picking stray female hairs from my pillow, with feigned disapproval. Mai Lee fancied me. She entertained me with the limitless saga of all the hotel guests who had propositioned her, and been refused, as Mai Lee did not bounce for money. She did not have a boyfriend, not even a Thai one.

'Why you not go with me?' she would pout, kneading my toes through the bedsheet. 'I look after you. Bar girl pas bien.'

One afternoon, I allowed nature to take its course; the sheet came off, and we bounced. It was efficient, not bad ... and free! As an afterthought, Mai Lee asked me if I could lend her 1,000 baht till payday. She would give it back at the end of the month, very soon.

'Moi bonne femme, not like other girls ...' etc., etc.

I handed over the money. The next day, I did not see Mai Lee, and learned from her replacement that she had been sacked, for *a* laziness, and *b* excessive bouncing with hotel guests, and had gone back to work at her Thai boyfriend's restaurant. Mrs Rolf had no objection to *b* in itself, except that it led to *a*, and the rooms were not cleaned. Bye-bye a thousand baht. Oh well. I would have dropped it anyway.

In a funny way, the older and more hideous you are, the better Patong is for you. There are plenty of century-old moneybags tottering around with sweet young things, and having the time of their senility, because they have given up any illusion that they are desired, or desirable, for anything except their mild manners and their money. There is no remnant of feeling that they are 'in there playing', or might offer physical attractions over and above some junior hunk. Being a plain and simple sugar daddy, or dirty old man, and rewarding lavishly the honeypot who provides you with pleasant, and possibly even orgasmic, company, is satisfaction enough. Arm candy is its own reward.

Plenty of antique geezers do genuinely enjoy themselves, and so do their honeys, because they both know the score. And Thai girls are not infected by squalid western youth-mania, where the first grey hair consigns you to the scrapheap.

You see plenty of cripples. Guys in wheelchairs, middle-aged thalidomide victims, whatever – a Thai girl will bounce with them, because their money is as good as anyone else's, and they most likely have 'good heart', due to their suffering. Her own good heart, in looking after such western sexual rejects, makes *tambun*, Buddhist merit, for her, too. Dino the Aussie barkeep told of one paraplegic in Fremantle who saved up for a visit to a brothel, but they wouldn't let him in, and then his wheelchair jammed, so he was stuck on the footpath outside the brothel ... shameful, we agreed. Years before, in England, I had listened to a pair of late-night females on a radio gossip show tearing into a millionaire rock star often seen escorting teenage beauties. 'He's over fifty!' one squealed. 'He's like something you've dug up! How does he get them?' – 'He pays them.' – 'Pays them? Yuk!'

A Thai lady has no problems that 'old man like young pussy', and it does not disturb her that old guys come to Thailand to get it, unaware they are unlikely to taste any at home. If farang women his own age find all sorts of unfair reasons not to tickle his aged balls, she just loves to do so. I can't remember many of those young honeys I enjoyed, even their names, or what they looked like, because they all looked gorgeously the same: long straight hair, serene face, with wide lips and big eyes, big rump and delicate breasts, and great big feet, suitable for pulling tree stumps.

Strolling down the beach road, by the post office, knots of girls would congregate on the plaza outside the jewel shop, late at night. These were streetwalkers, with an aura of danger. One evening, Porn shimmered out at me, and I plunged at once. Why not? I thought. Pornsuk, comic though it may sound to western ears, is one of the commonest Thai girl's names. Her face and torso were elfin. She had thin lips, knowing eyes, and a twinkly grin. Her behind was planetary, and I felt I was back in Nok territory. Porn had frizzy hair, and rather hippyish, scruffy clothes – actually a proper dress – a real turn-on, compared to the usual hot pants or sawn-off jeans.

And she spoke some English! Enough for copulatory conversation, at any rate. We went back to my hotel and she stayed all night, not sparing me the wrestling holds as she slept. Porn, too, was 23, had a baby, whose photo she promptly showed me, and was from Bangkok. She disdained the 'rice-pickers' who thronged the bars, and would never demean herself by joining their ranks. But in fact she did not fit the centrefold stereotype of bar girls. She had a big smile with badly fixed, irregular teeth, and was what the French call *joli-laide*, or ... 'not classically beautiful'. She was definitely a creature of the night (I mythologised) – romantic, wild, surging out of nowhere ... an individual! And plying her trade because she enjoyed it ... not a moper.

She was not a lush, like so many bar girls. She stripped with merry abandon, pranced around nude with that gorgeous brown bottom swaying, tantalising, as she inspected my hotel room, and thought showering together was just a great idea; we showered, and she soaped me, nurse-like, while hygienically but playfully inspecting my tumescence. She paused to squat, dripping wet on the loo, while I watched her pee – a hissing Niagara that was rather exciting – and was serenity itself as we resumed our shower, and then sat unconcernedly nude beside me, sipping a beer and giggling at the Japanese porno channel. It was about a bespectacled nerdy guy banging a bespectacled, sobbing woman with her head in the toilet. Those samurai! Porn was scornfully amused:

'Not take off grasses!'

Porn had a gorgeous, silky, coffee skin, and a derriere to die for. And that big, knowing – sophisticated – grin! Sophisticated was not a word I associated with Thai ladies, up till now. Her fee was 'up to you' – I mentioned a handsome sum – there was no question of her rushing off for another short time. Reality was, of course, prosaic. She got the bus down to Patong whenever she needed money, whored for a couple of weeks, then went back to Bangkok to live with her mother and/or sister, and sold T-shirts, or noodles. Or something. There was a brother, a boyfriend, maybe two boyfriends, or a jealous ex-boyfriend ... It was the usual convoluted, half-understood Thai lady soap opera. These stories are always the same story, and so humdrum, that if they are lies, and they usually are, it makes no difference.

I had whispered of a generous reward. So, as if Porn would not have done everything anyway, she did it all. She was – I convinced myself, and never wish to be unconvinced – genuinely keen on her professional duties. A regular 'monger sometimes wonders why he is doing the paying when he is doing all the work too, sweating away while she is happily horizontal. She squeaked happily, as I finally invaded her person, after going through my repertoire of acrobatic jollies. She did a bit of squirming and writhing, and so on, and I was perfectly happy if she was acting, for it showed she understood earning a fair wage for fair work. Condom on, of course (making sure it wasn't the wrong way round, hideous faux pas), one of the fruit-flavoured ones that are very popular, courtesy of Messrs Durex. Even with a girl who doesn't know you from a hole in the road, you still have this obscure instinct, or desire, to find out what pleases her, and do it. Porn, or her glorious bottom, even seemed to like a little playful spanking, and toe-sucking made her giggle '*chakajee*!' – 'that tickles!'

The reason I give all these details is that I actually remember them. I may have done similar things with my teenage beauties from the box bars, but I don't think so, for they would have been shy, or displeased: it was straight in and out. In any case they are all a blur, and I cannot recall any details at all. Porn remains detailed. After bouncing, and a bit more beer, it was established that she accepted, nay welcomed it in the back door. So we did that too, doggy fashion.

Now this was naughtiness! Tight and bony, but obligingly flexible, with the thrill that somehow you are trespassing in a private orchard. Sodomy, of course, is a dreadful crime in the Christian calendar, even between men and women, as it bypasses procreation. However, it is delicate pleasure, like caviare, an amuse-bouche rather than a meal.

While I was performing on Porn, I contemplated those marvellous brown buttocks, now beaded with lovely drops of sweat and shivering like nice big jellies. Wow! Power! She had her hand between her thighs, and was rubbing merrily, so I figured her moans of pleasure were only half acting. Suddenly, she hissed 'I come!' like a declaration of war, so of course I came too, noisily, into Mr Durex's fruit-flavoured product. Winningly, I told Porn that she now had a fruit-flavoured bottom.

In the morning, we repeated procedures, then at once Porn was a brisk and efficient Thai lady. As I still lay gasping and wheezing, she was showered, dressed, and ready to go, tucking her 'tip' into her purse. She politely refused breakfast, and away she went. She had that same inscrutable smile which they all have: whatever outrageous copulations may have taken place, they did so on another planet. Thai ladies have this unnerving speed. Post-bounce, they leap up, breezy for the next task. No lying in bed, cuddling and thinking sweet nothings, western style. One job has been completed and it is time for another. What could be simpler? A Scandinavian sentimentalist complained to me about his beloved that their phone conversations were unsatisfactory because she would simply hang up, without all the gooey farewells like 'love you madly' – 'bye, then' – 'bye' – 'mmwoah!' – 'love you too much' etc., which can take as long as the phone call itself. I explained that her phone call was over, no longer existing, part of the past, and she had moved on to her next reality, probably a phone call to another boyfriend. In the same way, when going to bed, Thais don't bid everyone 'good night', they just slide away.

Just after Porn left, it occurred to me that I didn't even know where she was staying. I was irritated she had not told me, but then, maybe she was irritated I had not asked. I assured myself that there were plenty of Porns in the ocean, and I was still at the stage where machismo suggested a different one every night. Many guys remain at this stage forever, and it is not a bad thing, for both parties. It keeps matters businesslike, and precludes 'she's-differentism', dormant in even the hardest male heart. But Patong being a small town, I still, sort of, hoped I might bump into Porn again ...

9. BAR GIRLS

Even within the innumerable ranks of full-time Thai midinettes, there is a class system. Go-go girls are the top of the trade – in their eyes – since they actually do something that could loosely be described as work, namely, gyrate inanely on stage in bikinis which the law forbids them to remove (although they do, of course, especially for the lesbian shows), and acts like handless dart-chucking, or insertion of beer bottles in places where other bottles do not reach.

They are actually paid wages, and must bring in the equivalent in bar fines, say at least ten tricks a month; they look down on disco freelancers, who look down on streetwalkers, and they all look down on bar girls, which most farangs end up with, since they are most accessible, and most easily inspected in the light. Bar girls in turn look down on streetwalkers and freelancers, because they are unemployed, and on go-go dancers most of all, because they immodestly show their underthings.

The bar girl scenario offers a kind of security to both partners, since each knows where to find the other – unless she is taking the dawn bus back to Nakhon Si Nowhere forever (or at least until her swag money runs out, and she can come back to town, knowing her victim has left). Bar girls can size up customers in a pseudo-normal setting, and do not go with just anybody, although supposed to: if a type is too drunk or obnoxious, they will take refuge barside, or in the bathroom. A streetwalker has to make a snap decision in the shadows; the lustful male will not know where to find her if she turns out to be a wrong'un and makes off with all his money. If she murders him for his money, whether or not he could find her again would be academic. Every bar has a mama-san, a stern lady of riper years whose task is to keep everything shipshape. This is one of the few areas in Thai life where ladies over thirty are visible at any job more authoritative than running a food stall. With males, her riper years make her forbidding, although some consider it highly macho to 'pull the mama-san'.

The girls are technically 'bar hostesses' whose job is actually, on occasions, to serve drinks, although they spend most of their time with customers, unless trying to avoid one. Otherwise, they take turns at the actual dispensary. In the bars which call themselves 'pubs' the barmaids actually are full-time barmaids, although they will still, of course, go to bed with you, and many farangs have a mistaken sense of achievement if they have 'persuaded' a drink-pourer to accompany them, as though this is more difficult than picking up the honey swaying on the stool beside you.

The girls are employed by the bar, and some bars have two or three dozen. They are often unpaid, except, occasionally, enough for a bowl of rice every day, but receive free barracks accommodation, a shack where they sleep, cook and eat together. Though successful girls may team up and rent their own apartment, most prefer communal living, sleeping, gossiping, and eating on the floor, just like back home. A mistake commonly made by a love-struck farang is to send his girl a wad of money, expressly to rent an apartment by herself, away from the squalor of bar life, meaning her friends. Solitude! He might as well offer her an igloo at the north pole. Thais hate to be alone, and the bar girls act as a platoon, looking after each other. Alone in an apartment, a girl freezes at every knock on the door, which is almost certainly the ghost of a jilted boyfriend who did himself in with a broken heart, or someone she owes money to.

The bar girls' tips come from their own pneumatic efforts, and are theirs to keep, although the pimp – sorry, the genial mine host – keeps the bar fines. If you remove a lady, even just for short time, a few hundred baht is added to your bill as 'bar fine', to compensate him for the loss of her valuable beer-pouring services. Prostitution being illegal in Thailand, if a girl chooses to go with a customer for a game of all-night backgammon, it is no business of the barkeep's. Bar fines for the more glamorous go-go girls are double the norm. Customers accept bar fines (rather than pimp taxes) without complaint; a fine is for some mild misdemeanour, like an overdue library book.

Since prostitution, like gambling, is illegal, it follows that every town has its neonless brothels to which Thai men proceed after, or for, a night's drinking and gambling. These premises naturally operate with the paid acquiescence, or indeed actual ownership, of the local police chief. A brothel in Phuket town was burnt to the ground one night – arson being a popular way of settling business rivalries in Thailand, as an alternative to murder. Twelve teenage girls were burnt to death. The owner was fined a small sum for negligence, in not providing fire escapes, and the law on underage sex workers (apparently there is a legal distinction between prostitution and sex work) was 'strengthened'. *Mai pen rai!* Under-eighteen girls simply borrow an older friend's ID card.

Of course a girl who does two or three short times in a night, returning to the bar, generates that number of bar fines. If the hoped-for sugar daddy materialises, and wishes to monopolise the girl for a week or two, then she must pay the bar fine for every day of her absence, or lose her place in the corral. If the geezer is mega-serious and wants to make her his steady squeeze for months, or forever, she may take the step of 'resigning' – but will make sure to drop in on the bar frequently, just to remind them she is alive and bouncing, and ensure her job, as and when sugar daddy melts away.

Bars in Bangkok have the ingenious concept of 'marriage fines', that is, when some lust-sodden drunk actually puts a ring on a girl's finger, the bar owner demands somewhere around $3,000 for the loss of her unique services. This, of course, is nonsense, since a bar girl is free to change employments as she pleases. However, the lucky bride does not disabuse her new husband of this notion, because the bar owner is slipping her a percentage of the take, which will end up in the gold shop or her purse. It rarely happens elsewhere; perhaps farangs are lonelier or stupider in Bangkok.

Bar girls are indeed free to move from bar to bar, and do so, as there is a shadowy grapevine of opportunity, and the usual intrigues. It is not done for (farang) bar owners to poach each other's staff; nor should a bar owner sample his own merchandise, without heating a cauldron of spite, jealousy, hatred, revenge, and broken beer bottles.

Bar girls are also the most eager, and their chirps of 'Hello! What you name? Where you come from?' almost drown the ghastly wail of 'Hotel California' by the Eagles, a song which, if it were ever to die a fervently desired natural death elsewhere on the planet, would live forever in Patong and Pattaya. It is a fair bet that most Thais are more familiar with 'Hotel California' than with their own national anthem, a weird, tinny wail, played at 6 p.m. every day on TV, and the most accurate timepiece in the kingdom.

Patong and Pattaya have countless 'pubs' with vaguely Australio-Celtic or German names: Kangaroo, Blarney Stone, Ned Kelly, Berliner Stube; places legitimate boozers might reasonably have an excuse to visit, to watch soccer matches on TV, or just get drunk. They have bar girls, but not as their sole function. But once you enter a bar complex, you cannot pretend you seek anything but sex. The open 'box bars' are back to back counter-tops, and sometimes you are not sure which bar you are technically in, not that it makes any difference. Etiquette is strictly observed. On your progress through the *soi*, all the bar girls will shriek at you; once you have settled your behind on one particular bar stool, only the girls from that bar shriek at you.

The bars are stacked up like cars waiting for a ferry: the Blue Dollar, the Blue Butterfly, the Blue Note, the Blue Lotus, the Blue Parrot: azure predominates. There is no reason to choose one bar over another as you stroll around with feigned nonchalance, other than the stridency of the invitations, the tenacity with which a girl may actually cling to your T-shirt (she has to let go, if you have managed to drag yourself to an understood limit of two metres from her home bar), or the actual charms of the viands on offer. You generally sink onto one barstool or another, in a kind of desperate surrender. There is no reason to choose, because the girls are generally scrotum-tingling – and whether you are slim, hunky and beer-swilling, or pudgy, balding, and beer-swilling, they want you.

If you have been cooped up in an aircraft carrier for twelve weeks, or an aircraft for twelve hours, or anywhere in the western world for a lifetime, you think you have died and gone to heaven. What the Thai lady sees is not a pallid, tawdry, sexually repressed, egoistic, beery nerd, she sees a money tree, in all its leafy glory. But who cares? These girls are so ... fabulous. And their smiles! When did you last see a beautiful western woman actually smile? Or one that really was beautiful? It's like being in the Playboy Mansion surrounded by a thousand centrefolds ... it's ... it's ...

'It's great fun,' said a young English stud, about to launch himself into the box bar maelstrom, 'but basically, it's just a glorified wank, isn't it?'

'Well,' I blurted, full of the joys of life, 'it's a bit more than that ...'

Is it? A glorified wank ... as opposed to what? An unglorified one? Lifelong devotion? The earth moving? How much bouncing on this planet, statistically, is anything other than live-model masturbation? At least, in the Thai demi-monde, all concerned know what it is. Except for the numerous demented, who fall in 'love' ...

Most frequently, a farang is cajoled into one bar or another out of sheer lassitude, like choosing the most advertised washing powder, just to put an end to dithering. The girls cluster round; they are shrilly excited by his presence; he buys one a 'lady drink', then another for her friend, and then another for her friend. Each lady gets 20 per cent of the price of her 'lady drink'.

Meanwhile, merry games are suggested, consisting of an extremely dull version of vertical tiddly-winks, or else the nail game, where nails are stuck into an upturned tree stump and girls and farangs compete to strike the nail head with hammers to see who can sink theirs the fastest. The bar girls always win at these games, since they have nothing else to do all day, except go bouncing. Oddly enough, these are not clip joints. These games are not played for money, the drinks are not watered and they all cost the same as in a non-girly bar. The demi-monde is scrupulously honest, because in an overcrowded scene, they want repeat business.

If you end up spending a lot of money, it is not because you have been robbed, but because you have been wheedled. Puh-leez ... one drink for my friend? One taxi for my other friend? Puh-leez, you buy me dress (wisp of cotton bearing fake designer name)? Bars have a ship's bell which is rung to signify that a farang, flushed with lust, drink and money, and proud to discover he is irresistible to girls younger than his grand-daughter, is buying a round of drinks for the whole bar. The *sois* of desire and loneliness shudder non-stop to the chimes of these bells.

If you have bounced with the same female for more than two days in a row, it means you are now her 'boyfriend' and are permitted to take her shopping. The wheedle-ometer needle goes up, since she hopes you are infatuated with her. Puh-leez, you buy me gold? Gold is the real McCoy. It can be turned into cash. All Thai ladies have an intricate knowledge of carats and gold prices, and the Indian gold merchants do a roaring trade in bangles and necklaces, which can be returned in a few days, or hours, with a premium deducted from the original price. The jewellers are really pawnbrokers.

Thai bar girls would be quite properly offended to be described as prostitutes. When one of the girls, perhaps one of the apparent millions under eighteen, chooses to visit your hotel room on the promise of a 'tip', why, who is to say if a sexual act is to take place? If you are following in the perfumed wake of some ravishing teeny-bopper, equipped with her big sister's ID card, it is obvious to the Thai policemen that you intend to spend a strenuous night playing chess. As for the tip you give, after the night's fumbling and panting, she rarely mentions an actual amount. It is 'up to you', and she will pout and shrug until your suggestions of reward become realistic. A good way to tease an over-zealous bar girl is to enquire after the health of her German boyfriend. – 'How you know I have *teelak* Gerramany?' – 'Just a wild guess ...' This can earn you the reputation of being a tremendous seer and wizard.

Many older farangs genuinely want a lady's company, but not bouncing. Others want to get strenuously naked and do the whole nine yards; it is up to you. Those with pacemakers might venture a cautious *chak wao* ('flying a kite'), or hand job. If you opt for that, or cosily watching TV à deux, it is up to you as well. A bar girl will give good service – she is, after all, a service girl. Do not be misled by her ravishing smile into imagining it is anything more than a service, and be thankful if she does not chew gum, or watch TV, while operations are underway.

It helps to have fluffy towels. Thai ladies love towels, socks, or anything fluffy, like the giant cuddly teddy bear you have bought her from the helpfully passing vendor, and which she can add to her vast collection. In their barracks, the bar girls sit and sleep on the floor. If any of these barracks actually possesses a chair, it is reserved for visiting farangs, i.e. anyone who has attained by two days' endurance the status of 'boyfriend'. A bar girl is at a disadvantage compared to a disco freelance or streetwalker, who will have a shack of her own, because her farang must have a hotel room to take her back to. If he has temporarily escaped from his own spouse, he has to spring for a short time hot-pillow hotel, where the rooms are rented on a two-hourly rate.

Bar girls are 'looked down on', but not like western prostitutes. Their job is not, as in western countries, a profession at all, still less a lifestyle choice, in a country without social security. A girl on the Rue St Denis or Hollywood Boulevard is a prostitute, the way others are schoolteachers or accountants, but Thai girls don't see it as a career move, just something to do for a while, until poverty goes away, which is usually never, unless she snares a rich foreign lunatic. Although, in Pattaya, a splendidly uddered honey of my platonic acquaintance ('in a relationship' at the time, I only went to the bar to buy smuggled American cigarettes) told me she was paid 4,000 baht a month, plus tips, food, gifts, and besotted scuba-divers; before, she made 4,000 baht a month for ten exhausting hours a day in an aluminium factory. No contest, really.

Being a service girl is not considered moral turpitude, merely something tiresome and grubby, in fact, low class. A girl with a tattoo, the mark of a prostitute, is unlikely to find a Thai husband, as many find out too late, when past the giddiness of their teens. Marriage, as in Victorian times, is a buyer's market. The respectable ladies consider service girls as we consider, say, lavatory cleaners: everybody has to earn a living, but rather you than me. Unless, reader, you happen to be a lavatory cleaner.

10.   THE WHORROR

Short time: man come, lady go.

There is a pleasing lack of uniformity in the denizens of Soi Saen Sabai, in the centre of which is Henry's Bar, since not all the beery tourists get this far, or know it is there. It is an eclectic shambles of drunks, bar girls, katoeys – or lady boys – and their client/victims, Chinese fortune tellers (the native population of Phuket, like that of other west coast towns, is largely Chinese), limbless beggars on carts, blind beggars playing reedy Thai folk tunes (here's-some-money-just-please-go-away), vendors of flowers, cigarettes and fortunes. I had to run the one-woman gauntlet of the Chinese lady of mature years who had the inexplicable hots for me, and would bawl 'Why you no come sleep with me? I want fuck you! Free! No money!' Inside Henry's Bar there is much the same thing. The street echoes to the thump of overturning giant motorbikes, inversely proportional to their rider's IQ or penis size, rented for huge sums by tattooed nerds who, back home, go to work by bus, or perhaps drive the bus.

The next street is for Thais only. One night there were fracas noises. ('It's only the Thais. Nothing to do with us.') Some oaf in a pool hall had acquired a knife, and was demonstrating his martial arts prowess; in his drunken gyrations, he accidentally slashed the new shirt of another oaf. The slashee went home, got his moped and a shotgun, and returned to blast the slasher into oblivion, making his escape, as is traditional, on his moped, and was caught two blocks away.

On the other side, Soi Sunset is the Heart of Darkness. It is Dante's Inferno, the Valley of the Fallen, the Lust Box of Losers. Here are the legions of the damned, those who have no place else to go when the regular bars close. Two dozen jam-packed bars and discos compete with each other to deafen inmates who sag, loll and shudder in wistful imitation of dancing, or just drink and smile ghastly smiles, avoiding each other's eyes. In these bars, all girls become freelance, so there are no bar fines. Gone is the false jokiness of the box bars, the stupid games of hammering nails into tree trunks, or playing incomprehensible forms of mah jong. No one clings to his moll to show off his new piece of arm candy, no one guffaws and belly laughs or pretends to watch soccer on the hundred unheard TVs.

There are no gawping 'straight' couples, in fact there are no farang women at all. Nobody is pretending to have a good time ... nobody is pretending anything, because if you find yourself in Soi Sunset, you have nobody to blame but yourself. Should you catch the eye of an acquaintance, you cannot grin feebly and say you are enjoying the spectacle, or are just sauntering past on your way to the bakery. There is no past to saunter through, for Soi Sunset is a dead end. Here are the loners, the losers, the drunks and doped-out has-beens and never-weres, those too ashamed of themselves to take a girl back to their room for anything more than the shortest of short times. The short time hotel near Henry's opens 24/7, and all through the wee small hours the couples wait, sheepish or exhausted, for other couples to descend, sheepish or exhausted, and vacate a pleasure palace.

'Five minutes, only five minutes wait,' the boy promises aspiring new lovers, and four minutes is more like it, as one delicious young monosyllable said to me while we waited for our room. And she was right. We waited four and a half minutes. Jeepers, do those chambermaids work fast. A room is stripped and disinfected in less time than a yawn, and you enter a spanking new hotel room fit for the greenest honeymoon couple, except that the bed only has one sheet, and the room shudders with adjacent rock music.

Tourists do actually stay here, booking from far away, and not realising what sort of people have used their rooms up to the minute of their arrival. You see them returning from a late dinner, staring in woozy dismay as they struggle upstairs past the hordes of monosyllables and their beaux, hoping they will not burst into the wrong room by mistake, or perhaps hoping they will. Nobody gets any sleep in the short time mansion, for the Heart of Darkness behind it beats until dawn.

Henry's is a tranquil haven in the midst of all this, and you can drink at his round table of doom, lurch into the Heart of Darkness for an hour or two (or a minute), stagger upstairs in the short time mansion for your four and a half minutes of passion, then, after performing with your selected receptacle, return to the round table for an alcohol breakfast, pretending (and convincing no one) that you have just been for a stroll. In the goldfish bowl of Patong, your every grunt and groan, and the type of farm animal your short time beauty most closely resembles, will be common knowledge on the street, and might even be in tomorrow's paper.

I should say resembled – for she, too, will be past tense, vanished again into the ear-splitting, stinking nightmare of Soi Sunset, to hawk herself for another four and a half minutes to another drink-sodden, lonely wraith. But in your four and a half minutes ... what delight! What burrowing, taupean ecstasy, as you nuzzle and gnaw at selected innards of your sweet thing!

She has stripped off her delectable undies, the padded bra and the two pairs of military police-style panties – always two, as if to keep the cockroaches out – and you have showered. She has, if a good girl, tweaked and rubbed discreetly at your genitals to see that nothing unhygienic is lurking inside, and there you are, naked as jaybirds, writhing and groaning in simulated joy, and both too dog-tired, or drunk, or both, to do anything except get the gruesome but irresistible ritual over with as soon as possible. For once, your intentions are the same as hers! You want to get your sorry ass out of here ASAP, but you feel obliged to put up a show, keep up male honour in general, and, darn it – despite everything – you are curious about her.

It is too much to hope, or even wish, to get to know her, and maybe that is part of the noxious thrill of it all. But, maybe, if you made a lucky pick, she might speak a little English, and you might learn who it is you are proposing to penetrate. It is always the same English. Yes, she has two babies, yes, she works in a beauty salon and sends money home to her mother in Ricepaddyburi; no, she has no regular boyfriend, neither Thai nor farang – and no, she does not like Thai men as they are all pigs.

You try not to laugh – she tries not to laugh. You both know these ritual words must be intoned, as prelude to orgasm. And as you are groping for that essential rubber skin (no wonder Phuket got rich) – strawberry-flavoured, a drunken impulse buy – she smiles at the farang's zany sense of humour, as though she had never even heard of such a giddy toy!

It is the smile of a mercenary panther, yet there is always something glorious in a Thai lady's smile. Whether in play or falsehood or derision, it is as if the sun has just risen, erectively, on you – and in fact the rays peeking through the window indicate it has. There is fumbling, and the semblance of a caress, and she smiles again, maybe half encouraging you to do exotic things to her. Then it is all a sweaty alcoholic blur, and you are a mighty Neanderthal subduing his mate; the shiny banknotes on the table are forgotten, or a mere afterthought, as she is doing all sorts of things that you could not possibly have paid for – for you alone! – and you are a king among men and ... you hear some apeman howling ridiculously, and it is you. The deed is done, you shower and dress, like a schoolboy in haste to reach class. No parting hug. Out the door you hustle, as the chambermaid darts in to fumigate your chamber of passion for the next bout.

Joseph Conrad wrote *Heart of Darkness*, and it was about a man's voyage up an equatorial river, seeking Mr Kurtz, the genius who had become a savage. In his house ringed by skulls, 'Mistah Kurtz, he dead.' The man carries his last words back to Mr Kurtz's beloved in Europe, lying that in his last breath, Mr Kurtz spoke her name. But in fact his last words were: 'The horror! The horror!'

You walk away, vaguely content at lust's sating, and lust's inconsequence. You scarcely remember her, nor she you. Thank goodness for the Heart of Darkness! There is no chance of falling in love in four and a half minutes. Is there? Flaubert declared that a man has not really lived unless he has staggered out of a brothel at dawn, wishing to throw himself in the nearest river. Mistah Kurtz, he dead. The whorror!

11. WHITE MEN CAN JUMP

Falling in 'love' with a Thai beauty is heartbreakingly easy, but not always jolly. After committing love, then seeing their dream vaporise, many farangs commit suicide. If you had never heard the word 'love', would it occur to you to invent it? It doesn't seem to have ever occurred to the Thais. Westerners have been conditioned for 'love', the moment of knowing that past life has been but a dream. Every banality, every vapid myth, is in their emotional baggage. Just waiting for a ruthless Thai goddess: you're the only one for me ... strangers in the night ... I want you only ... let it be me ... The self-centred libido! At last, the real thing, just as in the films and songs and storybooks. Love is exclusive – souls rattling together like two peas in a pod. Mutual possession! That is the logic-defying beauty of love!

The Thai lady assures her beau she will wait for him, while he jettisons his entire life for her, for she loves the hidden beauty he never knew he had. She freely admits that her life has not been 'pure', but the lithe torsos of youth hold no further attractions for her. She has been there and done it all, and with engaging frankness admits it, and is loved for her honesty. Although she is no butterfly herself (the ascending degrees of lubricity being 'butterfly', 'helicopter' and 'skylab'), she understands that a male needs erotic diversion, and claims not to mind ... until she gets him really hooked, for then he is her property, with serious grief for misbehaviour. Of course she wishes to have money, land and a car in her name, and maybe a beauty salon. But material things scarcely count when love conquers all, and 'we' belong 'to each other'!

Thais, and especially demi-mondaines, are above all realistic; if she bounces with another man, it is not that her love is 'untrue', but because she knows her beau will understand in the event her deception is discovered. Anyway, it is all his fault for not giving her enough money. She will mouth the monosyllable 'love' over and over, for incantation convinces. A male with any remnant of sense (although, after five years in paradise, most farang brains have turned to mushy peas) will realise that in her childish, skittishly cruel, and utterly adorable way, the Thai female is right. What matter banknotes when you are happy between her recently vacated thighs? Sex is an event like eating or sleeping. It means no more and no less than a bodily function.

Yet people die for love every day! Even teenage Thai girls, brainwashed into 'love' by TV soap operas. Usually they jump off the tops of buildings, as they cannot afford the appropriate pills. They know they will be reincarnated as a white-skinned princess, so they are not really dying at all; Thai suicide is just an extreme form of nagging. Foreign males also jump, or, in despair, at the end of the road – for where else can you go beyond Thailand? – float away on booze and pills. Another favourite trick is to crash your motorcycle when drunk ... just to show them. There are so many suicides, unreported abroad, though chronicled on the crime page of the local *Pattaya Mail*, *Phuket Gazette* and so on. ('After a fight with his girlfriend, and heavy drinking, with no money left, X fell from his balcony ...') To annhiliate yourself over love for a Thai honeypot, why, it's like plunging because the 7–Eleven has run out of chocolate chip cookies.

Instead of 'relationships', or passions, demi-mondaines have transactions. To love is to suffer? Thais do not like suffering. They prefer pleasure. Foreign males, entwined with the perfect, silky body, long to possess the teenage sugar cake, their heaven incarnate ... long to be part of her, or even be her. Of course that is impossible, and fruitless jealousy and frustration ensue. When the sweat and the stains have been mopped up, 'love' will not make breakfast or fix a drink, or clip fingernails. A Thai lady will – frequently all at the same time – because she knows a valuable property has to be looked after, for which her reward is right here on Earth. There is no sane alternative to pleasure. Jumping is for white men.

12. FUN

The top things in Thailand are *jai dee*, good heart; *sou-ai*, beautiful; and *sanook*, fun. Thais get *sanook* from things which elsewhere would be criminal, life-threatening or insane. That's what foreigners come here for: the fun.

Over the months I hung out at the round table at Henry's Bar, I listened in to the stories. They are proof that all farangs who remain in Thailand are pussy-dazed. Sport is occasionally mentioned – Formula 1 motor racing a real blast – but mostly it's sex, or, if you prefer, relationships. That is, amongst the regulars. There were semi-regulars from out of town, suburban types, who would ostentatiously park their Benzes and look at their watches all the time while hinting at 'business meetings'. The topic of conversation is mostly Thai ladies (venality, deceitfulness, heartbreaking beauty, and irresistibility of). Breathtaking stories of innocent perversion are swapped as casually as football scores. In the pub back home, lads discuss the latest goal; here they discuss the latest orgasm. They are eager to relate how they have been fooled, robbed, married to a girl who was already married, cheated out of their bar/car/ home because the papers were all in her name: like old soldiers displaying their battle scars. Yet still they come back for more.

Soft-spoken English Kevin had just arrived back with pregnant, new Thai lady. His former Thai wife had married him in England, where she was the soul of gentility. In Patong, she reverted to type. His laundry business a few doors down was taken over by the local mafia. Kevin wouldn't give up certain papers; brawling ensued, the cops pursued him to Henry's Bar and demanded these papers, secreted behind the mirror in the loo. An intimate search of his person revealed no papers; it did not occur to them that the first place an Englishman would hide anything would be the lavatory. The cops tired of the thing, and told Kevin not to disturb the peace of Patong again. But Kevin didn't get his laundry back. Now he had built himself a house up in the far northern boondocks, and had a proper girl. It, and she, were different. Thailand was still home.

'You can't beat this place,' he enthused.

There is a foggy, and rather comforting vagueness, about alcohol-fuelled expat yarns, so that you come away with the impression that you have gained some sort of valuable information, without precisely knowing what it is.

'That was the Swedish guy that bought the bar in Soi Katoey, and was living with that woman with the big tits that used to be in Soi Gonzo, wasn't it? And she ran away with his BMW and all his credit cards? About three years ago? And she ended up in jail in Chiang Mai for murdering a Norwegian?'

'Yeah, that's right. Only he wasn't Swedish, he was Swiss, or maybe Australian.'

'She didn't have big tits – you're thinking of the one with long legs.'

'And he wasn't Norwegian.'

'The guy she murdered?'

'I thought he opened another bar – you know, the Blue Pussy, down Soi Eric.'

'No, that was a French guy. Not the one that owns the

swimming pool, the one that had the St Etienne restaurant, before he sold it to Clueless Peter.'

'She didn't murder him, she ran off with his BMW though.'

'No, it was a Shogun. She crashed it.'

'And he didn't have a bar, he had a restaurant on the beach.'

'Who, Clueless Peter? Or the guy she murdered in Chiang Rai?'

'No, the guy that wasn't Swedish.'

'It was Chiang Mai, not Chiang Rai.'

'She was arrested for drunk driving when she crashed the Shogun into a tree.'

'How can you have a beach restaurant in Chiang Mai?'

'You're thinking of that other one, who had the Belgian delicatessen.'

'The bloke she did in? Or stole his Shogun?'

'No, not him, the other one.'

'Which other one? The Swiss one?'

'No, it was a different girl. From the massage parlour, opposite the Holiday Inn. She stabbed that Finnish bloke who used to have the Turtle's Neck bar in Soi Bangla ...'

'Now I remember.'

A definite result is signalled by: 'I saw him the other day in Soi Bangla! With Guenther's ex-girlfriend!'

Wise nods of bleary incomprehension all round.

People wondered where 'Squeeze' was. He was an Aussie of middle age, and legendary sexual exploits and appetites. Retired early from the Australian navy, he was called Squeeze because he liked to be squeezed between two girls at once.

'A fackin bod sandwich,' Fackin Douglas explained.

Squeeze also liked fellatio, and in order to get girls to 'swallow the kids', as he put it, he would successfully persuade them that this ingestion would make their skin whiter. He was reputedly quite rich, in cash-under-the-mattress mode, and sported monogrammed silk underwear. Squeeze's absence suggested that he had been suffocated in one of these macabre combos. Henry averred that he would not die without paying his bar bill. Like all rich people, Squeeze thought that paying cash on the nail was unseemly, and ran tabs everywhere. Or maybe he wasn't rich, and ran tabs to suggest he was, and had done a runner. The Squeeze question was put on hold, though in idle moments it would crop up.

'I wonder where old Squeeze is?'

'You mean where in fackin hell?' Fackin Douglas would say.

I suggested that being squeezed to death by naked women wasn't the worst way to go, citing the late French president Félix Faure, his name honoured by numerous boulevards, and who died of a heart attack while being fellated by a midinette.

'Fackin frogs,' said Fackin Douglas. 'I hate the fackin bastards. One beer and four straws, and they keep the straws to shove up their fackin asses.'

Fackin Douglas was a diabetic, who had to inject himself using syringes and needles, and occasionally got busted by the cops, who thought he was a junkie. He further explained that 'the fruits in fackin Sydney' practised 'felching' in their homosexual orgies.

'All the fackin Poms do it too,' he assured us.

I sarcastically said I assumed that things in Perth were more righteous than sodomitic Sydney: Fackin Douglas being from Western Australia.

'Fackin Perth! That's worse!'

Fackin Douglas, it transpired, was not even from continental Australia at all, but from some offshore island.

'New Guinea,' opined Two-Ton Tony.

Gerry, the burly Dubliner who ran the Irish Bar on the beach road – another jive bar, despite the usual Irish republican decorations, and Celtic cross outside made of Guinness cans – suggested that you could get a bod sandwich at Kristin Massage, sure it's aisy enough, if you were willing to part with the cash.

'Not,' he added hastily, 'that I've done it myself, mind you.'

Cries of 'oo-hoo'.

'I've been inside the bar,' he explained carefully, 'just to look. You go into this darkened bar, and look at all these motts with numbers on their skirts, and sitting behind a big glass window, and you pick a number, and go into a hotel room with air-con and all, and she gives you the business, a hundred per cent. They say you come out of there feeling like a new man.'

'Sir Mervyn always feels like a new man.'

Sir Mervyn, for reasons of parsimony, lived in a cheap guest house in Vaseline Alley, amongst the gayboys.

'Yanks go there to have fackin bananas shoved up their ass,' declared Fackin Douglas.

'You mean Vaseline Alley?'

'No, Kristin fackin Massage.'

Fackin Douglas was obviously an authority on all things anal, and I felt my own expertise to be modest. Nevertheless, I sensed that my input on Félix fackin Faure established me as a man of learning and, incipiently, one of the lads. No one ever admits to using uber-expensive Kristin Massage, but everybody knows somebody who knows somebody who went there. The name is constantly invoked, like a holy of holies: 'You can always go to Kristin Massage' – 'I've half a mind to try Kristin Massage' – 'One of these days –' etc. I put Kristin Massage on the mental back burner. One of these days ...

Pat, from Devon, feisty and fortyish, opened a chic little guest house and restaurant up the street from Henry's. A cordon bleu cook, she had grand schemes of a different plat du jour every day, pressed duckling with wild rice and herbs or something, to attract the gourmets of Patong. Her husband was toiling in Saudi Arabia as an engineer, and she had quit the dusty kingdom to come to Thailand to be near her laddish son, Leon or Alphonse, one of those sort of names, who ran a bar in Bangkok along with his Thai wife. Meanwhile her daughter, a one-parent family, stayed in the bijou family cottage outside Plymouth, bringing up her young son, of uncertain paternity, with no visible means of support. They all came to visit at one time: the husband, a nice, rather bemused soul, the bar-owning son amiably boozy and thuggish, the daughter a vamp, fond of reading pornography. They were the modern non-nuclear family. There was also Pat's mum, a dear old soul in a wheelchair, much disgusted with the hookers traipsing up and down outside, or sometimes inside, her daughter's abode, and the Burnts who associated with them.

'Why do they pay them?' she wailed, uncomprehending.

'Well, they don't work for nothing,' I replied, adding to the incomprehension.

I hung around because Pat was good company, and, familiar with her neck of the woods, I could tell Plymouth jokes in a Plymouth accent. Of course, it was soon inaccurately rumoured in Soi Mai Sabai that Pat and I were a romantic item. Also hanging around was a youthful lesbian from Yorkshire called Dilys, because her live-in lesbian girlfriend, Noot, worked as Pat's waitress, and the jealous Dilys wanted to keep an eye on her. Not without reason; Noot was no more a lesbian than she was Queen of Sheba, and flirted outrageously with the male customers and guests, sometimes sneaking off to a guest's room for a short time. Pat was in the unhappy dilemma of many hotel-keepers in Thailand, attracting a horde of deadbeats, frequently of smelly personal habits, who occupy a room but can't pay for it until some mythical cheque arrives, so that they cannot afford to leave, and she cannot afford to throw them out. Clever Trevor was one such, aiming to make it big in computers, discussing a half interest in some crappy bar, the usual nonsense, meanwhile holed up with his Thai girlfriend, fighting and bouncing and living on beer and crusts.

Dilys owned a house up the street, and had some sort of business, making tie-dyed T-shirts or whatever. Her presence in turn attracted Fascinating Frank, the Norwegian, who had the hots for her. Frank, who also had a house up the road, and a house in Norway, would show you the photo album illustrating the progress of his garden shed overlooking some fjord, a photo taken for every plank nailed, and describe in excruciating detail the ancient Norwegian art of building sheds. He was a fisherman, fishing the fockin big prawns. Except he wasn't actually a fisherman, he was a cabin steward. Nor was he really a Norwegian, because Norwegians said they couldn't understand what he said. He didn't come from Norway proper, but from Spitzbergen, the Arctic coal-mining island. Frank would burble on about not much, fascinating everyone to death, while he aimed lecherous leers at Dilys the lesbian, and ignored the glamorous Noot, who would drop her panties for sixpence. No one had the heart to tell him that Dilys was a lesbian, and off the menu, until I did.

'No, she is not,' he said. 'I can tell. She fancies me.'

I disagreed.

'Well, then, she is only pretending to be a lesbian, to make me jealous.'

In fact, apart from the bit about fancying him, Fascinating Frank was probably not far wrong. Dilys was on the rebound from some failed marriage and, having read the right-on feminist literature, had decided to be a lesbian.

'All that fackin bitch needs is a tube steak up her cunt,' was the judgement of Fackin Douglas.

It was continually frustrating to her that Noot did not take the thing seriously, did not act like a lesbian, and whatever obscure caresses they exchanged, Noot, like a good Thai hooker, was only doing it for the money. The whole scene was fakery built on fakery. T.I.T. Eventually, disappointed with the reaction to her cuisine, i.e. none, Pat gave up and started to bake meat pies, which were such an instant success, she took to supplying other bars with them. Eventually, she gave up the guest house and restaurant too, and just hustled pies for a living.

Much later, when I was in Henry's Bar, Fascinating Frank dawdled up, after several months' absence. I was sitting at the same place on the table of doom that I had occupied during his last visit, when he had entertained us with an explanation of why Norwegian matchsticks were much better than Swedish matchsticks. Now, he asked:

'Are you still here since the last time you were here?'

'Yes, Frank. I couldn't have put it better myself.'

'Do you not find that after a long time in Thailand, the brain gets sleepy?'

'Yes, Frank.'

Meanwhile, for several months, I continued to use, more or less mindlessly, girls of the centrefold class. I began to get disconcerting cries of 'dahling!' as I wandered Soi Bangla. Was this one I had had, or one who wished me to have her, or the girlfriend of one I had had? One night, bored, I took a girl back to the hotel, more out of a feeling of duty than anything else – I was here to have 'fun', wasn't I? She was a sweet young honeypot, fresh off the bus from Cabbageville, and gave me the whole shy schoolgirl modesty trip, locking the bathroom door when showering alone, then turning the lights out. Then, in bed, she draped herself in a towel. I undraped her; she redraped, moaning. This reverse striptease continued for a while. I was unstimulated. Is she, I thought petulantly, a bar girl or not? I mean, why does she think she's here? I paid her something, and told her politely that I wasn't in the mood. She got out, shy and indifferent, as if we had just bounced the ceiling down. Most farangs have had this experience and, on encountering shyness, asked the question, well what are you doing in a bar, then? Poor things, they are driven by necessity, and dumped into the maelstrom by their parents.

It was 3 a.m. I was disconsolate, as this had been my first unsatisfactory experience. I wandered out into the cross-roads of Soi Bangla. The discos were blaring in the Heart of Darkness as the unbounced bar girls traipsed in; the noodles were steaming, the girls were squawking happily, and the beer-bellies were dancing the boogaloo, clutching their bottles of Heineken. Everybody, it seemed, was having fun except me. Should I venture into Soi Nightmare for a rematch? No! I didn't want any fun! Fun sucks! I wished I knew where that damn Porn stayed. Just so she'd be no fun, either. Suddenly, I heard my name called. It was Porn, shimmering in the night, sitting alone with a plate of noodles. I took her arm and, without a word, steered her towards my hotel. Rolf, comatose over his umpteenth nightcap at his open-air bar, nodded in wistful envy. She asked me why I was laughing. I said, thank you, God.

13. AU REVOIR, PORN

I slept with Porn for the next two nights. Daytimes, she would go off on her own, no doubt to turn further tricks; she did not relish the idea of being arm candy, like some bar girl. I didn't care, as long as I could run my coarse farang paws over that bottom as she slept in the moonlight, while she unconsciously garrotted me. She had sparse down on her pubic mound; when I suggested she shave it, to stop hairs getting in an admirer's mouth, she went to the bathroom and came out gleaming bare and, next evening, turned up wearing split-crotch panties and fishnet stockings. In Thailand, home of bashful modesty! My worship knew no bounds. Insane with self-delusion, I felt that I knew her now; was familiar with her little quirks and foibles. As she must be with mine ...

Like many Thai girls, Porn understood more English than she let on. When an unwelcome question is posed, 'Not speak English!' saves face. Of course, at first, like everything else in Thai ladies, this seems charming and coy. Such laughs you get from these amusing misunderstandings! When she said I was nice, not like ski, I was puzzled, and thought she meant some farang swine had inflicted water-skiing on her at the beach. Ski came up again, only this time, at my enquiry, she frowned, shook her head, said 'not speak more', and it dawned on me that Ski was a person – Norwegian, Swiss, somewhere ski-infested perhaps. Apparently Ski had been too sexually offbeat. I bought her trinkets, the traditional fake watch (she had hundreds, of course); took her to restaurants; could this be lurve? Somehow, I kidded myself, she was, just a tiniest bit, in my power – or, even more deliciously, she enjoyed having me in hers. I dreamed that Porn was 'mine'. Or a mine. Banging, knocking, shafting, rooting ... digging for entry. Somebody has to possess somebody, grub out the pleasure. Porn was great, and I am sure still is, because in her smiling, gap-toothed beauty she cured me quickly and painlessly of she's-differentism and all the afflictions of the romantic farang heart. She had to go back to Bangkok on some obscure mission involving noodles, or T-shirts, and, no doubt, boyfriends. I had her phone number and address.

When I first visited red-light Patpong in Bangkok, bang opposite (as it were), on the main Silom Road, was a branch of a well-known English retailer, as on every British high street. What were they doing here? Scouring the *Bangkok Post* (a local, already!), I came across interviews with starry-eyed eurosuits whose supermarket decided the time was right 'for expansion in Asia' with Thailand as their hub. Always retail: nobody seemed to want to manufacture anything in Thailand, although in Malaysia you see the huge plants of Siemens, Bosch, etc. Even Thai cigarettes come from Malaysia.

Granted, the Thais spend a lot, and Thailand is relatively stable. Granted further that billions of sex-starved geezers come to spend their money. But what about Hong Kong, Singapore, Taiwan, all filthy rich? Japan, for heaven's sake. Thailand the hub of Asia? The core of Asian retailing? Lord Suit, the chairman of the company, was visiting Thailand at that time, and predicted over a hundred stores open in two years and, by then, the chain should be trading at a profit! Thailand was not, in fact, the core of their Asian activities, but their only Asian activity. Lord Suit was thinking of 'possibly' opening a store in Japan. I looked at his beaming face, and thought, I know what you're up to ...

All those solemn suits in their dank homelands, poring over spreadsheets, and drooling towards the eminently logical conclusion that the ramshackle Kingdom of Smiles is the perfect business venue! And all thinking of the same thing – luscious brown girls. Just the place for lots of high-level fact-finding missions. A few years later, the company sheepishly announced the closure of most of their stores.

One night at Henry's I stayed up till dawn drinking and talking with Gino from Fremantle, the laid-back Aussie, who came up to Patong for a week every now and then for a bit of golf and sex, nothing strenuous. He told of the street riots by the outraged Fremantle males when the pussy-hungry US Navy was in town, so that, for a while, US sailors were barred from going onshore. We agreed that it was so much better in Thailand, where dudes cheerfully sent their girlfriends out to sleep with whoever they could snare, and bring back the cash. I was still gushing on about how fabulous Thai girls were, and all the wonderful bedroom things you could do with them.

'Yeah, it's true,' drawled Gino, 'but you know, mate, sometimes don't you just want to take a break, and nip outside for a smoke?'

My moment of vérité.

'You're right,' I gasped, horrified. 'You're absolutely right.'

Gino told me of the time a friend asked him to 'look after the missus' while he was absent for a couple of weeks. She was a luscious Thai girl, hot, and apparently willing, but Gino obeyed the code of mateship and left her unsullied. When his friend returned, there was a squawking match and they both turned on Gino. 'What sort of a mate are you? Two fackin weeks, and you didn't give her one!' Turned out she was a hooker from the gold-miners' pubs in Kalgoorlie. Gino felt mortified, although I opined that this was perhaps carrying Australian mateship a bit far.

I went back to the box bars and there I met Wing. At the time I was 'partying' with Jimmy, a ring-a-ding ding good ole boy from the USS *Winnebago* or something, about to finish fifteen years of duty. He now makes lots of money selling Fords to the Ford-hungry of San Diego. Jimmy had been through two Filipina wives, been in every girly bar in the world, thought life was a party and we (the Americans) should nuke everybody. He loved the nail game and the tile game, and all the fun in the bars. He had a cutie named Chew and, rather than take her back to his hotel for prompt bouncing, he had to drag her round other bars to party. I was a draggee, really, because Jimmy thought it refreshing to find somebody who could speak English.

Chew was a real honeypot, and Jimmy described their couplings in graphic and unwanted orgasmic detail. After only one night together, Chew was already 'special'. Jimmy went back to San Diego and took his golden handshake from the US Navy; then I began to get these really sad letters from my all-American buddy. He was lonely, pining away without his honey, his little Chew that he loved so much. He would send me money: would I rent a house and put her in it, and give her enough money so she could stay chaste, and not have to bounce for a living? Would I please give her these photos and letter to remind her of her own true special love, while Jimmy would busy himself getting her a US visa, to marry him ...

I dutifully went to Chew's bar and gave her the photos and messages, and she smiled in that embarrassment of a Thai caught unasleep. Only by the photographs could she even remember Jimmy, and then only as some vague phantom. I wrote several times to Jimmy, each letter less diplomatic than the last, to the effect that he had rocks in his head, or had been smoking too much Mexican dope. Did he not realise that he was in California, seething with *Baywatch* babes? That Chew was a bar girl with a capital B, who had enjoyed half the US Navy before Jimmy's arrival, and the other half since his departure? Eventually my logic struck home, and Jimmy thanked me for my brutal wisdom. He had discovered a singles bar in San Diego, whence he had obtained the bouncing favours of a couple more – Americanised – Thai ladies.

'It's OK now, I know how warped they all are ...'

But that took place after I started living with Wing as my concubine, about six months into my Thai saga. At the bar, she was fending off some geezer with gold chains; Jimmy was playing nail games. I watched and, thinking myself James Bond, waited for her to ditch the goldy character. She did! I congratulated myself on my fantastic telepathic power of seduction. Wing was older than the other girls, without the careless T-shirted look that a nineteen-year-old affects. She was dressed to kill – European-elegant, too good for the sleazy box bar ...

She was different!

I took her back to my hotel and she sort of raped me, or so, to my delight, it seemed. Then she settled down to a good night's sleep, which lasted most of the next morning, too. I was charmed! This was the real Thailand! Not some bimbo who wanted to go to discos and dance, but a solid country girl – beneath all the warpaint – who wanted nothing more than to stuff her face with food and then settle down to a nourishing 24-hour sleep, leaving me valuable quality time to read a book. But Wing was satisfying – she liked all the things I liked, because I liked them!

'Up to you! You happy, Wing happy.'

You can do worse than hearing that from a female person. So Wing stayed with me for the next few days until I had to go back to London for a week. In the meantime, I rented an apartment in Patong, and went away with the keys to my new home in my pocket. Wing was definitely a concubine possibility, but I had plans for Porn ... insane with egoism, I figured I was king of the hill: two eager females to choose from, my toys, to do with as I liked! You always want to have your cake and eat it, yet, with plenty of cash in Patong, enough to enjoy a different monosyllable every night, you still feel the urge to bond with just one, who gets to know how you like your breakfast. Power! Then, of course, the town is all yours for 'extra' ... that male ego.

Thankfully, Porn knocked me off the heap, politely and efficiently, when we got together again in Bangkok, as I was en route for London. We did all the things she liked, without sloppy kissing, though, for which I was relieved. Thais do not kiss, which is unhygienic, instead they smell each other's hair, and say 'hom'. Meaning fragrant. A Thai girl who kisses (where have those lips been?) has learned it from American movies, to please the knuckle-draggers, or else from the knuckle-draggers.

I tremulously invited her to shack up with me in my new apartment, and I would look after her baby daughter and all ... was I ever noble.

'No! Ha! Ha! (or Ha! Ha! No!) – I be bored dead in one week,' said Porn.

As she slept I was vastly thankful. Had I really been such a dope as to say the farang things? Lurve, and all? Yes, I suppose I had. And Porn, bless her honest little heart and silky bouncing bottom, had not done what a Patong girl would do: move in, drain your bank account, then move out. But then Porn was classy, a Bangkok girl. Rather later, after my return from London, Wing moved in with me. Or rather, she just, sort of, didn't move out. There were no trembling declarations, nothing heartfelt: just breakfast, washing clothes, gymnastics, and a lot of sleep. Permanent summertime, where the living is easy. She had a big bottom, too.

In the meantime, I went back to London, and explained I was decamping to Thailand. London was full of beautiful, but oddly awkward women. They never seemed to smile.

'What the fuck do you want to live there for?' said the landlord of my local pub.

'What the fuck do you want to live here for?' I said.

Everybody who stays here has a similar story: the gaping disbelief and incomprehension of friends and family, that you could just up sticks and leave, to settle somewhere hot and cheap and sexy. How irresponsible! I imagine Columbus heard the same when he set off for India the wrong way. But if you think out of the box, it's easy to liberate yourself from the familiar paraphernalia, from things. Just do it. I didn't stop to reflect and, five days later, I was back in Patong. Home!

14. WING

Wing was there in the bar, waiting for me! I was jet-lagged and starry-eyed.

'Good luck for me!' she said, adding that she had just that afternoon said goodbye to some 'Australia man' who had vowed the usual eternal love.

She said this with the same big smile as when she announced the contents of her stomach: 'Wing eat three times today!' 'Wing eat five times today!' 'Wing make poo today!' – knowing I would share her joy. Packaging is the thing: everything neat, easily defined, tactile, whether chicken feet, soup, or boyfriends. This Switzerland man, this Sweden man! Eat! Make poo! Simple! Wing showed me a photo of her Australia man.

'Have company, big money,' she said brightly.

Charming innocence, to show your swain the photo of the swain just departed.

'Australia same America?' Wing asked.

'No,' I said, 'not same – long way across sea,' and she frowned, so I made hand language, which meant, 'It's sort of the same.'

I was, however, not the fervent farang any more, I was Joe
Cool. Wing could pick and choose, hey, so could I. So she
came back to my new apartment, promptly began exhaustive
housework, unpacking and tidying, and I had the unnerving
feeling that she already lived there, especially after a trip to the
market for essential household items I must not be without,
such as nail polish, shampoo, and skin whitening cream. She
stayed on, I think, because it did not occur to either of us that
she should do anything else. I still felt rich.

Wing did not comment on my arriving home at 7 a.m., and
so I thought it ungentlemanly to mention her own arrivals at
the same time. She never complained about lack of money ...

Actually, it was rather amusing to be living with a real working
girl, who did not want me to suffer the embarrassment of being
a cheap charlie, and so nobly went out and earned her keep.
What a lucky guy I was ... and, actually, I was. For Wing, it
was just work. She could have ditched me any time for some
loot-loaded German, but didn't. After a while, she realised my
ghoulish comedian's interest in her cavortings, and would leak
a few details: have German man, Belgium man. I was getting
sloppy seconds, a buttered bun. However, I was a pimp, living
off immoral earnings! I had a certain arrogance of ownership
at sending Wing out to 'work'. She liked the glitz and the noise
of the bar, and playing these stupid games, and chattering to
her friends, and maybe (dutiful prayers to Buddha, and King
Rama IV of the 104 concubines) 'good luck', and a nice farang
banknote. She had two daughters to support, up in Nong Kai,
next to Laos. Wing spoke Lao, like most people in Nong Kai,
and was very embarrassed about this; a distant dialect of Thai,
it sounds crude and unschooled to Thai ears. It also gave me the
equally arrogant assurance that Wing was with me because she
wanted to be, and not because I was her money tree. There were
no stories of hair-raising oriental orgies, no Caligulan excesses
with porn star studs. I was not permitted the agonies of jealousy.

Wing insisted that I was free to have a *mia noi*, 'little wife',
on the side, like most Thai men, and, like most Thai women,

assumed I had. But if she playfully asked what I had been doing until 7 a.m., I found that a mumble of 'Bar Henry' served all deflective purposes. Thais are determinedly nosy, and instead of saying 'hello', they say 'where you going?' And you are expected to answer. So you say 'supermarket' or something. Thai ladies want to know about your little wife, because they want to know how much money you have spent on her. If you insanely admit to having paid another girl, she will demand extra.

'You go lady short time ... you go Kristin Massage, is OK!'

Everybody seemed to venerate Kristin Massage as an icon of depravity.

The months went past, and we were comfortable with each other. Wing took off a few times, for a week, with some unbelievable story of visiting her family, and I didn't complain. She came back punctually, and I would admit that I had missed her so much that I had been impelled by my vast virility to have 'other ladies short time', or even 'little wife' during her absence. That was OK – as long as I was not 'broken heart' ... and use condom.

A stupid farang grieves that his girlfriend is lying to him. Why worry? It is her function to tell lies, just as it is her function to bounce. And she is going to do what she wants, no matter what you say, or how much you give her. In fact, she is paying you a compliment, by lying to save your face. You might as well return the compliment. Unlike our culture, it's unhypocritical hypocrisy. Wing told me, matter-of-factly, how she came to be a hooker, and I established that this story was true. Her husband had died of cancer, and she had nursed him through his final days, spending all their money on medicine, and when he died, she had no money left, so had to become a prostitute. At first she was very shy, but gradually got used to it. I felt pretty cheap, listening to her.

After a while, it became understood that Wing did not have to make up stories about her absences of a few days. In fact, I preferred her to say she had 'met' some ageing guenther. She liked helping safe old geezers enjoy their holidays, dragging her to scenic Ko Samui or Ko Phi Phi, the 'James Bond' island. If one seemed unusually obnoxious, she would play the 'have boyfriend' card, and actually offload him on to one of the younger girls, for Wing, a fervent housekeeper, liked to see everybody organised. If she was staying with a geezer for a few days, she would lie to him that she was visiting girlfriends, and come to the apartment every afternoon, to make my meals, do the housework, and check, I supposed, for signs of extra female tenancy. She bought, and paid for, all my food, drink, the newspaper – I didn't even have to leave home. She also came back for a bounce, because she got fed up giving oldsters a *chak wao* – 'flying a kite', or hand job. Farangs always suspect their girls of feeding a clandestine Thai boyfriend. To my horror, I had become a Thai boyfriend.

I took up with a *mia noi*, 'little wife', a freelance named Suk, whom I met in the street (no bar fine!) for an official whole two weeks of Wing's absence 'honnabeach' somewhere. Suk moved in, and moved out again, punctually, the day before Wing's return. She did not wish to see my steady lady – not that I suggested she should – lest there be 'boxing'.

Suk was great, a 27-year-old hottie, nymphomaniac, and maniac generally. Instead of shortening 'Pornsuk' to 'Porn', she shortened it to 'Suk', equally tee-hee I suppose. She was tall, thin, bony: big bottom, narrow waist, hard conic breasts. She lived in some little box apartment, which cost her a staggering sum, a tenth of my own rent. That, she explained, was why she was always broke. She 'worked' when the mood took her, and had not the slightest idea how much she made in a month, nor what she was going to do with her life a year, or a minute, in the future. She drank when there was drink, but didn't do drugs. She enjoyed the Japanese porno channel on TV, but complained that the Thai TV censored out the naughty bits, which was 'bullshit'. Suk enthusiastically used 'all holes' as she put it. 'No bullshit' ...

She had the usual sackful of letters from 'Italy man', 'Germany man', 'Sweden man' etc., all of whom wanted to marry her and take her back to live in frosty European splendour. She couldn't make her mind up: were they sincere, or talking bullshit? Were they secretly cheap charlies, a species for which she had a morbid detestation? Being a 'sexy lady' was so confusing ...

When I met her I suggested bar-hopping, and that we might go to the Irish Bar. She made a horrible face of disgust and cried 'Irish Bar! No!' with stabbing motions.

I realised she had understood Alice Bar, Alice being at the time under house arrest for allegedly persuading her lover to commit suicide by stabbing himself forty times. With leaden facetiousness, I said I hoped she wasn't going to kill me.

'No, no,' she assured me very earnestly, patting my wrist, 'I not kill.'

She said this as though expressing a preference for white wine over red: it would be perfectly normal to kill me, she just chose not to. Suk was completely illiterate, but street-smart, and could speak quite good American English, picked up from sailors she met at the Banana Disco. When she first arrived at my apartment, she went straight to the kitchen and rearranged everything, including the contents of the fridge. Everything was replaced somewhere else, moved from A to B. Having ascertained that Wing was from the Isaan, she announced what useless housekeepers Isaan women were, Suk herself being from Bangkok. Apart from that, she replaced the calendar featuring the king's portrait at the head, rather than the end, of the bed. In Thailand it is a grave mark of disrespect to point your feet at anyone, especially a revered figure, and I supposed it was even more disrespectful to have him watch your arse pumping up and down.

Suk and I had a pleasant two weeks; she departed, richer, and I saw her again a few times, going back to her shoebox apartment for a short time, although I did not wish her to reassume the status of 'little wife' – and nor did she wish to be thus reassumed, as such things were 'bullshit'. On Wing's return, I did indeed, under interrogation, admit I had had a temporary little wife, for her occupancy of the kitchen was obvious.

She said she had not been to Ko Samui or similar, but to Germany! She had always wanted to see Europe, and accepted the guenther's offer of a holiday up in the dunes and pines, in Schleswig-Holstein somewhere. She was afraid I would be angry, bless her heart, and not let her go, so I assured her to the contrary with much loving attention.

Then she showed me her holiday snaps, and it made me all nostalgic for good old Europe. There was one poignant photo of Wing, that plucky girl, all alone on a vast sandy beach, looking out at the grey Baltic. You could almost smell the dunes, and the sea grasses, and salt spray. So Effi Briest ... It made me feel sad, and wish I had Guenther-type riches, to make her life happy. But you look at all the Thais, smell their glorious food and adore their glorious beauty, and they are happier, in their strange way, than you can ever be. Your heart aches that you can never be one of them. It's easy to feel homesick in this life, but Thailand is the only place I know for which you can be homesick while you are still there.

All business, Wing reversed the *mia noi* procedure, rushing into the kitchen and arranging everything all over, back from B to A, then expunging every trace of Suk – a rearranged cushion, a shifted chair – from the apartment. When I said that Suk came from Bangkok, Wing assured me that Bangkok women were rotten housekeepers. Neither girl ever expressed the slightest interest in whatever gymnastics I had been up to. There was no 'Was she prettier than me?', 'How big her bottom?' etc. A Thai lady accepts that other women are desirable, and it does not concern her. She is only worried about her own prettiness, her own bottom. It was perfectly normal that in Wing's professional absence, I would require another girl to 'take care me'. Both ladies were concerned that I was, or was not, being properly fed, and looked after, like a water buffalo, or watered, like a money tree.

Mind you, such lack of jealousy is far from the norm. Penis severance while asleep is a common fate of the errant. This happened to an unfortunate Bangkok police captain, amongst others, whose ever-loving spouse drugged his soup and gave him the snip while he slept. Awaking in agony, he rushed to the hospital, where they know all about both snip and unsnip, while his police colleagues grilled his wife as to where she had dumped the meat, obviously necessary for the unsnip. She held up under questioning, and refused to talk, but kept looking at her watch. When exactly three hours had passed, she leered, and indicated the appropriate refuse bin, where they retrieved the conjugal penis. But by then it was too late. The wife knew that after three hours, unsnip is impossible.

On that disagreeable note, I shall mention another cause of dismay, which is the annual April 'water-throwing festival' known as Song Kran. This originally lasted two days, and was a religious ceremony, designed to encourage the rains to come. People trickled little cups of water over family and friends, and it was all very delicate and nice. I experienced it once, in Patong, when Wing paraded me round town to be decorously sprinkled by her bar-girlfriends, with much giggling and *wais*, and it was pleasant, in the traditional spirit of the thing. But that was the day before the festivity officially started. It now stretches to a week – nine awful days in Pattaya – and has become a water war, the streets being infested with hideous tattooed hairy-backs armed with water pistols like machine guns, who spend twelve hours in a plane just to knock people off their bikes and make everyone miserable. I mean, get a life!

Thai hooligans patrol the streets in pick-up trucks, equipped with barrels of water and hoses with which they soak the hapless. It doesn't matter if you are a mum taking her baby to hospital, you get soaked just the same. Then they fire bombs of face powder. The thing is scary and manic. Everyone is drunk, and road fatalities approach 1,000 for that week. A few years ago, a cop in Pattaya was faced with a hooligan carrying a giant water pistol. The cop was carrying his baby, and told the hooligan to back off. The hooligan squirted, and the cop shot him dead. Verdict: justifiable self-defence. Hooray.

Wing and I once saw a young fellow in his business suit getting soaked and splattered – *mai pen rai! sanook!* – and punching his assailants, and Wing was on the side of the hooligans. Song Kran makes you despair of Thais and, even more so, of white people. You think, Thailand has no culture. Then you visit back home, see the horrors of trash western life, and think, what about ours? Reality TV, debt, obesity, poisoned food, random slayings, raving loonies on the streets, and the 'war on terror'. Sixteen per cent of Brits told pollsters they would like Elton John to sing at their funeral. How soon do the assholes want to die? Have we corrupted Thailand with materialism, greed, hatred, folly? Well, no. Evil and stupidity are not the monopoly of white men. Song Kran is fun, the morons squeal. Yeah.

15. MONEY

In western society, money is mysteriously equated with work, thrift or acumen. If you work eighteen hours a day you will possibly make more money than if you work four hours a day. If you are very smart, and double-click your computer with panache, you can theoretically make millions on the money markets. In every case, a certain amount of input is required from the person enjoying the largesse. In Thailand this equation is absent: money arrives as a result of good luck. There is no western work ethic: here, 'work' means back-breaking labour in the rice paddy. Gambling, even on private premises, is outlawed in a country where gambling is the national sport, precisely because it is the national sport. All along the border, a few metres into Cambodia, there are huge Thai-owned casinos, where Thais go to lose their shirts, and, since most of them have no passports, the casino bosses obligingly cut holes in the border wire, so they can sneak through unmolested.

A lady friend won several thousand baht at cards. Four of

them were playing; another had won a lesser sum. I asked who, then, had lost money.

'The bank,' she replied.

Impossible to explain that in a four-person game where two people win, it follows that two people must have lost. There was no celestial 'luck bank' to take the fall. Yet in their hearts, they know that is where money comes from. The farang has a head start because white skin is already evidence of money, good luck, or virtue in a past incarnation. Hence the obsession with lethal 'skin-whitening' creams, which, after repeated use, make a face look as if it has been dipped in emulsion paint; TV bombards the audience with actors who are as white as possible, and children of mixed Thai-farang unions are prized. Many Thai ladies marry farangs simply because they want designer babies, for success.

There is no point in showing off possessions, in the brand-name fatuity of the west; it is assumed you have them, flaunted or not. Thai ladies do not care about brand names, because in Thailand they are probably all fake; only a Thai wants to wear a real gold Rolex watch. Gold should adorn a lady's person, and a farang should keep his money in an ATM for her to get at.

A Thai lady is unimpressed by your achievements, qualifications, your big car or hideous motorbike; these things are a given, whereas a Thai man must display them, otherwise he is a nobody, without 'face'. It does not matter if you, a farang, own a dozen companies or speak a dozen languages, or are a professor at Oxford. Even a bus driver is unimaginably rich by her standards, as is anybody who can afford to travel in an aircraft. She simply assumes you have money and, whether it is a million or a billion, it is still science fiction to her. The main point is that you spend it on her. You are, refreshingly, taken at face value, rather than for your 'background'. She is only interested in your foreground. Pale skin and bulging wallet are all the face a farang needs. A Thai lady establishes whether he has a good heart or not, and is not too repulsive to contemplate bouncing with. If he can make her laugh, is not too drunk, opens his wallet at regular intervals, and does not slap her around – or not much – so much the better. That is all she asks, and it is nice to be liked for your immediate self, not for your status. There is no soul, no special 'I' – you are what you possess, do, or look like.

Once, during my two years' concubinage with Wing, an Australian lady friend, met on nudist-friendly Naxos, came to stay, vivacious and fortyish, with grey hairs, and who liked to be naked. This in itself was an object of fascination, but it really stunned the modest Thai ladies that she did not dye her long tresses black.

'I am me,' she explained, 'you take me as I am.'

Nobody understood. How could you be anything, without clothing and jewellery? Nor did they understand that I could sit there unconcernedly, without signs of arousal. Wing's bar-girlfriends would sit on the floor, goggle-eyed, placidly chewing fish, leaves, raw onions, mangos and other healthy things doused in chilli peppers, and gazing at a naked European body, while my Australian friend, herself a rich retired call girl from Queensland's gold coast, would have cosy chats about their common profession, with advice to the mystified Thais about buying property, stocks and bonds. The boyfriend of sweet little Foon, of whom more later, would hover at the door to make sure Foon wasn't getting up to mischief, but refused invitations to join the party. If he espied a nude woman, I was told, he would automatically get an erection, which would cause him to lose face.

After a while, a farang realises that he is just a penis with a wad of money attached, no different, in fact, from being dignified as 'breadwinner'. Thai ladies are not hypocritical about it. The more thoughtful farangs reason that, while they may be just another fish in the sea, at least they are in the sea. And yet, every day, girls receive letters from Europe in fractured English, promising and demanding eternal love and devotion, recalling the good times (i.e., bouncing) which were so special, and how can Pim or Om stand her lover's absence 10,000 km away?

Shown these letters, I am asked to translate the untranslatable, usually summarised as 'farang big love Pim, broken heart not see she'. And from the envelope, hopefully, falls a banknote of large denomination. Once the sender has been identified, by means of a photo album, or, more normally, left a mystery ('Sweden man? Gerramany man?'), the banknote is pocketed and whisked to the moneychanger, with the letter frequently trashed unread.

An outgoing letter may explain that she is unable to wait and marry Guenther, or come to live in Bremen, Swansea, Adelaide or Omaha, because 'I have boyfriend' (surprise), but there is no mention of returning the banknote, indeed no thank you – any more than you would thank the ace of spades for turning up in your poker hand. The banknote is hers by right, part of her unassailable patrimony. It is her due. And as Guenther is dimly aware, it is his way of making merit, his *tambun*, his offering a duck to the monks for good luck.

And yet ... you know, you just know, as surely as night follows day, that tomorrow the banknote will be history, as though it had never existed. It does not matter if it is for $100 or $1 million: it is a law of physics that a Thai lady cannot hang on to money. No one knows what she has done with it; she does not know. She lends it to her friends; she loses it at cards, she buys something (anything) for herself, or for somebody else; she gives it to the monks for *tambun*. One thing she does not do is deposit it in the bank, or, if she does, she promptly takes it all out again, to show off her shiny new toy, an ATM card. Ask almost any demi-mondaine how much she makes in a good, average or poor month and she cannot tell you. All she knows is that she is currently broke.

A girl I knew in Patong was given $5,000 by a lovelorn Dutchman to go back to her home village and 'stay pure' till his next visit. It took her six whole days to lose the lot at cards, something of an endurance record. A ladyboy who got

$1,000 to buy herself an air ticket to Frankfurt, and join her paramour, played the whole lot away in a single evening. A girl with whom I spent an agreeable few nights was met by chance at the taxi stand, late at night. All she had in the world was one taxi fare to the Banana Disco. She had spent her last few hundred baht buying a duck for the monks, for good luck. Would it not, I suggested, have been wiser to retain the money until a customer had added to it, thus ensuring she could eat? Then she could afford the duck by way of thank you. Why no – it worked, because you came along! There is no untwisting the Moebius strip of Thai lady logic, and it always leaves you with the curious feeling that you have been wrong-footed. You cannot dent that loop.

The same girl proved very fond of bouncing in all imaginable ways, and a good cook too. We were relaxing by watching the half-witted late-night Japanese porno channel on cable TV, on which the Thai censor fuzzes out the naughty bits (front taboo, rear OK). This annoyed her, as she wanted to see what a Japanese pussy looked like – she was already familiar with the male Japanese organ. One episode featured a faceless lady on a bed alone, masturbating.

Thai Lady: What she doing?

Me: Uh, make self come, with hand.

Thai Lady: Why?

Me: She not have man.

Thai Lady: Why not?

Me: Uh ... Japan lady not same Thai lady.

Here was a twenty-year-old serious nymphomaniac lush, adept at every erotic art, and sincerely hor-nee, who had never heard of female masturbation. Why, on reflection, should she have? She had probably been bouncing since she could breathe. Yet, despite her pneumatic prowess, she had no money. It is the great Thai mystery: Thai ladies are obsessed with money, they will scrounge and beg and whinge quite shamelessly for the price of a breath mint, but when they get money, they are actually frightened of it. Having money will attract thieves, or worse, malign ghosts. It is bad luck. Better spend it, for there is always more money, sometime soon.

The farang money tree grows in Thai cyclical time, not western linear time. There is only eternal summer, punctuated by rain. There is always heat and always fruit on the trees, fish in the sea and rice in the paddy, and the money tree grows indefinitely. You don't need to make pickles or buy warm clothes or salt pork for the winter, because there is no winter. You don't need to think ahead, or think at all. If – as soon as – you blow one farang's loot, why, next day, another jet plane arrives to disgorge a fresh load of money saplings. And they all want to fall in love with you, they all want to take you home to Gelsenkirchen – they want to want to – they all send you banknotes and buy you gold and cars and houses ... if you are lucky.

And what are a male's motives in sending banknotes? Does he think he is buying a sort of timeshare of the heart? Simply giving himself the masochistic thrill of being a fool for love? No one knows. But it is arguably more dignified than jumping off the balcony with a broken heart. Once, at dawn, there was a crash, then a kerfuffle of voices, and Wing roused me from sleep to come and look. Not at my best in the morning, I snarled, 'Come back to bed, it's just another Swede jumping off the roof.' I was wrong: he was Swiss.

As soon as a Thai lady has gold, cars and so on, their provenance is forgotten: they are simply part of her good luck. So, if you decide to be a sugar daddy, and give her a ludicrously large banknote every day, once it has disappeared into her purse it no longer has your name on it. The banknote is simply part of her accoutrements, like her bottom, or hair. If she gets a car, or gold necklace, or anything at all, she loses interest in it, and immediately wants another one, like a new hairstyle. If she gets a banknote, she wastes it and wants another one.

So the Thai lady with the sugar daddy, who is keeping her in expensive luxury, will sit around gossiping with her girlfriends about men, gold, clothes and money. (Ring any bells?) One girlfriend got so much for a 'short time', another got so much for an overnight ... she thinks, why, I could be getting some of that action! It doesn't occur to her that S. Daddy is giving her twice that amount every single day for doing nothing, while remaining his faithful possession, like some suitcase with only his clothes inside. The Thai lady is nobody's suitcase, she wants to make her own gossip. So she sleeps discreetly around ('discreet' means putting up only a small neon sign); grief and woe ensue, and it is nobody's fault, and everybody's.

He: I pay you to be mine alone – because I love only you!

She: I am yours alone, and I do love only you, so what does it matter if I go bouncing with younger, richer, handsomer guys? It's only for money! I don't mind if you go bouncing with other girls.

He: But I don't want to! (a lie) ... So why should you? Why must money come between two people who love each other (etc.)?

She: If you love me, give me more money and I not go bouncing (etc.).

She doesn't know what any of these words mean but hopes they will keep S. Daddy happy: they rarely do. He too is at fault, for trying to graft western concepts of love, fidelity and possessiveness on to an alien culture based on practical, opportunistic sensuality. In protesting that he gives her so many thousands of baht every month, or indeed every day, he forgets that no Thai lady can understand any sum larger than 10,000 baht. It is just 'big money'. A seafarer of my acquaintance, a black guy from New Orleans, who spoke the most beautiful Jeffersonian English, told me had been squiring a honeypot for a few days, and, now his ship was about to sail, had promised her a small gift to remember him by. 'I want a car!' she said promptly. When you say a car or house costs some millions of baht, you might as well be talking about the moon.

He also forgets that Thai culture sets a price on beauty, for being *sou-ai* is all-important (a farang gets 'Oh! Handsome man!' just for having his shirt tucked in), while virginity is a marriage asset, a safeguard of male face, and an assurance there is no offspring waiting for cash handouts. Virginity is a kind of moral beauty. But, miraculously, to the farang, it isn't! Many stumble-wrecks who marry bar girls even get a thrill from their bride's previous intimacy with the entire US Marine Corps, but that's a sexual terrain best left unexplored.

A party girl from Patong or Pattaya who returns to the village disillusioned and broke, but covered in the latest faddish tattoos, will not find a husband, for tattoos are the insignia of a prostitute, and, moreover, are ugly. No point paying for devalued and *mai sou-ai* goods. However, this culture does not regard sex as sacred, or venerated because its owner is so tantalisingly coy about offering it. It's an asset, meaning value added, or, in the case of a grande horizontale, subtracted. In western, Christian culture the vagina became an object of worship, longing and terror precisely because it was so difficult to get near one, or at least a respectable one. Thais are not hypocritical when it comes to bouncing. 'Cock want pussy, pussy want cock,' Wing sagely said to me one day.

One reason (alleged!) why most bar girls come from the impoverished northeast, the Isaan, is that in the 1980s, when the sex tourism boom really got going, the banksters invaded and made big loans to the subsistence farmers to modernise, like the carpetbagger banks in the American south after the Civil War. Now, the poor soil of Isaan is fine for subsistence farming, but unsuited for production agriculture. So the farmers who had mortgaged their land, and spent all the borrowed money on a useless tractor, or, more often, on whiskey, girls, and gambling, found themselves dispossessed when the banks called in the loan. They hadn't realised this was not free money, but something they had to repay every month. This was done to ensure a constant supply of poor village girls for the stews of Patong and Pattaya.

Was that special ... did the earth move ... was I the best ... ? Nobody does it better ... trills the happy warbler, while the sad one croons I wonder who's kissing her now ...? Or, more ruefully: A kiss is just a kiss … In our culture, sex has to mean something, even if it means nothing: to fit into some emotional category. Casual pick-ups must be classified as such, to give them any slight meaning they have. In western culture, a man 'possesses' a woman by the act of penetrating her sacred rose, her essence, her mystery. In Catholic Brazil, another high-sex country, the luscious babes of Copacabana like anal sex as it is no sin, no 'possession' of their sacred bit. But you never possess a Thai lady. Her body is hers and, if you are sufficiently infatuated with it, the Benz is usually hers too. Money comes between lovers only insofar as it glues them briefly together.

16.   CHEAP CHARLIES AND OTHER SPECIES

If the top Thai compliment is 'good heart' (*jai dee*), its opposite is 'cheap charlie'. Girls have a justified suspicion that young men, thinking themselves irresistible, are cheap charlies, who feel the girls ought to be paying them. This is not in a Thai lady's rulebook, and a 'never-paid-for-it-in-my-life' bore, who shortchanges her, may end up on the wrong end of a broken bottle. Old men (over thirty) have more money and are aware that female company costs, either in emotional turmoil or banknotes, and are grateful that luscious young honeypots should deign to be in their company at all. Old men haggle less, and take less time at slobbering, grunting and pounding, before they reach their feeble satisfactions, thus freeing the beloved to go and turn another trick, or get some shuteye.

Old men will not take the Thai lady windsurfing, bungee jumping, or to the beach, which she hates, because the sun will turn her 'black', when she wants a lily-white skin. Neither do they usually rent huge, stupid motorcycles to impress her. Old men show off, like all men, but do it the correct way, with their wallets, not their muscles, recklessness, or genital enormity. She does not mind old-age sex. Sex is a bit like a bowel movement. It is something she wants to do every day; it is healthy, even enjoyable, and its absence causes irritation. But it is nothing to get excited about, and it needn't last for hours. Neither does she read the women's magazines which test-drive the latest erogenous zones. Her attitude to copulation is basic: she wants eighty kilos of beef pounding on top of her, and properly rewarding her. She does not want to be led through the Perfumed Garden.

Brits, Scandinavians and Germans are quite popular, although the Burnts tend to be drunk, and the Germans a little too keen on compulsory windsurfing, bungee jumping etc. Italians tend to be cheap charlies ('one coke and four facking straws!' as Facking Douglas puts it), Americans tend to over-bargain. Japanese men are treated with caution, not because they are cheap charlies, but because they expect their money's worth and want to try every position in the book, frequently reading the book as they do so. They also have a reputation for wanting more slap than tickle; coitus with much squealing and moaning persuades them they have giant organs. The Japanese do not mingle with farangs, or even walk the streets. They arrive, travel, stay, shop, fornicate and depart in all-Nippon boxes, usually huge buses, and if they have to cross the road to get to the beach, they do so, all wearing identical swimsuits, under the supervision of a whistle-blasting group leader. They have their own clubs, Europeans barred, for whatever mysterious things they do.

Japanese-oriented Thai girls wear blonde wigs, for Japanese like blondes, Scotch, golf, and schoolgirls – western icons. Tokyo has shops and even vending machines selling schoolgirls' used panties, an important source of teenage pocket money, at fifty bucks a pop! You can have a Thai girl's for the price of a beer. And the rest of her, for a bit more. Many Thai demi-mondaines make the trip to Japan, and return very rich and very sore. 'Nippoon girls' are regarded with awe by their sisters, the envy evaporating as fast as the nouvelle riche's bankroll, until, in a few months, she has gambled, drunk or given it all away, and is back penniless on the street, so they can all be pals again.

The Thai lady believes that 'the man is king'. She feeds and massages him, washes and shops for him, and clips his nails too. For a man to cook, or – horror – wash his own clothes, is not just unnatural, but bad luck. Luscious teenage girls, skins silky as coffee beans, hang on the arm of some wrinkly male old enough to be their great-grandfather, with every semblance of delight. The uglier and wrinklier the sunburnt flesh, the more of it is exposed to the public; yet the nymphette accompanying some 190-year-old, rattling with Viagra, and in the *Guinness Book of Being Able To Walk Records*, is quite oblivious to the Arizona-wide folds of flaking brown skin, the slack jowls, bottle-bottom glasses and monster hearing aid, the cadaverous, liver-spotted arms and legs, through whose skin the artificial joints can clearly be seen, and the fact that this specimen of the living dead is clad in little more than socks and a G-string.

For this semi-sentient has a penis. And in Thailand there is a very simple equation: phallus = power. A semblance of erection is 'big power'. His beloved will feed him lots and lots of eggs, until he is more anxious for a bowel movement than an orgasm; she will urge him to eat deep-fried locusts, squid, or tadpoles, 'for power'.

Thai men tend to be lissom and epicene, but have no cash. Furthermore, the Thai lady has had her fill of drunks, however lithe, who beat her up, when even the ugliest foreigner will treat her like a princess. The Eurohasbeen whose wife has gone cold, or just gone, finds that suddenly his putrid physique is in demand, and that Thaiettes are not ashamed to be seen with him. They want him for his dick, symbol of power, luck and wealth. The phallic towers of Buddhist temples are there for a reason.

A young man's erotic demands distract the Thai lady from her TV soap opera, or sleeping. With an old man, the sex is perfunctory – both parties are delighted it can be managed at all – and both can get some rest. She does not want him to dawdle, however thoughtfully flavoured his condom may be; she wants him to thrust and bang and generally poke around semi-vigorously, until he groans a bit and releases his 'oyster sauce', satisfying her hygienic needs. She does not want it to last forever, any more than she wants her bowl of soup to last forever. Sometimes an 'old man' will engage a service girl just as arm candy, which is fine by her. But at the hint of an erection, she will insist on stimulating him to achievement, to make sure that value has been given, and his tip is therefore of correct generosity.

Buddha is the role model: jovial, paunchy, pale-skinned, fifty-something. Thai ladies actually like an older man of girth: as in the Victorian age, scrawniness is associated with disease and, worse, poverty. '*Pom-pooey*' – loosely translated as 'fatty' – is a humorous compliment. It means you can afford lots of food. Some young blades imagine that after 'going with' a Thai lady for three whole days, their charm is more important than their cash. After being with a Thai lady for three whole decades, the bedrock remains money. You get what you pay for, and you pay for what you get. A young, testosterone-fuelled male finds the Thai lady is not interested in his muscles or motorcycle, but in his dick, which may be bigger than Grandpa's, but does not enjoy the same credit rating.

17. LADYBOYS

One of the attractions of Thailand is the huge number of transsexuals, known as katoeys, ladymen, or ladyboys. Troupes of glittering performers in outrageously or gorgeously camp costumes frequently enthral the theatre goers of Europe, who seem as fascinated by the tranvestite phenomenon as the tourists are here. Thai society is tolerant of these in-betweenies who, in the west, would often be the target of prejudice or derision. Many Thai game shows, which is all of Thai TV except soap operas, girl-drenched-in-river comedies, and knife-'em-ups, feature an outrageous drag queen as presenter, great fun for all the family. People are polite to katoeys. It is illegal to discriminate against katoeys in schools, universities or workplaces. Except that the katoey is not a drag queen in the theatrical sense, cross-dressing to make the audience laugh. Katoeys do not want to be laughed at, but adored, and given money. Transsexuals believing they have been mistakenly born with a male body, katoeys insist they are genuine ladies, although of course they are not really.

'They ain't ladies, they're fackin poofters with two assholes,' as Fackin Douglas put it.

Those with money have their male bits cut off – 'the snip' – and I have seen a film of this operation which would turn the stomach of an abattoir worker. The doctor manhandles the vital parts, squeezes and skins and chops them, like a butcher dicing calves' liver. I dare say a calf would find a film of a butcher's shop pretty gruesome, too. Patong and Pattaya are packed with katoeys, almost all on the game, although in Bangkok and elsewhere there are katoeys who live normal working lives. They take female hormones to make the bosom grow and the figure soften; they have things done to remove body hair, and so on. Those that cannot afford the snip take drugs to make their genitals wither away, until they look like pimples, but to the keen observer they are still there, which has led to many a rumpus between a katoey and a disappointed matelot; whether disappointed at the presence of tackle, or its unsatisfactory smallness, it is impossible to say. Unfortunately for the katoeys, some male features are unchangeable, such as hands and feet (big) and hips (narrow). Nevertheless, some of them are so artfully made-up that unsuspecting lechers are completely fooled. You see them on TV, glitzy chorus girls, but they are the top end of the market, not the katoey-in-the-street.

They don't smell like women. They smell sickly, like a hospital room full of too many flowers. The scent glands betray them, poor souls. The folk wisdom on katoeys is: 'If it looks too good to be true, it usually is.' Katoeys swish and wobble and pout, like parodies of women. They are too feminine. Sometimes, they seem like artificial constructions, or plastic kits that you glue together. Most suffer from a genetic defect, called Klinefelter's Syndrome. These katoeys are exceptionally tall, and thin, with gravelly voices. A Klinefelter's katoey, as opposed to an ultra-feminine gay who has gone the full nine yards, has an extra female chromosome. They are not beefy tall, but stringy, like beanpoles, which makes their artificial bosom and bouffant hair look absurd, especially when accompanied by their typical grating whine; the docs are unable to feminise their vocal chords, though many of us wish they would snip them, too. Katoeys tend to be loud.

I've met plenty of feminine gay-to-the-max ladyboys, which the girls just treat as girls, and very pleasant they are, but with a certain sadness, as she's aware guys are only there to say been-there-done-that-bought-the-fridge-magnet, and it's unlikely to lead to anything long-term, although sometimes it does: when the bar girls cluster in the internet cafés, sending identical begging emails to their admirers, it is the katoeys who send the most.

Katoeys proper, with Klinefelter's, are six-footers with gruff voices and lots of attitude, prone to psychosis, skeletal deformities, and gland dysfunction. They die early. However, they lack the modesty of Thai ladies. Even the cheapest bar girl will not show anyone her panties, but a katoey come-on is to lift her skirt to show her lack of genital bulge: 'I real lady!' She must prove the merchandise is authentic. The most gruesome ones get the most customers. Klinefelter's affects one in five hundred male babies worldwide, but is partly curable with testosterone treatment. Thais don't have the money for that, or perhaps the inclination. A katoey in the family means matelot money.

Katoeys have a reputation for thieving, usually by picking pockets in a smoochy two-girl ambush (especially in Pattaya, with more shadows to lurk in) and for violence with knives, if miffed. Many, or most of them get AIDS. You rarely see a katoey over thirty; at that age, they just seem to crawl away and die. There are many cases of drunken tourists being 'fooled' by a katoey's ladylike appearance, but not so many where the 'deception' is discovered, or admitted, for the katoeys specialise in oral and anal sex. Well, those are the only holes they have, unless the doc has fashioned a false vagina. Sometimes, if she lacks the cash, the katoey gets the castration alone, and has no vaginal aperture. Oral sex is thus her speciality, which is precisely what many farangs, especially Americans, crave. They want katoeys. It is a new, dangerous thrill, and no one back home will know. Anatomical details are always a curiosity – full or partial snip? One dude told me of a ladyboy he swived who was snipped, but impenetrable on the foredeck, *sans* slot – she was saving up for the next op. No matter, he went aft.

Of all the alleys, or *sois*, off Patong's main street, Soi Bangla, 'Soi Katoey' is the one always packed full. The bars feature katoeys in outrageous and gorgeous costumes, sort of Busby Berkeley, whirling and dancing and panties-showing, and the most enthusiastic gawpers are female. There is also a must tourist attraction called Simon Cabaret, which is a glittering drag exravaganza, to which female tourists insist on being taken. Katoeys and ordinary gay rent boys seem to lead different lives, and have different clients. The epicene youths of Patong live and work in two downtown streets called 'Vaseline Alley' and 'KY Canal', full of gyms and massage parlours – while Pattaya's gayworld is proudly announced in neon, as 'Boyz Town' – and are seen holding hands with paunchy, middle-aged farangs.

The Patong katoeys congregate in the apartment block where I once lived, nicknamed Katoey Mansion, which seemed to contain more of them than it actually did, due to high decibels. Once they established that you were not a potential customer, they were perfectly polite, and minded their own business. My only invitation was when alone in the lift with a six-foot beanpole, who cupped her hand to her mouth, eyed me, and made sucking motions, as of a salami, or Cuban cigar. I made friendly but definitive 'no thank you' gestures. The exchange took place in silence. She shrugged: nothing ventured, nothing gained. There was actually no need for them to hustle, as they usually did good enough trade, especially when the fleet was in port. The katoeys' clients were not effete or pervy, they were strapping young hunks who knew perfectly well that their towering paramour was no ordinary lady. Funny thing is, in places where gossip is paramount, and every kind of sex on offer, I have never heard of any foreigner who has got AIDS, apart from one guy who was a junkie on the needle. And I know strapping, special-forces-type guys, or ex-cons (often both at once), who regularly have anal sex with katoeys, eschewing condoms, which is shivery.

When we later lived in Katoey Mansion, Wing woke me up – look! – ladyboy about to jump. Her Swedish boyfriend had just dumped her, because he had given her $1,000 to pay off her gambling debts, and then she went and lost it on more gambling. Plus which, she had just learned she was HIV positive. So we watched this poor young thing, naked but for a pair of black shorts, launch herself off a sixth floor balcony. Made a horrible dry slap. Everybody was at their balcony watching. Then, a collective 'Ooh!' Next week the *Phuket Gazette* ran a photo of the girl, pre-jump, only it was a fake photo, as this girl was fully clothed. Somebody had climbed off the balcony, and hung on, to get a few dollars out of the paper. Chester, with his American belief in the virtue of the press, was most indignant.

Cops arrived and dumped the corpse into the back of a pick-up truck. For the next three nights Wing put a plate of soup on the exact place where she had fallen, to feed her ghost. She also put on an impromptu striptease show in our apartment, for the statue of revered King Rama IV, who had 104 wives, so that he would intervene in the beyond to stop the katoey's ghost causing earthly mischief.

None of the girls in the building would go into their apartments alone while the ghost was still at large, and every night they clustered in the lobby, waiting for their boyfriends to come back from drinking. In vain did I assure Wing, as I have done with every girl, that ghosts won't come near farangs, because we smell funny. After three nights the ghost was appeased, and the proof of this, Wing assured me, was that the plate of food had disappeared.

Another time, she woke me up at some ungodly midday hour and told me to fetch my camera. We went downstairs to the parking lot, and all the Thais were there, shouting encouragement at a katoey who was going to jump from the tenth floor. A middle-aged lady who owned one of the boutiques shouted up something, translated for me as 'Go up on the roof, you'll get a better splat!' Fortunately a more muscular katoey arrived and wrestled the jumper back to safety.

As well as up for anal sex and fellatio, their main selling points, katoeys are generally aggressive and feisty and ready for anything, good loud boozy fun, free of hang-ups. Farangs tell you true lies of being too drunk to tell the difference, best shag of my life, up the rear, phwoarr, etc. What I witnessed living in Katoey Mansion, especially when the US Navy was visiting! And the straight couples, posing with a glam ladyboy for photos to show the folks back in Wollongong – only at midnight, Dad is back on his own with the ladyboy on his knee, and groping her in earnest. One notorious lush actually lived with a ravishing replica of a female for six whole months, without knowing she had a penis as big as his own. She always insisted on sleeping with her back to him, and all he wanted was anal sex, anyway. He was really mad when he found out his girlfriend's secret, and threw her out! People might think he was gay!

Only once was there a 3 a.m. fracas at Katoey Mansion. A German had his head split open with a meat cleaver after refusing to pay the katoey on the grounds of deception. Bleeding on the parking lot beneath my window, he protested: 'You say you lady – you not lady, you man.'

'I lady! You fuck me, not give money.'

'I not fuck you! I see you have cock, I go away.'

'You stay one hour, you fuck me in ass' ... etc., etc.

That was interesting, because it wasn't one of those grey areas, where truth lay somewhere in the middle and there was room for compromise. One had to be telling the truth, and one lying. The cops eventually carted both of them away. The German was not too drunk or befuddled, and there could have been no mistaking the giant gruff ladyman for anything but a ladyman. She lived on my floor; the next night, the German was back, knocking on her door for about an hour.

'Darling, I sorry, I love you, I pay for short time ... please ... I sorry ...'

She did not open the door to him.

One of the notable traits of ladymen is their fondness for knocking on doors, at all hours of day or night, and their equal fondness for sulking and refusing to open them. A distraught ladyman will bang for hours on another's door, and have a whole conversation of moans and whines with her, even though she will not respond, or has actually gone out.

What puzzles me, is whether Thailand has more transsexuals than anywhere else, or the same percentage, only they are just more open about it. It is estimated there are 150,000 katoeys in Thailand. Are there lots of secret wannabe katoeys in western countries, afraid to come out of the garden shed? The next time you see a tall thin man in a respectable city suit, just think – underneath, there might be a gruff-voiced beanpole struggling to get out.

18.   THE BUNGLE IN THE JUNGLE

After six or so months together, Wing and I moved into a big house downtown, 'the bungle in the jungle', in a Thai-style compound near the sea that was still jungle, as when Patong Beach was just a beach. It was ancient and wooden; the roof leaked, the bathroom overflowed, and, with millions of mosquitos, it felt truly Maughamesque. The trees gave shade, and the stews of Patong, just across the road, might have been on another continent. Nights chirruped with the croak of bullfrogs, as falling coconut shells thudded. When it rained, the waters lapped the floor of the house and you had to wade to the main road, though this never deterred the Buddha-mongers hawking their gilt statuettes. Monsoon is nothing like your western downpours. The sky is just a wall of water, the streets a lake, and everything stops for half an hour. Then the sun comes out again and the whole place is a steam bath.

The owner of the compound was M. Boulbet, the spry 74-year-old former French consul in Phuket, who lived in the largest house with his Thai wife and apparently hundreds of her relatives and children, including two boys of his own. Like many farangs, he imagined himself a patriarch, with two young French sons complete with passports. But they weren't: they were Thai designer kiddies with pale skins for the Thai wife. A sad spectacle often witnessed, the miserable, self-deluding patriarch (British, American, whatever) with a brood who despise him as nothing more than a sperm donor.

Boulbet was the very type of the old colonial; after serving in the French Resistance in 1944, he was drafted into De Gaulle's army and sent to Vietnam. After that, he just stayed, planting rubber and whatnot, and moving through SE Asia: Cambodia, Laos, Borneo, Malaya, and finally Thailand. And now he was headman of a colonial anachronism in bustling, sex-mad, glitzy Patong. He began the day with a bottle of Pernod, and carried on in the same way. Long periods of heat, boredom and loneliness in the tropics, especially in the military, drive you to drink. Not roaring bellyfuls of beer: just the steady drip of the spirit bottle, making the heat bearable, and decay and boredom seem rosy through a fug of alcohol.

Boulbet had not always been an old soak. He had written books, published by learned societies in Paris, on obscure hill tribes, full of photographs. He was showing me these one day, and I saw nude Cambodian girls tied to trees, and evidently whipped with real marks on their backs and bottoms, and real tears in their eyes; or else, giggling. The photos were captioned: 'Tribal justice'. Boulbet politely took the book away and sighed.

'That,' he said, 'is all the past.'

Later on, he became less reserved with me, and I asked if the Cambodians did not think nudity, even for a malefactor, was immodest.

'*Ah! Justement!*' he cried, spearing the air with his finger, like a Jesuit scoring a dogmatic point; but the girls preferred to strip for punishment, so as not to spoil a dress.

'And it is the custom in Asia for wounds, even deserved ones, to be rewarded,' he said solemnly.

It is indeed a custom in Thailand that if blood is shed, but not fatally, the wounded party may offer to ignore the police, if the aggressor hands over large cash. Under the Anglo-Saxon system of wergeld, you could quite legally murder a man, then pay how many pigs, cows, etc., he was worth. Some very cynical farangs believe that Thais will set out to provoke an attack, hoping to collect some wergeld. This might explain the frequency of traffic accidents where both vehicles are stationary at time of impact. On the other hand, an alcoholic bar owner in Patong ran over some pedestrians while drunk and broke their limbs. It cost him $20,000 to settle the matter and stay out of jail.

Boulbet occasionally did some howling at the moon; there were arguments with his wife, in Thai, but at the height of passion she would slam the door on him, and he would lapse into French.

'All you want is my money, you bitch! But you won't get a sou! Ha!'

Then he would address the Creator: 'God, why have you condemned me to this hell of she-devils?'

I reassured Wing that it was quite normal for farangs to talk to God, but figured, if Boulbet has been here since before I was born, and he's still getting grief, what earthly chance have I got? That was when I began to spy the cracks in the dream of paradise. Asia always wins in the end.

But don't get niedermayered. Niedermayer had been a US Navy dentist in the Philippines before the American naval base was closed, and was sent back to San Diego to be top naval dentist, with a house in the suburbs, a Filipina wife and kids, and in-laws. One evening he came home to find she had changed the locks. From behind the window, she said: 'We all have our green cards, so we don't need you any more, and you can go away.' Niedermayer returned to his surgery, opened the poison cabinet, and whacked himself. I heard that from Mike, manager of the US officers' club in Singapore. Of course, out here you never believe anything uncorroborated. Then I was in the Dominican Republic (which is a whole other story) and in the American bar, Herb the Nam vet and I would laddishly discuss oriental females. I started to tell the story, not sure if it was true, and he interrupted me.

'Was his name Niedermayer?'

'Yes.'

'Was he from St Louis?'

'Yes.'

'The story's true.'

Since we had a nice big house, we welcomed Wing's coterie of younger bar girls, and the house was perfumed with lithe-limbed squid-guzzlers, sleeping or gossiping most of the day. At that time, they were filming some movie about hippies living on a beach, and the town was awash with gold-medallioned cockney cameramen, gaffers, best boys and whatnot, spreading their loot around in swashbuckling fashion. The Italianate American star wouldn't put up in a mainland hotel, it being insufficiently ritzy, but stayed on his own yacht, to pursue whatever secret pleasures he favoured. Meanwhile my house was full of girls playing illegal poker, and trying to lose, frightened of the huge dosh they had received from the film crewmen. If you have too much money, the ghosts will come and make mischief.

I enjoyed this cosy paternalism: I had my own tribe. When listening to girl talk, a rudimentary knowledge of Thai is all you need, since most Thai conversations consist mainly of numbers, i.e. sums of money. The crucial bits are frequently in English, so you will overhear something like: '*Poon nerng song 2,000 baht, ding tong nang Gerramanny man, 10,000 baht, I love you too much, forn toot nong go away, pee whoo ping broken heart, Gerramanny man cry.*' The girls' erotic vocabulary is incomplete without melodramatic English. They all thought that the daily round of heartbreak and guys crying was tremendously funny, like a motorbike collision, or a drunk disappearing into a pothole. In fact, the Thais do express themselves with simplistic melodrama: the newspapers report 'broken hearts', 'life ruined forever', or 'shattered into a thousand pieces', whether over murder, exam failure, car theft, or constipation.

I sympathised with these girls. I still do. They were just sweet, homely village girls, away from home, trying to turn an honest horizontal dollar. Some of them were ravishing in full warpaint, but lust was absent as they were my guests in a domestic, not erotic, context. It was hard to remember all their names, especially as they kept changing, or swapping them, for good luck. Ong would become Phew, Chew would become Ook, and vice versa.

Walking around town alone had its pitfalls now, as I would be greeted with hoots and squeaks from various girls, and had to make split-second decisions: was this one I had had, and who was just being friendly, hoping for a rematch; one who was newly offering herself; or a 'niece', whom I did not recognise in uniform? Girls usually remember you, sometimes from years ago, and are indeed friendly if they do: partly because they want repeat business, like a mechanic asking after the health of a sports car he once had occasion to repair.

Mostly, they don't steal, although the ladymen are notoriously light-fingered. You can leave a girl i/c your precious wallet, camera, etc., while you shower, and they will be untouched. What they do is cajole, beg and wheedle: 'Please, you give me … ?' One delicious centrefold picked up a silly-looking calculator watch, which is also an address book, that I bought in Turkey for small change. I duly explained its magical properties, and how much it cost, about 400 baht, or $10.

'Please, you give me?'

'Sorry, can not.'

'Only 400 baht!'

I tried to explain that the information it contained was the whole point of this particular, special, individual watch: all alien concepts. Nothing – jewellery, a photo, a gift of any kind – has any sentimental value. All that matters is what it cost, and its resale value. Farangs get upset when their girl wheedles a gold necklace out of them, as a token of undying love, and the next day it resurfaces in the gold shop, with the cash in her purse.

'Please, you give me? Only 400 baht!'

I kept my watch, but of course tipped her 400 baht extra.

Concubined life became a domestic routine, if you can call it routine to live with a girl who disappears occasionally for the night, while I equally disappeared to see Suk, or Porn, who would turn up at the most unlikely moments on a street corner having decided to come down on the bus from Bangkok for a week's streetwalking. If I went walking, anywhere at all, there would be the lovely Porn, as if by magic. The delights of her bottom began to seem agreeably routine. I did not see Suk too much, although, eagerly nude, she was hard to resist, when I did. Wing was a wonderful housekeeper: I sinfully lolled, like a king. Conversation at Henry's Bar, on the fickleness of Thai ladies, always admitted that they looked after you. And they were at least predictably fickle.

Money is central to the erotic life in Thailand, just as elsewhere, though we pretend it isn't. I gave Wing little money, and got a lot in return. She had a nice home, and a *teelak* – boyfriend – who had 'good heart'. I understood what she meant. Farangs would get insanely, angrily, jealous if their girl wanted a couple of hours to 'go shopping' with her friends, because they assumed she had another *teelak*. They would not let them sleep, but drag them out for windsurfing ('fun') instead. They would call them seagulls: 'eat, sleep, squawk and shit'.

My good heart was just laziness, or writerism: anything for a quiet life. I figured that no Thai girl would, or indeed should, be stopped from doing what she wanted to do, so, if you made a fuss, the only loser was you. I even pointed out to Wing that, one day, she would run into a gold-plated guenther and he would make her an offer she couldn't refuse, whisk her off to a castle in the Alps, pay for her daughters to go to college and become world-famous brain surgeons and so forth, all of which were unlikely to flow from my modest

THE BUNGLE IN THE JUNGLE

purse. My fantastic indifference seemed the purest evidence of 'good heart'.

Farangs get confused that Thai ladies do not separate love and money. They will bounce enthusiastically, so it must be true love – but they want to be paid for it, so it cannot be!

'Sure, do they know the meaning of the word love at all?' asked Gerry of the Irish Bar, after some marital drama.

'No,' I said.

The girls nattered, and I picked up bits of gossip, tantalising because half-understood, like the foggy alcoholic bar tales. Sweden man ... or England? Australia? Have company! Big money! The legendary Ski cropped up, causing twitches of distaste, and vague mention of girls he had mistreated, including Henry's missus, Porn, with whom Henry was still officially in love, after years of storms. She seemed rackety even by bar girl standards: certainly a butterfly, probably a helicopter, possibly a skylab. Henry's Bar was legally hers, as she was Thai, and Henry, despite his thirteen years' residence, had just a stamp in his passport like the rest of us. Nor was he officially married to her.

Henry's Porn might perhaps have male Thai friends, who wanted Henry out, to get their own hands on the bar. The very sexy Porn, at 32, after a notable and ongoing horizontal career, was now an 'old woman', but with a desirable property attached. Henry, after a few beers, would look on the bright side. She was still there, tactile, most of the time ... once every six or seven weeks, he would put on some gruesome 1960s pop at top volume and chortle: 'I just gave her one!'

The delight of living with a woman whose English is limited to the basic bodily functions is that you cannot have arguments. On the other hand, you cannot have conversations either. I wondered how long Wing and I could realistically last, given the increasing cash demands of her distant offspring. That is partly why, for selfish reasons, I was happy for Wing to live 'her own life' – on parting, I would spare myself a guilt trip. And I knew she had no shortage of besotted guenthers on the back burner.

Every other day there would be an anguished phone call from one of Wing's daughters, Om or Oy, begging for money. But if she sent money to one, to share, that one would keep it all. I understood why Wing was always broke, and ventured to suggest that, given the importance of family, it was time for them to look after Mother. But no, they were at school, which was sacred. What they studied there, or proposed to do with it, was a matter of luck, not planning. Just 'go skoon' was glorious enough. The Thai educational system is designed to keep girls submissive. Mere literacy gets you a high school diploma. What you read or write doesn't matter. Learning is by rote, and questions are discouraged, for that would suggest the teacher has not adequately explained something, and thus the teacher loses face.

One day, Wing opened up a suitcase and poured out a junkheap of letters from Sweden man, Gerramanny man, etc., etc, all previous amours. I read some of these, the same corny phrases, 'my one darling', 'our eternal love', and, generally, broken hearts: 'Why do you not reply to my letters?' It seemed that many of these swains actually revisited Patong, just to find Wing. They made the rounds of bars, even knocked on the door of her girl barracks, to be told by her friends that Wing had gone back home. She said this had happened quite a lot, and her friends were very loyal in lying to protect her. The most persistent suitor was a German named Helmut, who had visited her home village promising marriage, land, house, car, etc. Helmut was seriously gold-plated.

Unfortunately, he had failed to pass the Daughter Acceptance Test, which I had apparently sailed through. Wing's two teenagers found him arrogant, and sans good heart. Wing had wished him to purchase her a piece of land back home, for a house surrounded by other houses, with everybody on top of each other, the normal Thai village life. But Helmut insisted on a Colditz-style fortress, surrounded by electrified fences and Rottweilers. So, Helmut was history. Nevertheless, he kept writing, promising undying love, and coming back – five times in six months! He even had 'Wing' tattooed on his arm.

Thai ladies have no idea, or image, of an absent 'boyfriend', which is why they keep mountains of photo albums as visible memories. The absent lover is in a foreign country, and might as well be in a distant galaxy.

Farang concepts are a mystery to a Thai, which is why she uses phrases in English. Farangs are 'in love' or 'angry' or 'have broken heart' or 'cry too much'. It is like trying to read a book upside down. She can recognise us, but she cannot read us. This is what I tried, with eventual success, to explain to Jimmy, in San Diego. 'His' Chew did not remember him, because he was not here.

Wing took the pile of letters outside and burned them.

'Finish boyfriend,' she said.

I felt I had scored a small point.

19. FACE

In Thailand, face is everything. You have no individual 'soul', but are just a molecule in the great flux. The opulence of your vehicle, the heaviness of your jewellery, the number of your servants, the magnificence of your bling, and the banality of your pronouncements say everything about you (how different from our own celebrity culture!): as do your politeness, good manners, and respect for others, which means agreeing with everything they say, unless it is appropriate to stab them with a broken beer bottle. A Thai should never lose face, or cause someone else to lose face. Hence, arguments and shouting matches are avoided. This is misinterpreted as serenity. First of all, you might actually lose an argument; secondly, by losing your cool, you are losing face; thirdly, if you shout at someone, they lose face, and this will bring you bad luck, and someone else again will shout at you, with further loss of everyone's face. So it is better to smile, until beer bottles or shotguns become necessary.

Thailand would be broke without sex tourism, but given the obsession with saving face – that is, lying – they claim they want wholesome family tourists instead. Families are space-hungry, requiring tennis courts, golf courses etc., benefiting the landowners, who lease big land to big hotels. Independent sex travellers don't need many square metres, just a bar and a room. For that reason, the ruling classes don't like sex tourism, and also because Thailand loses face, and too much money gets into the hands of the lower classes, thus upsetting the divine order. Girls are supposed to be in the village, picking rice, and bowing to the boss-in-a-Benz, not driving Benzes themselves.

Joe the American cocaine smuggler (who had arrived with two months' supply of Viagra, after being 'impotent for ten years'), once hobbled into Bar Henry all bandaged up. He had been eating in Mr Boon's seafood restaurant, and had partaken of a small lobster, and they had tried to charge him for a large lobster, which he had not had. He unwisely opined that this was 'bullshit', and the next thing he knew, he was flat on the floor, Mr Boon himself having whacked him with a wine bottle, though not a broken one, as Mr Boon's is a classy establishment. Joe required $200 worth of stitches, which Mr Boon paid for, along with grovelling apologies, and Mr Boon was now Joe's best friend. Mr Boon had lost face at the accusation of bullshit, but had lost even more face by losing his temper.

A Thai will sit for half an hour, until a taxi fills up and starts moving, to deposit him a hundred metres away, for walking is a loss of face. A Thai girl would lose face if she beckoned customers by showing her intimate garments; she says 'up to you' when asked her price, because to name the sum which she knows, and you know, is the accepted norm, would suggest that she is a prostitute! Which is of course illegal, and a cause of lost face. National face consists of great pride that the independent Kingdom of Siam, now Thailand, was never colonised by a foreign power, unlike Malaya, Indonesia, etc. During World War II, the Japanese occupied Thailand. That is, they did not exactly occupy it, but after the Thai Army had resisted them for five whole hours, they were admitted as tourists, and their army was permitted to come and go as it pleased, and build the death railway over the River Kwai using allied POWs, while the women of Bangkok were obliged to dress in Japanese kimonos. The Kingdom actually declared war on the USA and Britain in 1942, though they didn't actually tell them in so many words, for that would have made them lose face, and no Thai would wish to make possibly generous farangs lose face, and become less generous.

A few years back, an American periodical published a tongue-in-cheek piece rating SE Asian countries, and concluded that all Thailand had to offer was 'sex and golf'. There was a diplomatic uproar and the rag was banned until they made an abject apology. A European TV network aired an exposé of the sex industry in Pattaya, with the same shock-horror. The tourist ministry sent a young lady to report on Pattaya, and she dutifully assured them she had seen no evidence of sex in Pattaya, which is like seeing no evidence of sand in the Sahara. Despite the hilarity thus inspired, face had been saved. Of course, a good Buddhist, she was telling the truth: you don't see sex in Pattaya, you just see bars called things like FUCKU2, where consenting adults converse chastely.

Sex toys like vibrators are totally illegal; in the 70s, the makers of the erotic movie *Emmanuelle*, partly set in Thailand, had great trouble with the cops – arrest, confiscated film, etc. – when it was suspected they were not in fact making a movie about wild flowers. Particularly blasphemous was filming a nude bathing scene at a sacred waterfall belonging to some monastery. But it was OK, once money changed hands; they should have paid up before committing blasphemy. In 2006, HM the Queen (bless!) voiced her distress that young Thai bar girls were performing 'the coyote dance' (left to your imagination), thus causing Thailand to lose face. The august lady is several decades old, and one wonders where exactly she has spent them ... imagine Buckingham Palace being shocked to learn that the British like drinking beer.

The 1950s Hollywood musical film *The King and I* is still banned in Thailand, as any depiction of the Thai royal family, especially revered King Rama IV of the 104 concubines, is considered a loss of national face. It shows the king taking a bath (!) and eating with chopsticks, which only poor people do. Recently, filming of a remake was proposed. They wanted to shoot the film in Thailand, with footage of the royal palaces and various temples, and assured the Thais that it would not be disrespectful. The Thais would have vetting of the script. The sum of $20 million was mentioned. Now, if a film company wished to shoot in, say, Buckingham Palace, or the White House, they would be given a polite but firm 'Don't even think about it.' It is not Thai to say anything so negative; nor to refuse $20 million. We have a culture of right and wrong; they, Buddhists, have a culture of face and shame.

So, the script was vetted and refused, rewritten and refused again; film executives jetted across the Pacific Ocean to talk to one ministry after another, one committee after another, whose key members were always, inexplicably, on holiday. Eventually, the film people walked away from this interminable stalling and buck-passing, and built a replica of the royal palace just across the border in Malaysia, where they could, and did, film *Anna and the King*, and say whatever they liked about Thailand. Nobody in the vast apparatus of Thai bureaucracy wished to lose face by approving a film which, by even depicting lustful old King Rama at all, would be automatically scandalous. Yet nobody wanted to lose face by being the man who turned down $20 million. So they all went on holiday. Thus saving face.

20.   SOAP AND SUPERSTITION

There is a daily astrology forecast on TV; ghosts and spirits abound, and most buildings have a 'spirit house' in front of them, like a doll or bird house. This is where the displaced spirits lodge. So now they have somewhere to live, with the usual elephants, Buddhas etc., and are given flower garlands and bottles of beer to keep them happy and stop them disturbing the peace. Every home has its little shrine, as does every bar, where the girls pray for good luck before starting work. In Thailand, as in the west, newspapers run astrology and horoscope columns, but nothing like the vague, halfwit stuff of western tabloids. The typical Thai horoscope goes like this:

Q: 'My daughter was born in Bangkok at 11.30 p.m. on 22 August this year. What are her prospects in life?'

A: 'Your daughter will have a slow start at school and you will weep tears of despair, but teaching her to play the tuba will trigger her latent brilliance and she will get an excellent degree in agronomy. She will marry the conductor of a Swiss symphony orchestra and have two children, a boy and a girl, but he will be a cruel husband and beat her severely. She will return to Thailand, marry a police general in Chiang Mai, and own a fish farm and 25 noodle stalls. She will have 3 more children and 11 grandchildren.'

Thai TV is really no more idiotic than any other, except that kids' shows are actually prime time TV. British kids' shows *Bob the Builder*, *Thomas the Tank Engine* or various cartoons are shown at the peak hour of 8 p.m., watched just as avidly as Thai soap operas of betrayal, ghosts, revenge, murder, suicide, slasher bloodbaths and hopeless love, which are confusing to the farang, because the same male and female actors appear in all the shows. So, just as you are wondering why Mr Nice Guy is suddenly waving a dagger at Miss Nice Girl, you realise that this is a different show altogether. There are four main types of Thai TV drama: *pi* (ghosts), mafia, broken heart, and *talok* (comic), with combinations such as *pi talok*, mafia broken heart, etc.

Thai soap operas mirror Thai life, especially the fear of gangsters and ghosts, with alarming accuracy. They mirror everybody else's life too, only we won't admit it. Bar girls pray to the Buddha for 'good luck' in their evening's copulations, and we farangs smile at their superstition. Yet inspect the forests of love letters (collected in book form) written by hapless farangs, whose hearts have been twanged by some luscious Thaiette, and you will find the same posturings, pleadings, incantations, and the same offerings for good luck. What is a girl supposed to do with offerings of 'undying love'? The offering of devotion, and perhaps a banknote, is a palliative for the giver's aching spirit and testicles, not really expected to serve any practical purpose: just as the bottles of beer by the spirit houses remain unconsumed.

The gist of farangs' love letters is cosmic: no cute nicknames, no 'my little bunny rabbit' or anything. Thai ladies serve us as the goddesses in which we have forgotten how to believe, and as the stars, and their alien denizens, in which we long to believe. Unlike the godless west, there are no 'UFO landings' or 'alien abductions' in Thailand. There are quite enough ghosts already. The imagery is corny – Thai ladies are the moon, the stars, the sun, the firmament, though I have yet to see a specific comparison with, say, the Horsehead Nebula, the Rings of Saturn or, more appropriately, the Martian moon Phobos. Thai ladies are the ancient goddesses: inscrutable, fickle, cold, aloof, distant, but at intervals heartbreakingly warm and sensual. They fulfil our ancient and unsatisfiable need for terror and loneliness, as the plaything of a goddess.

'What a fool I am to love you so!' – 'You must think me crazy!' etc. But, 'I know your love for me is true, and my heart belongs a hundred per cent to you!'

The answers being 'Yes', 'Yes', and, 'Up to you'.

In a masochistic role reversal, it isn't the girls who get soppy and fall in icky love, it's the boys. In the bar girl scenario, the farang is the sentimental one. He wants to be enslaved, owned, dominated by a cruel goddess/slavemistress, who becomes ever more desirable the more heartless and inscrutable she is. He wants to suffer, and weep – just like girls, the lucky creatures!

'They' – their essential selves – are infinitely unattainable, yet their glorious bodies, the silken brown expression of those unattainable selves, are yours for the asking! Which makes it all the more deliciously, heartbreakingly frustrating, because you are not the only worshipper at your adored one's shrine.

'I cannot bear the thought of you sleeping with other men'; 'I do not want you to make love with strangers'; 'I want you to stop working as a bar girl' ...

Sweet surrender! Sweet torment! Sweet self-pity ...

Thai ladies are our UFOs, Kalis, Freyas, Virgin Marys, our malevolent aliens and imps and trolls and succubi, all our beloved nightmares. They are wonderfully distant, invisible, inarticulate, and frequently not even literate – all of which is essential to their glamour.

These love letters could be written to a woman in the writer's own country. But where would be the fun in that? Where the distance, the anguish, the unknowing frustration, the very unspeakableness of it all; the thrill of agony, as the ugly green dragon of jealousy tramples our spines?

A Thai lady is our own personal Gaea, our Earth Mother, who offers us such wonderful bounty, but is superbly indifferent to our fate and our feelings. I am the stuff of life itself, she says, I don't want to speak your puny human language, and I don't care about you as long as you take care of me. And we do!

All the motion and commotion, inventing the steam engine and the electric toothbrush and searching for life on other worlds (when all you need do is go to Thailand); all the striving, the things we do to kill time, while time is killing us, are suddenly made meaningful by her, our goddess. We come to Thailand to have our hearts broken, in a writhing frenzy of short times, because a short time is all we have, and a broken heart is better than none. We give her gold of the earth, and gold of our hearts, and we keep on giving as she swallows it and sings her mocking siren's song for more. We want to be stroked, ignored, frustrated, humoured and despised by her because, deep down, we want to give ourselves to beauty. She makes us feel alive and we want to suffer for it. So, weeping, pleading, smiling, sobbing and grasping at the airy, desperate stuff of fantasy, as our clock ticks towards ashes ... we get what we want.

21. THAI DELIGHT

It is a truism that the sex tourists flock to Thailand because they are too old or hideous to get laid back home. Like everything else in Thailand, this is half true; Patong and Pattaya are crawling with beer-bellied drunks in stained T-shirts, furtively clinging to bored honeypots. However, there are plenty of trim, fiftyish, gold-plated guenthers with a real Rolex on one wrist and a bit of teenage on the other, and also virile young hunks, who strut unashamedly, their glowing poise and suntan announcing: 'I have plenty of squeeze back home, only this one is brown.' What are they doing here?

Say you are middle-aged, thin of hair and thick of paunch, not as happy or successful as you expected, stuck in Duisburg, Leeds, Wollongong, or Omaha. Your sex life is mostly frustration, either because you are single-o, or have been married for thirty years to the same female who has wizened even more alarmingly than you. The best you can hope for is arduous courtship of an acronym your own vintage (WLTM M w/GSOH, etc.), who blames all her woes on men in general and you in particular.

Suddenly, desperately, you come to Thailand. You find that breathtakingly, mouth-wateringly gorgeous women, with silken brown skin to die for (which farangs frequently do), and young enough to be your daughter, actually smile at you, flirt with you, want to be naked with you! You find that Thai ladies like your paunch because it reminds them of the Buddha, and indicates that you have plenty of money to enlarge it with. They think your larval, pallid skin is sexy! So much so that they will let you buy them carcinogenic skin-whitening creams to make theirs the same colour. They like your big veinous nose because it means good luck. You discover another truism: women age, but men mature. The geezer d'un certain age falls in lust with Thai honeys because they are so accessible. There are no dates, no chatting up, no singles clubs, no lonely hearts columns. It is all so simple.

'Where you go, sexy man?' – 'With you, sexy lady!' – 'Up to you!'

From the Thai lady, you receive no confusion and uncertainty, no broken dates – she pursues you! – no wondering what it all means. Of course your Thai honey is going to turn up because if she doesn't, her best friend will. A western male and female are not really dating each other, but each other's dossiers. Conversation is mental sparring. What background? What accent? What school? What prospects? Should I be enthralled/ashamed to be seen with this person? What will my friends think? A Thai lady doesn't care whether you are a rocket scientist or a hole in the road. She doesn't care what her friends think, for it is the same as she thinks. She wants you – solid flesh, here and now. What she doesn't want is for you to get savvy. A Henry's Bar acquaintance told me he got grief from his live-in girl because he spent all the time drinking with farangs.

'Well, who am I supposed to drink with?' he replied. 'I am a farang.'

'Not those people,' she said. 'They live here! They know too much. They are the enemy.'

I had the reverse experience in Pattaya. In the bookstore, a teenage honey struck up conversation in an American accent. Her English was perfect, and I assumed she was American, of Thai parents, but no, she had been brought up in an American convent and never left Thailand. Despite her luscious availability, I decorously fled. She was the enemy. She knew too much. She would know what I was thinking.

Of course, in the west we are liberated and sex, as we all know, was invented in the 1960s. We bang and shaft every hour of the live-long day. But we are self-consciously liberated. Thai ladies are not self-conscious, because they do not have centuries of guilt and sin to be liberated from. In her childlike, greedy, devious innocence, the Thai lady is more mature than westerners who worry if they are 'getting enough', or 'too much' or 'average' or the right kind, or just worry. She knows that the mammoth blast-off (as Middle-Class Charles put it, see below) is only part of what we must gruesomely call a 'relationship'.

'Man happy' is much the same as 'clean floor' – part of a properly kept household. A Thai lady, busy with mop and broom while her farang lolls in kingly indolence, wondering if he has lit the right end of a menthol cigarette, will pause to check his parts for activity. It is part of a good girl's housework. If she detects seismic genital events, she will complete her mopping, and then mount, or be mounted by, the unruly member which needs to be tidied, like the rest of the house. After the job is done, she mentally checks her 'bouncing' box and proceeds to the next domestic task. Bouncing becomes part of housework.

Of course, I was not idle. I used to help Wing's friends by typing and printing their love letters to distant 'fiancés'. This saved the cost of the translation and calligraphy bureau. In Bangkok, some of these places specialise in helping a girl frame the most effective pleas. They'll remind her she had a kidney transplant last year, and not to claim appendix removal, as he'll look for the scar. Some girls invent a new baby (his!) which of course requires large cash, and when he arrives to see it, she borrows one from another girl. There are girls who make a comfortable living just renting out their babies. Eventually I made up the letters myself, especially in German, making them as pornographic as possible, and steering them away from sobbing and aching hearts to wetness, erect nipples, etc. The girls would trip in with the reply, and out would tumble a shiny new banknote. 'Oh! Papa! Good heart!' they trilled, hugging me.

Wing's hottie friend Foon would arrive every so often with a black eye and all her belongings, and share our bed for two or three days (politely pretending to be asleep during our gruntings and groanings), swearing that she would never go back to her whiskey-drinking man. He had bashed her up because she had been turning tricks from the bar where they both worked, and she turned tricks because he didn't give her any money, and he wouldn't give her money because she was turning tricks, and anyway the bar was owned by this rather sordid gold-dripping gangster, who only paid wages when the stars were auspicious. (In 2005, soon-to-be-ousted Prime Minister Taksin took refuge from a barrage of press criticism by refusing to answer any questions at all, as his stars were not right, and 'Mercury was in the wrong place'.)

Foon always did go back, though, especially when Wing and her other girlfriends took the battering boyfriend's side. He had good heart, he only drank whiskey because Foon was too mouthy, too crazy (ding dong), and she richly deserved a spanking. Once, she won 8,000 baht, about $200, at poker, and entertained a dozen of us to lunch, when we could have had it sitting on my floor at a fiftieth of the cost. She had a farang called Roberto, and had even stayed with him in Rome, but hated his mamma, hated Rome as it was so cold and boring (!), and couldn't understand the TV. The Italian girls hated her, for she was much sexier than them, and they were jealous of her body. Now, in one of her splits from her live-in boyfriend, Roberto phoned to offer her a week in Bangkok, all expenses paid, and 1,000 baht a day fun money.

'Thousand baht is for short time. I say, fuck off, cheap charlie!'

I thought it a pretty good deal, food, gifts and lodging, plus petty cash, but held my peace. There is frequently friction between long-standing partners, where he thinks he should get a bit of a discount, but she, as an irresistible beauty queen, is still charging him by the taximeter. So she blew off Roberto and, needless to say, a week later, she was round asking to borrow a thousand baht, as she was stony broke.

Another time she came in, sat down, and wordlessly spread ten thousand on the bed. Winnings from a new poker school, to which she was lucky to have been admitted, for it was run by a fashionable, elegant bar-owning lady. The next day, she won another ten thousand. The next day, she was to have the honour of attending an all-night serious session at the grande dame's house! In vain did I warn her about the oldest trick in the book. Off she went, and came back owing fifty thousand, with threats of severe maiming if she did not pay up. There was a panic, until her gangster overlord did the decent thing and settled the matter, whether with money or muscle I don't know.

When I earwigged conversations about troublesome (or ungenerous) boyfriends, they were full of phrases like 'cry bitter tears', 'broken heart', 'love you forever', 'cannot live without you', 'I will always be true' and so forth, in English. A popular book of lessons in English correspondence consists of sample letters, which the student is supposed to learn from, but which they simply copy. I would concoct much the same for them, only with a lot of triple-X stuff thrown in. Here are some examples, quoted verbatim: –

Dearest –
How are you? I hope you're getting on well over there. I'm very glad to tell you that I no longer have to work in a disco bar as my parents were able to clear all the outstanding debts with the job placement agency which arranged the working contract for my father in Saudi Arabia. As I told you earlier, I

had no desire of working as a bar girl at all, but it was due to my parents' heavy debt that I decided to take this unsavoury and risky profession. After returning home I plan to start pig farming and if possible run a beauty salon of my own. To be quite frank I am fed up with this boring life and I feel very embarrassed when I have to pretend to enjoy it while entertaining the customers indiscriminately. At first when I met you I thought you were similar to other customers I have. But I noticed you seemed to be totally different from them since you're very gentle and polite to me, and made me crazy about you. You said you'd marry me after I quit this job. Now I've done it and would like to know if you still remember it. I really love you and want to belong to you only. Please let me hear from you soon. – Yours lovingly ...

Dearest –
I've already received your letter of last week and it burnt my hands and heart. I don't know who told you I wasn't true to you. I swear I have never had any Thai boyfriend while you were away. I agreed to be your wife, not because of your money but the love I have towards you. I love you so I agreed. Even though our marriage is not legally binding, I prefer to be your wife only. I think sincerity is very important and both sides should not have suspicion of one another, otherwise it'll be harmful to our sweet relationship. I would like to tell you frankly that most of the money I got from you has been sent home to my parents, and I never use any of your money to feed a Thai boyfriend as you mentioned in your previous letters. I was shocked to read this. I couldn't close my eyes in the night. As you know very well, I love you so much, why should I do that since such a lie will surely lead to the end of your trust in me and you'll desert me for being unfaithful. – Your very own true love ...

Dearest –
I am reluctant to send you this letter as I don't know if it will be convenient for you at this time, but you told me that whenever

I need more money to buy necessities I should let you know. Darling! Now basic items such as soap and washing powder are going to be finished very soon. You are coming next week, aren't you? Do you want anything else? Please let me know and I'll prepare it for you, OK? Actually I want to go shopping with you when you are here but I decided to do it myself as this is only little thing. I hope you don't mind, do you? – Yours lovingly ...

My Dear Husband –
I am writing this letter while my eyes are full of tears as you don't know that the pimp for whom I worked before told me to work for her while you are away. She said that you didn't pay her in full when you wanted me to quit this profession for marriage. I certainly feel unhappy about it and want to know if it is true or not. If it is true I may have no choice but to work for her again. I love you so, I want to free myself from these people and stay with you forever if you still regard me as worthy. Now I am able to save some money which will at least let me open a small beauty salon in my native province. It has always been my dream to do this, as I know very well that the life of a service girl is not permanent and is looked down on by people. We have no social status. Please tell me what I should do and if possible come over here urgently. – Yours passionately ...

Dearest –
I don't know if what I'm telling you will make you feel pleased, as I plan to purchase a town house on the monthly instalment basis which will cost about 4,000 baht per month. I think the monthly payment won't be a problem for me since my salary could cover that amount. The only problem is the deposit which is about 100,000 baht. I don't think I could save my salary up to that amount and even if I could by that time the deposit would be double the current amount. That is the reason I need your help. As you know, my rent goes on increasing. I don't think it's a good idea to live like this throughout my life

without ownership of a single inch. I hope you'll agree with me and when you come to Thailand you need not stay in any hotel. Here will be your second home away from home. Please urgently let me know. – Only yours ...

Peter! Darling!
What's happened to you? Why have you not sent me any letters at all? Do you know I worry about you to death? I have stayed awake for several nights. Our children keep asking about your return. Darling! I'm short of money now, and as you know my salary alone is not enough. If your money doesn't reach me at the end of this month I shall have no alternative but to work at the same pub in Patpong again. You are the one who wanted me to quit this career and I'm obviously much disappointed that you left us behind without a single letter for several months ...
– Your loving wife ...

George! Darling!
I'm writing this letter to apologise for using harsh words against you without knowing the exact truth. I thought you married me just for the sake of your convenience in running a business in Thailand. Though my past life has not been as pure as other girls, I have never associated myself with the life of a service girl again. I want to be a good wife to you and a good mother whom our children can be proud of. I don't want to damage your reputation as a businessman. Only during this business trip I did realise that you're a great man and beloved husband. I'm so sad because I should not listen to other people too much as it will never bring any good to the family and may even ruin our love life as well. George! I think of you very much and I hope you'll forgive your wife and return to Thailand soon. Father didn't know you had left the country so he bought bananas which are your favourite fruit for you. Take care! – Your loving wife ...

No, really. Or, as Lenin said, 'Who, whom?'

22. DEATH, LUCK AND OTHER MATTERS

Life is cheap in the Orient, meaning death is cheap. Thailand has an incredibly high homicide rate, those that anyone bothers to record. The police are fond of 'extra-judicial killings' and in a campaign a couple of years ago to purge the country of dope peddlers (those not in the police) killed nearly two thousand undesirables. The high-ups cried that they didn't expect the police to do that, without explaining what exactly they did expect the police to do. Even more recently, in the Muslim deep south, an entire football team, suspected of being separatists, was shot down in a hail of bullets while playing a game. Seventy demonstrators who protested this were arrested, tied up, and piled into the back of a police wagon, where they died of suffocation.

You can be wasted for pocket change, for the tiniest gambling debt, or for scuffing some apparatchik's son's Gucci loafers in a crowded disco. His appalling loss of face must be avenged, and the scuffer will find himelf shot *instanter*, or bundled into the back of a car by heavies, never to be heard of again, except as a plop in the canal. There is also an incredibly high rate of road carnage. The Thais drive cars and bikes with what appears engaging insouciance, until they smash into something. It is the Buddha who is really driving, and if you have a crunch, why, it is simply bad luck.

Putting out a contract on someone is a simple matter, and costs not much, unless you have to go through the local police captain, who will charge a little more. The job is traditionally done from the passenger seat of a motorbike, usually in a traffic jam, after which the cops will arrest the nearest motorbike rider. After getting 25 years in the monkey house, he will protest that he is part of a conspiracy, and can name names in the highest echelons of police and/or government. Only the prospect of suffering undue torment, or disappearing altogether while actually in jail, prevents him from naming these names.

However, Thais are too polite to cause scandal, or have a muck-raking newspaper tradition. Unseemly matters are handled discreetly. Some bigwig, caught with a carload of crystal meth and underage girls, is not disgraced (for he might lose face), but promoted to an 'inactive post'. The newspapers bleat about 'setting a good example', with the name of the miscreant blurred by a fog of pieties. Not 'let's nail the bastard'. That would be impolite.

Yet another abbot of a large Buddhist temple, or *wat*, was recently under investigation by the High Council of Buddhist Things for 'irregularities', notably: dealing in land, claiming to perform miracles, and being alone with female worshippers (sic). The worst that could happen to him was to be promoted to be Abbot of Wat Nakhon Si Nowhere. Even if he were derobed, nothing would stop him from robing up again, under another name, as a novice at some other temple. The monkhood can be joined for as little as two weeks or two months, and is a convenient way for felons to lie low for a while. The courts sentence minor offenders to serve six months or so as monks, in lieu of jail time.

Buddhists dispose of corpses by burning. In Patong there is a small Muslim cemetery, down a back alley, and the Thais avert their gaze if obliged to pass this burial ground as they fear that ghosts may be lingering in the mould. However, most of the time, the morgues and hospitals in Phuket overflow with unburned corpses, and the place stinks. The municipal crematorium charges a corpse's family to burn it up and, since Phuket is the richest province in Thailand, it attracts many unidentified moochers. The private crematoria refuse to burn these stiffs for free – also because riff-raff smoke would lower the tone of reincarnations – and the provincial government refuses also. Hence Phuket is becoming the stink-bomb of Thailand. Life may be cheap but death is not free.

A local English character in Patong, named Roger, was murdered for his money, allegedly by the aforementioned Alice who served me in Alice's Bar. He was in his fifties, quiet and modest, and not a 'monger. Suddenly widowed, and having made his pile of money in Hong Kong, he retired to Patong, of all places, to play golf. Not for the girlies – he didn't approve of that, like a guy who settles in the Yukon but doesn't approve of snow. He had a collection of gold pieces and valuable antique swords unwisely displayed in his home. Though no bar-hopper, he became smitten with Alice, a decade younger, and lived with her as his concubine for a good ten years. Alice was too old to be a regular working girl, but she had plenty of toyboys, and in particular a police captain, who said she could chisel more money out of her beloved than he was actually giving her. Roger, in return, wanted her to give up 'mongering. As well ask a turd not to float.

Eventually he threatened to cut off her money, a dire mistake. The fait accompli is the only sure thing. When you ditch a Thai lady, make sure she is a hundred per cent ditched, and change your locks, if possible your domicile and name, and consider plastic surgery. Roger was stabbed forty times with one of his antique swords, and Alice claimed this was a clear case of suicide. However, somebody had hired three hitmen from northern Thailand, who were promptly arrested when they went into the gold shops of Patong the day after the murder and tried to sell these distinctive gold pieces – speaking their northern dialect, almost a foreign language in southern Patong. The British tabloid press covered the case as though Roger was an old lecher who had fallen for some doped-out teenage bimbo: but no, he was (allegedly) done in by his long-term concubine.

His funeral was an odd mixture of Buddhist and Christian. He was burned, Buddhist fashion, but in a coffin, Christian style. His funeral took place at the Buddhist temple, but the oration was given by a missionary type, who lectured the assembled girls and farangs that they were terrible sinners for living in Patong, like him. The girls wore black, as they were told this was the Christian colour of mourning, though for them it would be white, and black is what they often wear on duty in their girly bars. So they all turned up dressed in their sexy little black numbers, which was highly convenient for them as they could go straight to work without changing clothes.

The coffin was left open for the moments before being consigned to the flames, supposedly in Christian tradition. The farang mourners, thinking they were following Buddhist tradition where the dead are accompanied by bottles of beer, bags of instant noodles, packets of condoms, and other things useful to them in the beyond, began to throw coins into the coffin. The girls, thinking that throwing coins was a Christian tradition, did likewise; eventually, the lid was closed, and Roger proceeded to the flames a bit richer in cash terms than moments before.

Now, in a Buddhist funeral, you are supposed to watch the chimney for billows of white smoke – like cardinals choosing a new pope – to indicate that your loved one is well and truly ashes. In Roger's case, all that emerged was a sickly wisp of greasy black smoke. Some intrepid farangs went backstage to investigate. They found the funeral staff gleefully scooping up handfuls of coins from the floor underneath Roger's funeral pyre, where bits of Roger's smouldering bones stuck out from his charred coffin. Unused to coffins, the morticians had doused it with the same small amount of benzine as would be used on a Buddhist stiff, who would be naked but for a shroud. Thus, the coffin had rather vaguely caught fire, and Roger's internal organs had melted somewhat, but not his muscles or bones, nor the coins. Eventually, more money changed hands, and somehow, Roger was propelled correctly into the beyond.

His actual assassins got life sentences, while Alice herself, her policeman boyfriend not as powerful as she imagined, was nevertheless under house arrest, meaning 'don't leave SE Asia'. Her trial kept coming up every three months, and being adjourned for three months, when yet another witness had disappeared, or lost his memory, so by now she is merrily serving drinks behind her bar again as though nothing had happened, and doing 'short times' for those macabre or lustful enough to want to go with an aged, alleged murderess.

A few years ago, two dangerous gangsters, let's call them Ping and Pong, were brought from the jail in Bangkok to face trial.

Judge: You are Ping and Pong?

P and P: Yes.

Judge: Armed robbery is a serious crime. How do you plead?

P and P: But we were arrested for stealing a watermelon!

The police colonel in charge admitted that he had released two petty thieves, Ping and Pong, a week before, as their crime was so trivial. Oops! He must have got them mixed up with the armed robbers. His excuse was that all these little brown people looked the same! The judge said, well, yes, such an honest mistake could be made by anyone.

There was a Belgian named Fritz who had a butcher's shop, retail and wholesale, in Patong. He was an alcoholic sex maniac who used to dose himself with testosterone, and boast that he had four girlfriends at any one time. He never made any money, as he would pay for all his girls and Stolichnaya vodka with chunks of meat. Anyway, Fritz was carted off to the monkey house to stand trial for murder. His 'trading company' had collapsed with huge debts, morphing into his one-man, flying-by-the-seat-of-his-pants butcher shop. His Chinese-American business partner suspected embezzlement, and was going to blow the whistle on Fritz, who bought him off with cheques totalling 800,000 baht. The day after they bounced, the American was shot dead at his home, the hitmen escaping on the traditional motorcycles. The American embassy took a dim view of somebody shooting an American, so eventually prodded the cops into action, and Fritz was arrested. But after a year in clink, he managed to make bail, and everybody expected him to do a runner, although he couldn't go back to Belgium, where he was wanted for something else. Fake passports are easily obtained in Bangkok, on the Kao San Road. Yet there was Fritz, swigging Stolichnaya and swanning around with girls on his arm as if nothing was amiss. I think he bought himself off the charge in the end.

There was another, less fortunate Sri Lankan bloke, who had arrived in Patong with a suitcase full of traveller's cheques, presumably stolen from the Danish bank where he had been working. He partied with gusto until the money ran out, at which point he tried to commit suicide with an unsuccessful overdose. This meant he had to spend a couple of expensive months in hospital, during which his passport was running up 'overstay' fines of 200 baht a day, so when he got out of hospital, he was vastly in debt. Gerry of the Irish Bar led a whip-round amongst the worthy farangs of Patong, and they managed to get him on a plane back to Sri Lanka. Such collective good heart!

Dave the oil engineer is a regular at Henry's Bar, when he is on self-appointed holiday from the Persian Gulf. He looks like an all-in wrestler, with a gift for philosophy, due to his having lived in Thailand for most of nineteen years. At one point, he tried to settle down and live with wife, kids, and his own bar, in the southern seaside town of Song Kla.

'There were three gangs in Song Kla, and I kept a .45, just to let them know not to mess with me. In those days there was a lot of Vietnam surplus in Song Kla, and you could get an M-16 for $200, or anything you wanted. Anyway it all fell apart, my wife got the bar, it was in her name, but not the house. She came round one night and wanted the cash as well. She made me write a cheque for $15,000, which was a big chunk of what I had. I wrote the cheque because my .45 was upstairs, and she had a live grenade, with the pin pulled and her thumb over it. I gave her the cheque and she said if it bounced, the grenade would come through my bedroom window. I put a contract out on her, and had her warned to get out of Song Kla. It was only $500 down and $500 to come if they did her in. She got the message and fucked off. I went back to England and hated it. I was in a pub in Birmingham and offered to buy a girl a drink, friendly like, and she said "Fuck off, Granddad." I got the first fucking plane back to Bangkok. Now I fuck a different girl every night. You give them a decent tip and they smile, then piss off happy and don't shove hand grenades in your face. It makes life simpler. Thailand is home. Treat 'em right and they don't kill you.'

Thailand is fertile: in the central plain there are three rice harvests a year. Everything is constantly swelling, growing, sprouting, blossoming, à la D.H. Lawrence. Life is cheap because it is plentiful, and because death is an integral part of the process of blossom and mould and reincarnation. Buddhists have no special tailor-made souls, which is why they are different from us. They have cyclical incarnations. If you 'make merit' in this life, your bit of vital essence will re-emerge from the cosmic ooze for your next time round as something higher up, like a police colonel, or owner of your own bar. You make merit by good deeds: giving money to the monks, or, better still, giving money to the rich. Giving money to the poor gets you few points. In the Thai school of Buddhism, being rich or holy in this life means that you had super merit in the last one, and being poor means the opposite. In theory, if you accumulate enough merit through the cycles of earthly existence, you will achieve nirvana, and join Buddha in everlasting sleep. You easily get used to living in a country where nothing means anything. Only nirvana is real, everything else is just light and shadow. *Mai pen rai*!

No sooner are you burned, or bleed to death by some roadside, or disappear full of bullets into a convenient river, than some plant or tadpole is sprouting from your ashes or goo. Your ghost may be around for three days – proper (i.e. rich) Buddhists observe mourning for a week – but after, your ghost should have been reincarnated as a noodle-seller, abbot, or bar girl, depending on merit, and it is business as usual. Or you could be a plant, animal or bug. Reincarnation, as well as being transspecial, is conveniently transsexual, too. So you might come back not just as a slug, but as a female slug, or a ladyboy slug. There is no actual chart listing the number of merit points gained by this or that good action. You just have to trust to luck. Nor is it explained how worms can make merit, to jack themselves up to fruit fly.

The twin concepts of luck, and making merit, explain the whole girl economy of Thailand. Western grandees like Messrs Rockefeller and Carnegie got where they were by doing something. Thai grandees get there by luck and bribery. When Thai Airways advertised for a new president, one of the qualifications was: 'Has never been sentenced to imprisonment except for the charges caused by negligences or petty offences.' Thai role models are not adventurers but monks, who depend on donations from the celestial bank of luck, i.e. poor people. Girls and large-scale bribe-takers are lower down the scale, but the concept is the same: smile, and somebody will donate goodies. A particularly popular demi-mondaine is envied, not for her athletic prowess, but for her good luck, due to past merit, otherwise she would have come back as an earthworm, or fertiliser.

That is why the Thais are always broke. Money doesn't come from effort, it comes from luck. It's like permanently being on the dole, you don't have to save for a rainy day, because there are no rainy days. There's always another donation.

On the jungly, mostly undemarcated, borders where Thailand meets Burma, Laos and Cambodia, there are firefights between various armies, private or national. These are politely called 'incidents'. There is a decade-long, forgotten war between the Burmese government and the Karen hill tribe, who number a quarter of a million, and do not wish to be Burmese. Neither does the Burmese government want them: it simply wishes to kill them all, clear the area, and have a monopoly on the drug agribusiness. Few have heard of the Karens, and fewer care. In Thailand, the policy towards unreconstructed hill tribes is more benign, and more typically Thai. The aim is not to destroy them, but to make tourist money out of them. This is done by bureaucratising them out of existence.

Few hill tribesfolk have birth certificates, for which they would have to travel a long way to the nearest hospital, or government office. Hence they have no ID cards, sacred in Thailand, and hence they are not Thai citizens at all. They have lived on their land for centuries but, being foreigners, they cannot own it, and anyway they have no title deeds, and could not read them if they had. Having no ID cards, they cannot move to cities, or get jobs. So they are relocated for 'humane' reasons, out of the war zones, to showcase villages, where busloads of air-conditioned tourists come and gape at the ring-necked women. It is estimated a million tribal Thais are not legally Thais, doomed to be mere tourist attractions in their own country. Who cares? *Mai pen rai.*

I went with a teenage Patong girl a few times, and was getting to know her quite well; mainly, I got to know what pleased her sexually. She always wore 'sexy' underthings – purple, pink, lime-green and so on – and one day she turned up wearing white bra and panties. Then she demanded anal sex, and we both enjoyed ourselves. Afterwards, she explained that the white underwear was mourning dress for her grandmother, who had died the day before. It was her thoughtful way of making merit.

23. BOILING NAIL CLIPPERS

After about a year, Wing and I had to vacate the bungle in the jungle. Boulbet announced that everybody, including himself and clan, had to go. He had sold the whole property for a million dollars to Marc, the Frenchman who owned a couple of girly bars and restaurants next to Henry's, and who was known as Napoleon because his ambition was to 'conquer' every female in Patong; no comment. Boulbet was deep in debt, I heard through the women, the bank calling every day. I figured that the site, prime downtown land, would promptly be flipped, and fetch four times as much, for a hotel.

But no – Marc, who was, or is, apparently the front man for certain mysterious Swiss interests of the money-laundering class, wanted to turn it into yet another cash-haemorrhaging dive school. As soon as we left, I watched the Hollywood-style swimming pool take shape, and the houses refurbished into cabanas. Subsequently, the place was immaculate, and noticeably free of residents or divers, the purchase price well laundered. Our eviction was at the height of the tourist season, when rentals were hard to find, as the island of Phuket was packed with knuckle-draggers. I pointed out to Wing that I had arrived on a plane with a holdall, and could just as easily depart the same way. Rather than motivate a Thai girl with the threat of another woman, it's best to threaten her with another continent; she can't compete with a continent. Wing rushed to speak to crucial squid-sellers, and, next day, thanks to the Thai grapevine, we had an apartment on the sixth floor of the Sky Inn Condotel, aka Katoey Mansion, a few blocks away.

The girls moved house for us, like a swarm of bees. I was not permitted to do a thing except pay for the two tuk-tuk taxis into which Wing's mountains of worldly goods, mostly dresses, were loaded, then weighted down by the delectable bodies of half a dozen teenage girls. Riding in front of this strange convoy, I felt like Caesar leading his troops into Rome. A few of these girls lived in the building and were now neighbours. They would arrive at any time of day or night, for eating or sleeping purposes. If they had no one to sleep with, they would come and share our bed, in fear of ghosts.

Om was a lovely girl, hard as nails, veteran of numerous abortions at age 26, with a couple of the unaborted stashed with Mother, upcountry. She was an alcoholic, woke up with the shakes, and had to have a half-bottle of Sang Tip whiskey for breakfast. (A German informed me that Sang Tip, which he was drinking, was banned in the European Union as it contained twenty chemicals harmful to human life.) Om took pills, any pills, and would lift her skirt to attract customers, showing her panties, a no-no in modest girl etiquette. She would trash hotel rooms when miffed, stoned, or drunk. She had spent several months in Japan, enduring unspeakable erotic practices, and came back with $50,000, which was gone in six months, along with her new car and apartment in Bangkok. Om was never without a boyfriend. Never. She was fun.

Once, she brought her latest boyfriend with her, and was fluttering around serving us things, anxious to please, in a pretty flower dress, all girly and simpering, although I gathered she had trashed his hotel room a couple of nights ago in a fit of drunken jealousy. It seemed she was sweet on him. He was a genial enough fellow from Jersey, in the Channel Islands, and said he liked Om for her dainty suckable feet. I said I wasn't averse to a bit of toe-sucking myself, so we made agreeable guy talk on that and related subjects. Then he said she had a terrific pussy, shaped like an orchid or a rose or something. He assured me that, such was his experience of Thai girls, just by looking at her face, he could tell what a girl's sex looked like: various flowers, molluscs, or French pâtisseries. The majority were in fact like flowers. I didn't quite see the practical value of this talent of his – do you go up to some girl in the bus, and say, 'I bet your snatch looks like a dandelion, fancy a shag?' – but hey, here we were, two strangers having a cup of coffee, and chatting about herbaceous borders. Just another day in Thailand.

When Om visited, she was relatively sober, and was the sweetest, homeliest girl next door. She would sweep the floor, dust, tidy, for 'Papa'. She was always borrowing Wing's nail clippers and, each time, Wing would throw the nail clippers, and any cutlery Om had used while eating, into the waste basket. I assumed this was some nice-girl hygienic ritual, until I asked her why she discarded perfectly good utensils. It seemed the other girls, while fond of Om, thought her likely to be HIV positive, since she did everything, with anybody, and was too spaced out to use the sacred condoms. After eight or nine repetitions, Wing finally agreed to pretend to believe my explanation of sterilisation by boiling, 'same doctor', and after Om's visits we would solemnly watch boiling spoons, forks and nail clippers, which is more exciting than watching paint dry.

Once, Foon came in with a ferocious bruise on her thigh, which I took to be the boyfriend's work. But no: she was giggling. She had ridden the 'bump cars' in the fairground for the first time, and had been injured in a duel with a ten-year-old boy. The best part was, she had made him crash, and bloodied his nose! It was such fun! Rivers of tears and blood

... but it was OK, because she gave him 50 baht, as his injury was greater than hers. His tears dried, and he was happy and laughing! *Sanook!*

Yes, life became the same old humdrum Thai routine. Even Suk and Porn, on her rare cheering visits to town, became a kind of routine. Henry's Bar, and the ongoing stormy saga of Henry and his missus became a kind of soap opera (his). Porn was gone, Porn was back ... gone ... back ...

The *Bangkok Post* continued to provide amusement: 'German researchers found that two-thirds of the German visitors to Thailand agreed that "the local people somehow belong there, and are no trouble at all, as long as they don't come too close".'

A Thai got twenty years for murdering his next door neighbour, a Scotsman. They had a deal to share one water pipe, splitting the bill, and thus cheating the water company out of precious bawbees on the standing charge. The Scotsman's pipe started to leak, and he neglected to fix it, so the Thai cut off his supply, suspecting that the Scotsman was stealing from him as well as the water company. The Scotsman then called him names and the Thai shot him.

The *Bangkok Post* solemnly reported: 'A former German soldier faces deportation after he threatened to kill the ambassador and other German diplomats in Bangkok. Michael Hoffmann, 43, was arrested at his home in Phanom Sarakham district on a charge of intimidation, which carries a maximum three year jail sentence and deportation. The arrest followed a complaint by German consul general Carlsten Titz to police on July 16. He said Mr Hoffmann telephoned him at the embassy and asked him to find him a new wife to replace his deceased Thai wife, and to lend him money. When his request was refused Mr Hoffmann made threats, Mr Titz told police. Police said Mr Hoffmann has been living in Thailand for more than 10 years on a military pension paid by the German government. After his Thai wife Boonlon died, he took a new wife named Somporn, who later ran away with his cash and ATM card.'

A Finnish girl was murdered by a Bangkok taxi driver for money, haul: $10 and a camera, the instrument of his undoing, as he forgot to remove the camera film, and the buyer found photos of the victim. Another Thai, in a wheelchair, couldn't pay his $20 bar bill, so robbed a jewellery store, which he could enter only with assistance. When he had done his stuff with the sawn-off cucumber in a paper bag, he didn't understand why no one would assist him out again.

Wing's two daughters arrived for a week at New Year, and stayed three. They were two delightful teenagers of fourteen and sixteen, spoiled rotten, the younger one smart, and maybe able to get a career, the older, luscious one quite brainless, perhaps destined to be Soi Bangla fodder. I asked what she learned at school, conveying the concept 'learn' with great difficulty. 'Basketball', was her answer. Neither girl seemed embarrassed that their mother was 'working bar'. As for any idea of what the pair would do after school, they didn't understand the question, let alone have the answer. Wing's brother arrived unannounced on the same bus, having 'no money', to my surprise. Equally to my surprise, he stayed somewhere else and didn't mooch off me. But when I asked Wing what he did for a living, she said she did not know, as if nobody could be expected to know something so stupid.

In the west, people will say they are bricklayers or mechanics, even if they have been unemployed for twenty years, just to establish an identity for themselves. That is our sort of packaging: you are what you 'do'. In Thailand, since nobody does anything special, it is meaningless.

However, Om and Oy were the drain on Wing's economy. At first, farangs are impressed by the Thai respect for family: it is your sacred duty, for merit, to help your family, and old folks are looked after, not off-loaded on the social security, as there isn't any. There is something called social security, but only for those who are employed. Thus, you can only ask for unemployment benefit if you already have a job, which naturally disqualifies you. The whole girl economy is nevertheless based on handouts. You are generous, because some day you will need handouts yourself. Saving, planning – boring things – are unknown. Luck is what counts.

In the bar, the conversation was often, of course, about vaginas, and the tricks Thai showgirls do: making pingpong balls, canaries or mice emerge from the labial cavern, bursting balloons with darts, and so on. Thai women, like others in SE Asia, choose to have children by caesarean section, so as not to impair their suctive powers. Cowboy-shirted Nebraskan Larry described a visit to the musical *Miss Saigon* in New York, which depicted a red light district. At one point a lone pingpong ball rolled symbolically across the stage. Larry, according to Larry, was the only one who got the joke.

Swashbuckling Chester, Patong's own Errol Flynn, enthused about his recent week in Bangkok, claiming he had been 'good'. Being good included visiting the Paradisia Club, where a naked girl gyrated upside down, her legs clinging to a pole, then parted her thighs and invited him to position the contents of a bucket of ice cubes.

'What do I do now?' said Chester.

'What you like,' said the thigh-spreading lovely, so Chester stuffed her pussy full of ice cubes, and she gyrated some more, until they had all melted.

Then she asked for a towel to wipe herself, like a good clean Thai girl. Briskly pleased at a job well done, she joined Chester and his English friend at their table, and gave Chester a hand job, while her girlfriend was giving Chester's friend a hand job, with Chester's friend's fingers in Chester's girlfriend's pussy, while she was hand-jobbing Chester, and Chester's fingers in his friend's girlfriend's pussy.

'This is as good as it gets!' enthused Chester's friend, Brian the Arsehole, a dopey English know-all and bar-emptier.

Meanwhile Chester's steady flame was home asleep in Patong.

'That is what you call being good?' I asked Chester. 'Ice cubes up her snatch, and a hand job?'

'I didn't sleep with her!' he protested.

He enthused that this girl was intelligent, professional, etc., and didn't give him the water buffalo spiel like 99 per cent of them. She said she was well paid, had no moochers to support, and enjoyed her job, but didn't take her work home with her. Party-pooping, I said she was a turn-off.

'Huh? Come on … !'

'When you asked what you should do with the ice cubes, she should groan, Please, stuff them in me, or, better, please don't. Saying "what you like" is a cop-out. She was saying, this has nothing to do with me – my body does this because I'm paid.'

Pedantic, moi?

Larry, boss of Patong's raunchy, high-glamour Rock Hard go-go bar, countered with a story of a hard-boiled US Navy officer who had taken home one of his top girls, a real nympho and gold-digger. The next day, the officer said he hadn't done it with her, though he had amply rewarded her for telling him her water buffalo saga.

'She is a virgin,' he said. 'I do have some moral standards. She promised me she was a virgin, and I knew she was telling the truth.'

I have to admit that I have always admired US forces encountered, they are always jovial, polite, intelligent, and on their best behaviour. But you wonder about those seadogs. Gerry of the Irish Bar said that American sailors and marines were his best customers, unlike the Australian sailors, who were always puking and pissing and getting into fights. I said, surely the officers do something to stop them.

'That is the officers!' Gerry replied.

Unlike the comfortable Australian Navy, US sailors sometimes spend six months with no shore leave, and maybe that does something to the brain. O was another of Wing's friends, a serious serial copulator, not so much a skylab, more the international space station. Funnily enough, she wasn't the traditional Thai glamour princess, with long dark hair and so on, like Wing, but quite mousy. She just had magnetism, she looked dirty, as the Welsh say. One day I met her carrying a sheaf of papers. She informed me brightly that she was about to get married, and go and live in America.

This was a letter from her intended spouse, second-in-command of a US warship, and she was going to the translation bureau. I offered to save her the hundred baht and translate it for her. There was a photo of the dude, Commander somebody, resplendent in his white uniform, with five pages of gush: I love you forever, our love is special, and on and on. He was going to divorce his wife and kids in Indiana, and he and O would be so happy in some idyllic island hideaway. He had sent $5,000 to her bank account, so she could be a good girl back in the village, awaiting him, and they would be married ASAP. I translated as 'He big love you, send five thousand dollars.'

'Five thousand dollars?'

O's face lit up. She crumpled the screed and threw it in a waste bin. A couple of months later, I saw her hanging on to some spermed-out Burnt. Out of his earshot, I asked what had happened to her marriage. What marriage? The American sailor. Oh, that one. That was finished. Did you get his five thousand dollars? Oh, yes. So you still have it? No, she answered, shaking her head, as to an idiot. I thought, this gung-ho superbly trained naval guy has at his disposal enough firepower to start World War Three! Yet at the first sniff of Space Station O, his brains go out the porthole. I mean, where do they get them from?

At the Rock Hard, Larry did employ a professional virgin, who sold her virginity once a month, with real blood on the bedsheets. Twenty thousand baht for a short time, as opposed to the normal one thousand. Not even the sleaziest sleazebag suspected that her virginity recurred every month. After a while here, you get pussy-dazed, and the brain melts, just like ice cubes in a lady's vagina. However, Chester and his ice cubes sum up the yin and the yang of sex paradise Thailand, where girls will do anything. It is wonderful, because nothing is naughty, and it is depressing, because nothing is naughty. It is only a job, and they don't care: pussy on a cart, stacked up like squid. There is no prominent fetish scene in Thailand, whips, chains, rubber, etc., for there is no need of sexual fantasy: Thailand is one already. Who needs imagination, when her pussy is always open, for bouncing, or ice cubes, or ... what you like!

24.   GIRLS R US

Asleep, a Thai lady is blissfully content, her smile unfeigned, a picture of utter beauty. She is free of desire and frustration; she has temporarily attained nirvana. There is no time when sleep is not advised. If you enter an apparently empty store, look down and you will find the owner or assistant stretched out, strategically asleep. There is good sense in this, for mosquitos react to movement, and so inertia keeps them away.

Once at the Hat Yai airport, I wished to engage a taxi from the desk in the airport, marginally more expensive than the hurly-burly of freelance taxi drivers outside. There were three gorgeous Thai girls in smart blue uniforms, all with their heads on their neatly folded arms, and asleep on the counter. There was no flight due for another hour. What more logical than sleep? I tiptoed outside and sat down for a smoke, and a Benz pulled up. The chauffeur opened the back door, and a mafia dude in sharp suit and shades stepped out, fumbling with his cigarettes. He dropped some cigarettes, and at once, all the porters rushed to pick them up for him. Shades, suit, Benz, cheesy grin, abject proles, power. Only in Thailand. Or, only in Thailand?

Money to a Thai lady is like air. She knows she needs a constant supply, but has no idea where it comes from. Like air, it disappears as soon as it arrives, and she has no idea where it goes, leaving her 'very am poor'.

A Thai lady has a bank account and ATM card (just the same as she has a nose job, or an unused passport), because all the other Thai ladies have them, so she must, too. She will deposit money in the bank and promptly go to the ATM and withdraw the whole lot out again. Or, she will go to the ATM and put her card in, just for the fun of seeing all the lights flicker and the sign read 'Insufficient Funds' in two languages. Try and avoid getting stuck behind a Thai girl at an ATM, for you will wait ages while she juggles various cards and PINs, trying to find a stray 500 baht somewhere.

Or, she will use her ATM card hoping that maybe, while she was asleep, some money materialised in her account, from Gold-Plated Guenther or Sentimental Sven or Lustful Luigi. Guenther, Sven and Luigi are constantly sending some paltry banknote, with advice: be careful with money, stop smoking and drinking and taking pills and bouncing with strangers. Try to melt Antarctica with a candle. She has no word for 'budget'. One day, I said to Wing that we should get some oysters. Instead of taking me to the market, where they cost 150 baht a dozen, she led me to a restaurant, where they were 150 baht for three. We feasted, but I gently reminded her that the point was to get them cheap, and cook them up at home. She was genuinely sorry, she hadn't realised.

Every demi-mondaine knows that she is currently 'very am poor' and will actually take out her purse and show you its emptiness as proof that she 'speaks sure'. She is equally sure, like my agreeable nymphomaniac, who had spent her last banknotes on a duck for the monks, that soon, some male will come along and fill it.

Thai ladies are sharp, and know exactly where you have hidden your traveller's cheques, whose hair is clinging to the neck of your T-shirt, and what will make you feel good. But they believe in ghosts, consult soothsayers, cannot be persuaded that the world is round (if it is, we must live inside), or that Australia is not the same as Belgium. They are convinced that the slightest ache or pain means imminent death, and must go to the doctor, who for his 500 baht-plus fee, prescribes paracetamol, which they can get in the 7–Eleven. The great Thai headache is an excuse for not doing, or comprehending, anything you don't wish to. Headaches are sacred. Wing once went to the doctor with various headaches, and came back with several packets of pills. Sure enough, they were all brands of paracetamol, and exactly the same. Each colour, she said, was for a different kind of headache. I insisted she read the labels.

'They are in English. Not can read.'

'They are in Thai on the front, you can read that.'

'Not can, because I have headache.'

Some farangs, disgruntled that girls don't seem to care about learning English, decamp to the Philippines where the girls speak English, and even have college degrees. But there, as in other sex heavens like Brazil, they are planning for a ticket out – marriage, and a farang passport. They have the Catholic church, baseball, and juke boxes, so they are already half acclimatised. In Thailand, it is the farangs who beg Thai ladies to join them in their frigid homelands – and weep when their sweet little butterfly refuses; or else spends a disastrous time in the west – cold, no Buddha, no squid, no fried locusts – and flees home. They don't want to leave Thailand for us. We go to Thailand for them. So who's stupid?

In 1855 British diplomat Sir John Bowring brought back to London the Bowring Treaty, in which King Rama IV accorded the British certain customs privileges, and so forth. Thus, the Thais retained their independence. The king said (as it were): 'Hey, Sir John, look at all this tasty totty! You don't want to go to war with us. Have some fun!' So Sir John, having been

British ambassador to Siam, went back as Siamese ambassador to Europe! Thai ladies are more persuasive than cluster bombs.

If Thai ladies are relatively straightforward, Thai bureaucracy is not, though you can bribe your way into, or out of, almost anything. A methamphetamine lord known as 'Bang Ron' was on the run. Eleven separate law enforcement agencies were allegedly on his trail, and said they could not find him, because *a* they were unfamiliar with anywhere outside Bangkok, and *b* they didn't talk to each other.

A rich German businessman with a Thai wife, and large interests in Thailand, was held in jail for months without trial, and even without formal charge, for 'illegally importing' his yacht, a heinous crime, and also being an illegal immigrant. Now, in most countries, if you are deemed an illegal immigrant, you are sent home. What could be simpler? Thailand could be simpler. In Thailand, an illegal immigrant possessed of big money is put in the jug until they think of some excuse for extracting all this money from him.

A police captain claimed to have 'secret information' from Interpol that this gent was wanted just about everywhere for 'drug dealing'. The German police reported him squeaky clean, and free to yodel. Then, Interpol said that nobody at all was after him. (The police captain was meanwhile disgraced, for having fixed it for his sons to join the police force as a way of avoiding their military service.) It then transpired that the interior ministry had the German's name on their computer blacklist of 'undesirables', which is compiled at whim (he had obviously juiced the wrong police colonels), yet immigration officers were happy to stamp his passport every time he re-entered the kingdom.

He ladled out a quarter-million dollars in bribes to try and get himself out of the slammer, but this largesse only made more Thai pots accuse more Thai kettles of being black, and added to the enthusiasm to keep him there. If he wasn't guilty of something, then he would not have doled out so much bribe money. And there must be more! Thailand, it is often said, is the easiest place in the world to make a small fortune – as long as you arrive with a large one.

Full page ads on the occasion of the Asia Games in Bangkok warned consumers against faked merchandise, with the forged 'official games logo'. The direst penalties were threatened for forgers. The same thing happened in 2006, for the sixtieth anniversary of HM the King's coronation. Everyone had to wear a yellow T-shirt, and the whole country was a sea of yellow. Big capitalists were accused of hoarding, forgery, and price-gouging. Yet it is impossible to buy shorts, baseball caps, T-shirts or jeans without emblazoning yourself in the faked names of famous epicene designers.

These things cost a fiftieth of what they would cost in your shopping mall back home, and are indistinguishable from the 'real' thing. Should you wish to tell the time (not advised), you can purchase a genuine fake Swiss ten-dollar watch. Patong, like Pattaya, contains numerous art galleries, where industrious Thais churn out copies of old masters and modern art. You can see them at work, copying from a magazine picture: Dali, Picasso, Renoir, Matisse ... all there, faithfully reproduced in oils. They will copy a photo or painting to order, so you can furnish your home with fake paintings, dress yourself in fake designer clothes, and consult your fake Geneva wrist watch, while listening to one of the thousands of Elvis impersonators. Thailand is probably the world capital of Elvis impersonation, and it is done stylishly. There is even a paunchy tribute band to Sir Cliff Richard and the Shadows, impishly called 'The Young Once'.

It does not occur to any of these copyists to create their own paintings, even if glorified picture postcards – water buffalo, temple, monk, river – for the tourists. Every seaside town from St Ives to Acapulco has its coterie of bearded 'artists', who produce just such harmless stuff – and it sells. But Thailand has copyists. To create your own painting you would need, if not an original idea, at least some sort of individual perspective.

But what is the point in having your own vision of the world, when the Buddha had it all for you, millennia ago?

The world does not change – there is no possibility of its changing – the monsoon always comes, the bananas always grow, the girls and noodles steam inexorably, and everything is always the same, forever. 'Great Thai Inventions' almost beats 'Great Welsh Philosophers' as the shortest book in the world. It consists of the words: 'fantastically', 'beautiful', and 'women'. This shopper's paradise has hundreds of shops, crammed, each one, with exactly the same merchandise: T-shirts, knives, carvings of buddhas and elephants and so forth. That is what the truck, or fate, delivered this week, and you don't question a truck. Why be original? Farangs buy the stuff because that is all there is to buy. *Mai pen rai*. Nothing this side of nirvana means anything, and that is why we love Thailand so: everything in this vale of tears is just a joke compared to the bliss of eternal unconsciousness, and it is great to live in a place where meaninglessness is a fine art, and where it is men who learn to fake orgasm.

The current boom in sex tourism was blamed on the Americans, who chose Thailand – specifically Pattaya – as a suitable place for the GIs to relax after combat in Vietnam. But they chose it precisely because Thailand already possessed an established brothel culture. Even today, it is estimated that ninety per cent of bought sex is Thai to Thai. Most Thai hookers never see a farang, and those in Patong or Pattaya are the elite. Cheap air travel put Thailand on the map, the biggest draw, apart from Japanese, being Americans, Germans and British, coincidentally the world's major paedophile exporters. They halfway tolerate paedophilia here, despite the hand-wringing TV specials in Europe. Thai cops think, if a vicious rent boy gets paid to let some old fart slaver over him, what's the problem?

Family tourists assure you that they come for the world's most glorious beaches. This is hogwash. Everywhere in the world, except Saskatchewan, has the world's most glorious beaches. What is a beach after all but a lot of sand and sun and some waves to pee in? The planet is crawling with them. The family tourists choose Thailand because it smells of sex. If not participating – though plenty of liberated couples prowl the bars seeking threesomes and foursomes – they come to ogle, in search of prurient excitement – look, Norm! Those girls are prostitutes! – and reassurance that whoredom is squalid, so they can feel good about suburbia.

Yet there is always that hope on Norm's part, that he just might be tempted by a thigh or derriere, and plunge in, if he can get away from the old dutch for a while. The couples sit in Soi Katoey, radiant with happiness – the females especially – as the drunks drool and fumble with their chosen honeys. Gosh, wait till we tell the folks back home! These are whores ... they have sex for money ... just like that ... and here we are, me and Norm, sitting right in the middle of it! And look, this is a snap of a ladyboy sitting on Norm's lap! I can't imagine what they do! (Norm can.) Of course, Sheila keeps an exra-tight grip on Norm as they negotiate their way back to the hotel through the barrage of bare brown legs, and Norm can but dream. That's a plus, finding you are still able to dream. Often, Norm does manage to sneak away when Sheila is snoring, and you see him down the Heart of Darkness with the same ladyboy, then checking into the hot pillow hotel next door.

Above the bare brown legs are often bare brown bellies with stretch marks, for the most teenage of teenage nubiles has a couple of babies stashed with Mama in Nakhon Si Nowhere, and her excuse for being a bar girl is her sacred duty to support her family. Thai girls give birth early, for somebody is always there to look after baby while they go on the game. They often claim to dislike the job, and only do it to support their aged relatives and/or infants. As for liking doing your job, who does? Does a taxi driver like traffic? Does a schoolteacher like noisy kids? But they choose that over the alternative. They like having a job.

In the welfare west, choosing to be a working girl is a bizarre and perhaps distasteful lifestyle choice, but not an alternative to starving. In Thailand, without social security, it is just that. Thai girls claim they 'work bar' because they have babies to support. Often, they have babies to support as an excuse to work bar as opposed to growing old respectably, with a pig of a husband in some poverty-stricken dump where the brightest light is the one on top of the police car. You can't eat respectability. You can't drink it, and it's not much fun in bed. They work bar because it's simple. A whole generation of kids grows up with Aunt or Grandma, supported by remittances from Mother, who is horizontal in Patong or Pattaya, and to this 'skipped' generation, whoring seems the obvious and most desirable way out of the rice paddy.

As and when they see Mother, she has gold, clothes, a rich wrinkly farang doting on her, feeding her, and not beating her up. If she is lucky, and has enough money, she keeps a lithe, subservient Thai toyboy or two on the side. Way to go, Ma! I'll have some of that! Thus, the eternal cycle continues. Meaningless? Up to you.

25. I LOVE YOU FOREVER

The 'fun' of squawking seagulls in their box bars began to seem banal, tourist stuff. Wing would be out at her line of work, or away for a week on Ko Samui with some gold-plated guenther. I once more became a night hawk and haunted the throbbing sewers of the Heart of Darkness, to return numbly home in the cold grey dawn. The Heart of Darkness offered the lure of self-degradation, filth, abasement. There I met Wow. That was her evocative name, Wow. She was small, bouncy, voluptuous, deliciously full-breasted – lovely big chewable nipples! – with long frizzy hair and an enchanting crooked smile, like Porn's. I started to take her to the short time hotel – avoiding the gossips in my apartment building. Cool! Desperate 4 a.m. darkness! Sin!

Wow was from Phuket Town, where she worked as a hairdresser. She had two babies, and motorcycled at midnight over the mountain top, down the corkscrew road, to earn an extra crust in Patong. Now, this was romantic, a night journey of lust and greed. She was my dark angel, coming to me! She liked my attentions to her generous breasts and rump, and, after I had taken her a few times, she opened up physically, squeaking what seemed genuine squeaks. She said she now came to the same bar every night – run by a genial drunk from east Vancouver – hoping I would be there, and when I wasn't, which was most days, her heart broke into the usual thousand pieces ... she said 'I hot for you', and insisted she was my *mia noi*, 'little wife'. She said that in some unspecified, but recent, good old days, she would take three geezers a night, but now I was her only boyfriend. I visualised her in a porno movie, her sweet little body humping away, all grime and sweat and smoking a cigarette, as a legion of Burnts pounded her. What a thrilling, dangerous woman!

After our tryst, she would get back on her motorbike and soar away back to Phuket Town. Her back and big squashy breasts were mottled with a dark-brown skin blemish, like old parchment, which I thought utterly cute, but of course it disbarred her from backless, strapless, etc., dresses, as worn by bar girls. Disfigured, she had to be a creature of the night. It was real Tristan and Isolde stuff, sinister, depraved, romantic. But even Wow, with her orgasmic writhings, got to be routine. She always wanted us to come together, which was sometimes impractical, and so I learned how to fake orgasm, just like a woman, before I had the real one. You learn that in Thailand. I got the usual story of drunken boyfriend, too much battering, her departure with infants. But she didn't give me the water buffalo treatment, nor hint at permanence. She smoked Marlboros, saying she was not allowed to smoke at work, so smoked at all other times. She smoked as I watched her pee, she showered with a Marlboro stuck in her gob! I thought this the acme of sluttishness! I got her to smoke while I bounced her, a cigarette seductively drooping from her lips, as I rutted slowly, sitting up, face to face, or when she was smothering me with her ample and very tasty rump. But ... Wow, too, was basically nice.

I persuaded myself, not inaccurately, that these night writhings in hot pillow land, haunted by furtive footsteps, grunts and moans, actually improved relations with Wing, as they made me appreciate domestic bliss. As we got to know each other (though we didn't really, for she had even less English than Wing), Wow would actually delay her departure for five or even six minutes while she smoked two or three cigarettes. Now, this was intimacy indeed. For a Thai lady not to fling herself into her clothes and rush off to some other task, either domestic or sexual, is rare. Was she ... different? A fantasy come true? We long for what we do not possess, what cannot exist. We want the dream itself.

In Henry's Bar, I met Tom and Cynthia: nice, English, well off, bon chic bon genre. On their previous visit, they had visited her nephew, who had been caught with his apartment in Bangkok full of smack. He got 25 years. For $5,000, he could get the sentence reduced to seven years. Tom and Cynthia coughed up, and his sentence was duly reduced. A month later, they went to visit him in the Bangkok Hilton, and learned he had hanged himself. Life is cheap ... they sell T-shirts showing the Bridge over the River Kwai, with DEATH RAILWAY in big letters. All that suffering and torture, for the prisoners of war to build the Japanese their railway, and it ends up as a T-shirt. *Mai pen rai! Sanook!*

The Blarney Stone, another Irish bar, is in the middle of Soi Bangla, opposite Gonzo's katoey bar, where you'd see Norm and Sheila posing for photos with the bewitching transsexual love dolls in their fab frocks; then see Norm slink back later for a genuine grope, and maybe more. One time, John the boss, a jovial Kerryman, had words with his barman. Why was he always loping across the road to talk to a certain statuesque ladyman? Was something going on here? No, the boy said, it's just that he was my sergeant in the army.

I used to get my visa done (illegally) by Captain Kolochai of Patong's finest, who swaggered around with his pistol at his belt, cowboy-style, and was rumoured to have performed numerous extra-judicial executions. He later got jailed for corruption, i.e. he wasn't sharing the visa loot up and down the line, as was proper. He used to come around with some girl in tow, introducing her as 'my sister', selling microwave ovens or something. Would I like a demonstration? No, thanks. Well, actually, she wants a farang boyfriend, how about you? I said I was already spoken for. Next visit, he would have a different sister, selling mousetraps, and we would have the same comedy. He used to drink – Johnnie Walker Black Label of course – in Gerry's Irish Bar, and was usually fondling one of these 'sisters'. Gerry's saintly Catholic mother berated him, on the phone from Dublin, for living in a den of prostitutes. Gerry replied, sure, Mother, d'you think there are no prostitutes in Dublin? She called back later and assured him there were indeed no prostitutes in Dublin. 'I looked up the Yellow Pages under P, and there wasn't a single prostitute.'

One night a fellow came up to Gerry and said that the girl he'd paid the bar fine for wouldn't step out with him because she'd been told to stay and serve beers. Gerry, off guard, said 'Sure take another one, they're all the same.' I never let him forget that. We watched philosophically as some Australian asked Gerry's top horizontale to marry him. ('Sure, she's been fecked from here to feckin Jupiter.') With much kissing, she accepted. I asked Gerry why he didn't give safety warnings.

'I used to, but they just get angry at you spoiling their dreams. That one'll be back here on the game in a few months, when she's had all his money.'

Another top performer was in conversation with a young fellow and his pretty wife. It seemed he ran the family printing business in Dublin, and had big money. The next evening, past midnight, the same dude was there, with the same girl, but minus wife, and they were definitely canoodling, prior to bouncing activities. Gerry shook his head in disgust. Fast forward to a month later.

'Do you recognise that lad over there with my hoor slobbering all over him?' says Gerry.

'Sure, it's that printing fellow from Dublin.'

'And do you know where he is now?'

'Why, he's over there.'

'No, he's not. He's on a business trip to London, and the wife doesn't know he's here. She also doesn't know he married that mott in the Buddhist temple, and bought her a restaurant in Krabi, and they're going off to live there.'

'How stupid can people get?'

'How long is a piece of string?'

Helmut arrived back on the scene, on one of his desperate pilgrimages. This time he actually managed to track Wing down. She had taken to frequenting the open air restaurant, where our friends sang Isaan 'mor lam' songs, a pleasant Irish-style folk music that manages to be melancholy and bouncy at the same time. He found her there, which I learned from her, and all the other girls too, who thought it a great joke. Helmut was down on his knees, literally, with tears flowing and in full whine, with all the usual broken heart stuff. Wing was embarrassed: it is not done to make a scene in public.

'I cannot go with you, have boyfriend,' she repeated ritually.

Helmut promised moon, earth, and various celestial bodies.

Then he moaned: 'Why do you keep calling me that name?'

'What name?' Wing said.

It turned out that she had been unconsciously addressing Helmut with my name! I was here, you see; Helmut was a creature from another universe. Hey! I was numero uno! Wing explained this to Helmut, and he did what any red-blooded German male would do, which is, collapse in a heap of Teutonic blubbing, then depart with eyes heavenwards.

'I love you forever,' were his parting words to Wing; he might as well have presented her with *The Times* crossword puzzle.

26. VISA RUN

The curse of staying in Thailand is the quarterly visa run. Every farang must do it; or (on suitable payment to a friendly policeman), his passport must, every three months at least. It does not matter which Thai entry visa he possesses, and they are as varied and bewildering as blood groups: a type O, type B, etc. It doesn't help that, as a South African air steward told me, 'they change the rules as often as they change their knickers'. Whatever visa you possess, the entry stamp on your passport only admits you for three months at a time, so every three months, you must take your passport to an international border and make the visa run. Farangs whose only home is Thailand, who have Thai businesses, Thai houses, Thai wives and children, may have spent more of their life in Thailand than in their native land, but they are mere foreigners, and, unlike most countries, it is almost impossible to become a permanent foreign resident.

Foreigners may not own land in Thailand. They may own homes, but only the glue and matchsticks are theirs: the land is leased from a Thai owner. They may own motor vehicles, under certain conditions. A foreign company can only trade in Thailand if 51 per cent of the shares in its Thai operation are Thai-owned. If you arrive for a holiday of less than a month, you are stamped into the country for thirty days, at no charge. Thirty days is the time they would like you to stay, because in thirty days you will have spent all your money, and then you can get lost. Otherwise, you must negotiate the visa maze. Long-term stumble-wrecks bombard the *Bangkok Post* letters column with whinges about 'our' police, 'our' politicians, 'our' railway system, etc. But they delude themselves. Those things are theirs, not ours, dummy.

Many countries have visa requirements, of course, on the understanding that you may become an illegal immigrant and a drain on the welfare system. Citizens of the 'first world' travel fairly freely, since they are presumed rich enough to go home in due course. Three months is about a normal 'tourist' stay – in Turkey, or Mexico, or Brazil or whatever – but if you desire to take root, retire, buy land, bring money into the country, they don't make it difficult, beyond a certain amount of paperwork. Thai immigration 'policy' is a labyrinth – no, a nightmare, a funny farm. Why not allow a simple tourist to enter for three months, like any normal country? Because you only need a month to drain your wallet. The Thai government wants your money; it could happily do without you.

You can retire in Spain, or Costa Rica, or Mexico, or Malaysia, with a minimum of fuss; they welcome you. A retired farang in Thailand, until recently, had to have 200,000 baht in the bank, or else a monthly income of 20,000 baht, enough to live comfortably. Suddenly – without warning or discussion, by mysterious decree – the retired farang had to have a monthly income of 65,000 baht, and 800,000 baht in the bank as well. Just like that. There are villages in Thailand which do not have a collective annual income of 65,000 baht. There is also a Thai saying, on sighting a farang, which trans-lates as 'See the pig come!' For pig, read sucker. They do not want some harmless old geezer pottering about in the sunshine, with a small pension, enough for his modest needs. They want Gold-Plated Guenther, who is going to spend!

Of course, it is complicated for a Thai to get a visa for the first world. Bar girls who marry farangs do not automatically get the magic entry visa to the west. The US thunderously refuses them on grounds of 'moral degradation', while the British question their 'primary purpose', i.e. are they going to work. (We have our own masseuses and strippers, thanks.) The *Bangkok Post* headlined a 40-year-old English garage owner, who had married a 17-year-old Thai bar girl, and spent 5 years, and £40,000, on trips to Thailand, her family, and her. When he finally succeeded in getting her an entry visa, she spent two whole weeks in their new home, before disappearing. His only comment was that he should have listened to the immigration people.

Immigration absurdities do have their own brutal logic, which is to keep poor people out of rich countries. In Thailand, it is the opposite – a poorish nation seems to be doing its best to keep out rich people, whose money it needs. Thailand is a rich land, with a first world lifestyle at third world prices, yet, as in nineteenth-century Europe, the wealth is not evenly distributed. Most people live on the breadline, and the elite have millions. When Thais say they have no money, they mean no money, not even the price of a postage stamp. Thailand is proud that it has always been the independent Kingdom of Siam. So they are paranoid about 'letting foreigners take over the country'. At the same time, they thirst for more foreign investment, more tourism.

So, like everything else in Thailand, the visa nightmare becomes a charade; the letter of the law is obeyed, but not the spirit. The uniform at the airport stamps your passport yet again, as he has done for the last decade. He does not ask you why you come to Thailand so often. He knows you live here. He smiles! It is all a big joke that keeps him in a job. It helps if you arrive by air, not some grungy bus, for air travel in SE

Asia means you are already one of the elite. To get a Thai visa, all you do is fill in your name and birth date, with perhaps a photocopy of some bank account. You may be a member of a dozen terrorist organisations; you may have a humongous jail record; you may be a dope-dealing paedophile; *mai pen rai*! All they want is your money.

Why, then, do we give it to them, keeping our profiles low, and our whinges restricted to letters in the *Bangkok Post*? Why do we not take off, and spend our money in some more grateful tropical paradise? Why do supposedly civilised men put up with the Thai system, which would be corrupt even if it were not insane, and insane even if it were not corrupt? Girls, that's why. We are too pussy-dazed to complain. We would gladly spend eternity filling in visa forms, and trekking absurdly back and forth across borders, for one sweet taste of a Thai lady. And the Thais know it.

27. AS GOOD AS IT GETS

I partially get round visa nuisance by having, due to an absurdist quirk of fate, perfectly legal passports of different nationalities. One of them is Irish. If you have just one grand-parent born in the Emerald Isle, you qualify as an Irish citizen. Half the world is probably Irish. So I revolve passports, always have a fresh visa. One sleepy Sunday afternoon, the same immigration guy checked me out on one passport for the flight to Penang, then checked me back in on the Irish one.

'Not same passport!'

'Have two! Visa OK, yes?' (Shiver, visions of slammer.)

Many uniforms interrupted their doze to rush up, with much ensuing mirth that the same handsome geezer featured in two passports. I was introduced with tremendous ceremony to the police colonel commanding Phuket airport immigration, who saluted, bowed in a wai, and laughed. We had the usual surreal Thai conversation:

'Iceland! Very cold.'

'No, Ireland.'

'Iceland same Norway, yes?'

'Yes. Whatever.' (Don't fight it.)

'You have Iceland money? I collect money.' (There is perhaps a Thai cop who doesn't.)

'No have, very am poor.' (Police giggles.)

'You like boom-boom Thai lady?'

'Not understand.' (Mock puzzlement.)

'(stage whisper) You like fucky-fuck?'

'Oh! I very shy!' (Police hilarity.)

'Iceland lady like fucky-fuck?'

'Maybe.'

'Iceland lady no want fucky-fuck, Thai lady not shy, like boom-boom!' (Police collapse in apoplexy.)

The colonel proceeded to quiz me about my romantic arrangements, ignoring my assurance that I was only here for the temples. If I didn't want a common service girl, he could get me a nice, clean lady, very high-class. Gave me his card, and another salute, with an invitation to call him any time if I needed help, or a classy dame. Thai cops are keen to help you out of trouble, for cops usually cause the trouble in the first place. Well, it was better than 25 years in the monkey house, I guess, and I got home unscathed.

The Malaysians seem so nice, one is kind of embarrassed about using their country as just a visa stamp to go back to Gomorrah. The passport women are so cute and wear these blue headscarves ... but they don't have that innocent, salacious look of the Thai ladies. Still, those uniforms ... mmm! The point being that just as you are ready to despair, lose all patience with Thailand and the Thais, take your money to Malaysia and ogle those cute policewomen's uniforms, or, worse, write a whingeing letter to the *Bangkok Post*, the Thai loop snares you: they make you laugh. There is no escape.

Chester's friend Brian the Arsehole had long greasy grey hair, claimed to have been in the British Army, knew all about everything. He was another 'this is as good as it gets' merchant, the

usual loser. He had been holidaying in Thailand for six years.
He came for the scuba diving.

'No you don't,' I said, 'you come for the pussy, like everybody
else.'

'I admit I sometimes give way to my animal instincts,' he said
ponderously. 'But I love Thailand ... the relaxed atmosphere
... the fun.'

'And why is there a relaxed atmosphere? Because everybody
is getting laid all the time! You can go diving anywhere in
the world. You can go diving in England, for heaven's sake.
Malaysia is exactly the same as Thailand, except they don't
have a relaxed atmosphere.'

Brian conceded that maybe getting laid all the time had
something to do with the relaxed atmosphere. You bet. You
never see a Thai go scuba diving.

'I picked up a girl the other night,' he conceded further, 'and
we went swimming, for two hours, by moonlight! It was so
wonderful! We had such fun!'

'You mean you didn't bounce her?'

'Well, yes, I did, afterwards, but that's not the point. She'd
have been happy just to stay on the beach and go swimming.'

'Of course she would,' I said, 'and that is the point. She'd
have been happy to stand on her head with a banana in each
ear, because you were paying her.'

'A Thai girl is wonderful! She'll give you half the food off
her plate!'

'Quite true – but will she give you half her BMW?'

'You're too cynical,' whined Brian.

As opposed to what? As opposed to this is as good as it gets,
I suppose. These are the four stages of Thailand:

This as good as it gets!!!

New day, same shit.

Beam me up, now, Scotty.

This is as good as it gets.

But it never ceases to delight you with sheer weirdness. Always
little things ... like the choice urban myth, told in Bangkok,

Pattaya and Patong, that a local girl called Noi (= small, as common a name as Porn) had died after bouncing with a 'chocolate man', and being split open by his giant machine. All the girls assured you of this, with fearful grimaces of terror, although nobody knew this Noi, of course; a friend of a friend did.

Sir Mervyn of Beds looked ashen-faced one day. He had been to the jail, to see an ex-girlfriend, a lesbian, facing 25 years for murder. Eight years previously, she had been in a bar fight with another lesbian in Soi Bangla over another girl, and an obliging katoey had handed her a broken Heineken bottle which she slammed into the foe's ribcage, killing her. The killer fled to Chiang Mai. Some years later, in Chiang Mai, she met a guenther, and eloped to Germany for a year. Tired of Germany (surprise), she flew back to Thailand, where (more surprise), her name showed on the immigration computer as wanted for murder. So she was now in the monkey house in Phuket, and, without sufficient bribe money, her bar days were over.

Mervyn was one of those people who had been here so long he had almost forgotten how to speak English, and spoke a fractured Thaispeak, until you shook him and reminded him that he was an English gentleman. He'd had a bar, of course, and another bar, and it all went belly up, then a succession of jobs working for other people, who always fired him because he spoke his mind, or so he said. Now he was hustling 'translation services' and 'visa help', and bumming cigarettes. He wouldn't sit down in Henry's as he couldn't afford a drink, and he lived, ate and drank in this ghastly fleapit in Vaseline Alley, surrounded by rent boys, because he could run up a tab. There was a cheque in the post, of course, some protracted legal thing in England over an insurance claim, and when it arrived all would be well. Eventually, his girlfriend gave birth to his son, but of course had to be shipped off to the village, as Mervyn could hardly feed himself. Mervyn was an example of the Thai addict, who doesn't know when it's time to put his hands up, admit Asia has won, and return home to the dole.

One of Wing's friends was Goong (= prawn), who lived a couple of floors below us, and she spent a lot of time alone in her apartment, watching TV, eating, sleeping. One day I was invited down, to join and observe a cluster of girls, busy, as above. She was, literally, a beauty queen. Her whole apartment was a temple of her own glacial loveliness, festooned with cups, trophies, and photos of herself. She was a really handsome girl, an ice maiden, in love with herself. She had three boyfriends, Swiss, German, and Norwegian, each of whom sent her 10,000 baht every month. Yet I would still bump into her, as I staggered out of the Heart of Darkness at 5 a.m., preceded by Wow or somebody, and Goong would be arm candy for some new, enormous Burnt. Despite her vast income, she was always broke.

But the ice maiden, like all the rest, was so ... nice. She asked me if I was upset that Wing spent so much time in her flat. I said that on the contrary, I was delighted that Wing had friends 'for speak-speak'. She explained that many farangs, notably 'Gerramanny man', got 'angry' (the English word) if their honeypot spent so much as a minute away from them; got angry at the vast quantities of food their lady wished to absorb, squatting un-Teutonically on the ground; got angry at the aeons of time she wished to spend asleep, and not windsurfing. I said I did not get 'angry'! I was delighted for Wing to sleep, eat and gossip to the max. My gormless insouciance, yet again, was evidence of my good heart.

One day, Wing and Foon were out with Goong, and when they got back sweaty to her apartment, she stripped off and suggested they all take a shower. So the girls had a shower together, and Wing and Foon came back, convulsed with laughter. They had seen the ice maiden bare-ass! Without her carapace of finery, she had a wrinkly bottom and saggy breasts! Ha ha ha! She was ugly, *mai sou-ai*! It could only have been funnier if Goong had slipped and cracked her head open.

Goong used to go for sex trips to Singapore with some girlfriends, and once asked me to accompany them, to add respectability, all expenses paid. I wisely declined, even though she showed me her passport full of European stamps, saying 'I have beautiful passport' – meaning, she wasn't an indigent Thai bar girl. The Singaporean cops had the nasty but efficient policy, if they arrested a Thai girl without a work permit, of shaving her bald and packing her off home. It wasn't the bouncing that was illegal, for prostitution is legal in Singapore, but the lack of work permit. What the cops would have thought I was doing there was anyone's sinister guess.

One evening, Goong had just come back from a trip to Singapore and was flush with cash. She gave me a ride the kilometre downtown in her swanky Japanese rental car. I assumed she had some business and was going to drive upcountry to the home village, but no, she had just rented a car for the evening, to cruise around aimlessly, for *sanook*.

She was off the map for a while, and then she reappeared in the car park downstairs, looking less than glamorous, but with another car, this one her own. Her American fiancé had bought it for her. They were going to be married, and he was buying up land, to open a vast new resort complex, and we must visit. She also had a podgy eight-year-old boy in tow, her son from some previous liaison, which no one had known about. After that, there was no more heard of Goong until the grapevine informed us that her American had disappeared (wanted by the cops), along with his fantastic business scams, and she was heavily into dope, her looks ruined, living in her car on some waste land, and doing fellatio for 200 baht.

People fall in love with this place, and men weep when they leave. Some big gruff Burnt, weeping into his beer! It's pitiful. Because they are leaving themselves behind. People say they have fallen in love with Italy, Greece, or whatever, but as the plane takes them back to their grey homeland, they do not burst into tears. They have happy memories, and Italy isn't going anywhere. But with Thailand, men fear that their golden moments, their brown lovelies, their youth itself, are gone forever. They will never find the same Porn, or Noi, or Goong. Although they do. Take another, they're all the same.

A while later Foon reappeared from a visit to her mother upcountry with a charming, weatherbeaten lady of a certain age, who, it transpired, was her mother. She proposed to stay in Patong with her daughter, as she was broke, and couldn't pay the rent. Foon was carrying a six-month-old baby girl, and I thought she had somehow been pregnant without my noticing, but no, it was her new sister. Her mother, well past forty, had produced this delightful infant, much as a rice paddy produces rice. There was no mention of father, husband, or other fertilising agent. These things just ... happen.

The mystery remains of how these girls, even Goong, the many-suitored ice maiden, are always, almost as a religious duty, broke. If you take a western woman on a date, you assume she has got her life organised somehow, has food and lodging. You do not expect her to ask you for the bus fare home, or the socks you are wearing, or some money so she doesn't have to sleep in the park. In Thailand, the base line is different. Always wheedle, cajole, beg, for even a girl in a Benz, in her heart, is always broke, and the Benz will be repossessed, or riddled with bullets.

On my first visa run out of Phuket airport, I asked the police sergeant-major at immigration how many cartons of duty-free cigarettes I could bring back. Two cartons, he said. 'You buy one for me?' I said, some other time, so he gave me his card, offering the usual help with problems. I can't imagine an immigration officer at Frankfurt demanding a free bottle of schnapps. But who knows, I might have been a lottery winner, full of bonhomie. If you don't try it on, you never get.

Another English type was lamenting the passing of Thai innocence.

'Ten years ago, this was just a little village, the girls were so sweet, now they are hard and brassy. It's all this tourist money ... this isn't Thailand.'

Every expat says that. Thailand's innocence finished just after you got here. I say it myself. So guys who respectively arrived fifteen, ten, or five years ago, all agree that it's 'not the same'. Just as their reminiscences end at the moment they get to Thailand, when time and brain function stop. But it is the same. It's been the same for millennia. As good as it gets, or, new day, same shit.

28. ANCIENT MASSAGE

At long last, I made my own pilgrimage to the fabled Kristin Massage. It was awful. Supercool, smooth, efficient. You went up into a bar, shady, with discreetly placed tables. A girl brought you a drink while you looked at the far wall, a single glass window, behind which the masseuses sat in tiers, wearing evening frocks. It was like looking at fish in a fishbowl, and unnerving – not Thai – for they sat still, without talking. They were scanning the punters, with come-on smiles and winks. We were in a fishbowl for them.

After ten minutes, a Chinese man in a suit whispered, would sir like a full-body massage (adding details)? If sir was just gawping, that was fine. The girls wore numbers, by which you selected. Was there a factory producing number badges for massage parlours all over Thailand? You could even select a proper, non-erotic massage, but, opting for the full-body thing, I paid the enormous price at a cash desk, like a cinema's. My girl came out, took my ticket, and got a room key. We rode up to the fifth floor and entered a standard hotel room.

The first thing she did was decisively switch on the TV. It was some game show. Then she yawned, and apologised. It had been a long day, she had a headache. Now I felt I was back in Thailand. She stripped, writhing Houdini-like to get into her towel without exposing herself. I followed her example, and sat watching, as she inflated a rubber air bed and ran a hot bubble bath. She pinned up her long hair and wrapped it in a towel. Then she spread another towel on the bed, and placed a box of tissues and a condom – I swear it was strawberry-flavoured – beside it. Neatly.

It was fascinating to watch her work, nurse-like: erotic, not.

Then she took off her towel, and, nude, motioned me to join her in the bath. She soaped and inspected and rubbed me most efficiently, and spoke a little English. She was from Bangkok, had no money, got paid peanuts, could not leave the building without permission, so had not seen much of Patong, and what little she had seen, she hated. Her mother in Bangkok thought she was working in a restaurant, and would be horrified to learn she was a service girl.

Since it was low season, the girls in the fish tank were rationed to one customer each per day. So – this was evening – she had been sitting on her butt since 1 p.m., doing nothing, while her comrades filed away, like contestants eliminated from a game show. As soon as she could save the bus fare, she was going back to Bangkok. She was industrious, did what was required. I was laid on the airbed and had oil rubbed all over by her naked body, slippery like an eel. From time to time she checked me for an erection, and was surprised I didn't have one. This is Patong, I wanted to remind her. Naked women are no big deal. I've even got one at home.

Then it was time for The Event. I lay down on my back and she enquired if I wanted oral or regular sex. A blow job with a condom! Yuk! I managed to get the thing done the regular way, but I had to fantasise about various naked women before I could unburden. Tip demanded and given, more water buffalo stuff about how hard life was, and I was out of there. I didn't ever want to go back. The overpriced experience was clinical, and basically silly. I did not feel particularly rejuvenated, or particularly anything. The scuzziest bar girl is an individual, and your experience is at least an experience, but a masseuse is not even an individual. Still, at last, I had discovered the notorious Thai 'sex industry', and you can have it. I walked back to the seedy box bars, with their raucous inmates, and felt home again.

However, my visit to Kristin Massage signalled the end of an era. Wing's Schleswig-Holstein dude was back in town, she was seeing him for prolonged sprees, and it was evident he was smitten. He had serious loot, and was prepared to spend it on her; he could keep her daughters in the style to which they wished to be accustomed. After nearly two years together, it was time to part, free of guilt, I fondly imagined. But no westerner is ever free of guilt. That's why we envy the Thais. They never feel guilty. I set off, with Wing grabbing me for a desperate farewell bounce as my airport taxi waited. It was a bit teary, and a bit inevitable, with the usual lies about see you again, I'll come back, and all that. Have a nice life. I left Patong without knowing what had happened to Squeeze, or Ski, not that I'd ever met them. Squeeze probably did go the Félix Faure route, and I sensed from the rumours that Ski was seriously sadic. I had the worrying feeling that perhaps Squeeze and Ski were the same person. Nothing here is ever what it seems.

Anyway, I holed up in Montreal for a while, chatting up the cute girls in the university quarter, who were amazed to find an Anglo could speak French. I impressed them with my rantings about all the countries I'd been to, until I realised I was just a curiosity, a sort of ancient mariner. And the cost! Eight bucks for a lousy hamburger! When you first get to Thailand you are amazed at how cheap everything is, but after a while you take that as normal, and everywhere else seems ludicrously expensive. So, bowing to the inevitable (as we also like to think) I set off once more for Thailand, albeit by a circuitous Caribbean route. But even so ... Thailand lured.

The turquoise ocean, the smiles, the luscious brown lovelies, the flowers, the food ... tiger prawns or plump oysters at 60 baht a kilo; *tom yam goong*, the fiery shrimp soup (or *tom yam moo*, pork, and my favourite *tom yam pet*, duck) ... grilled honey-glazed chicken from a street stall ... tiny sweet clams and huge mussels; beef in oyster sauce, sweet and sour everything ... enormous, succulent pineapples and watermelons and pomelos, a sort of cross between an orange and a grapefruit ... all tastier than elsewhere, and absurdly cheap – apart from one thing, that infamous culinary delight the durian, called the world's most dangerous fruit. It is like a spiny football with a thick rind, and weighs about 3 kg. You have to hold it by its stalk to avoid injury from the spines. Anyone hit by a falling durian – from a 20 m height, for although durians are cultivated, you have to wait for them to fall – can be seriously injured or even killed. Inside the fruit is a custardy pulp that is smelly and not unpleasant, though devotees think it the tastiest food in the world. Wild animals are attracted by the odour of ripe durians and compete for fallen fruit, along with gangs of armed durian poachers who frequently have shoot-outs. The perfume-loving Thais are fastidious about smell, and in airports or malls you see 'no durian' signs. In authoritarian Singapore it is a crime to eat durian in public. But it's a fuss about nothing, as the durian smells like a ripe Camembert cheese, scarcely life-threatening. In every way, Thailand makes the mouth water.

It is curious that Thai restaurants in our northern world tend to be expensive, trendy, glitzy. The stuff they serve can be whipped up by any Thai housewife for a hundredth of the cost, and with a hundred times the taste. It is common to see Thaiettes in Patong or Pattaya glumly dining with a guenther, who, to show off, has spent on one meal what would feed her family for a week. I can make this myself, and eat it off newspapers on the floor, she silently screams. Give me the money instead, you dolt.

A favourite Patong conversation piece is the dreadfulness of rival Pattaya, the sleazy big brother of tasteful Phuket.

Tsunamis aside, the southern island increasingly regards itself as a sort of Asian Monte Carlo, for the discerning traveller, not the sweaty masses: more Thai hypocrisy and wishful thinking. Phuket means yachts, fabulous beaches, rich folk in blue blazers, studied elegance; Pattaya is drugs, paedophiles, Arab and Russian gangsters. So I resolved to sample this sinful place, and was pleased, if not surprised, to find it much the same as Patong, only larger, and without the small town snootiness. Eventually, both Chester and Chris the Cybernaut surfaced in Pattaya, too, tired of the Patong cauldron of doom. I often thought of Wing, another drop in the little bowl of sadness you carry inside you, and which never goes away. But Wing was not the woman in my recurring dream. Blame everything on dreams, like the Thais. I don't pretend I'm not a heel.

29. WAYNE AND CHARLES

Another trip halfway across the planet; the airports, no longer places of romance and excitement, just sweaty, clogged despatch centres. At least, on the plane to Bangkok, I had the satisfaction of knowing where I was headed, and, with tongue ever so slightly in cheek, could assure the newbies how wonderful their holiday destination was. At Don Muang (now superseded by a glitch-ridden new airport), the heat and beauty struck full blast; the girls, the girls, the girls. A bus crawl through the choked Bangkok traffic (true to form, the divinely uniformed airport girls pretended there wasn't a bus downtown, and I should take a taxi; after I pointed at the sign saying 'bus', they grudgingly admitted there was, but, truthfully, warned it was very slow). At last, a bus got me to Pattaya in three clanking hours and, before boarding, I was one-upped by a German stumble-wreck. Quizzed about hotels, he replied smugly, 'Oh, I wouldn't know. I have a house there.' Dial L for Loser. As we crept into the straggling outskirts of Pattaya, there was no feeling of wonderment. A larger version of Patong: home ...

If Patong was the thrill of discovery, Pattaya was the nod of recognition: horizon-to-horizon girly bars. More bars spring up every week, or every day. Given Thai hypocrisy (or charming unpredictability), there are phases of puritanism, restricting opening hours or nudity. Farang boozers in Bangkok undergo random urine tests to check for drugs. Protests are made, the rules then relaxed, or the cops bribed, and the whole cycle starts up again. On the innumerable Buddhist holidays, when bars may not serve alcohol, they serve it in coffee mugs, to reassure prowling cops. One disco was shut down when a visiting politico found a condom on the floor, used or unused was not specified. Yet government propaganda encourages condom use. T.I.T.

My life in Pattaya was, and is, rather different from that in Patong, simply because it is a city as opposed to a village, without the cosy ennui of seeing the same people every day. Entertainment-wise, Pattaya consists of a beachside rectangle about 7 km long; beyond are vast suburbs, but inside it, the narrow streets pullulate with girly bars, discos, and katoey cabarets like Tiffany's, and the Alcazar, near the Big C supermarket, up where I used to live. There, along with the Carrefour and Lotus supermarkets, you can get washing machines, computers and TV sets, as well as the latest western fad, whether tricycles, skateboards or scooters. You would think yourself in any American suburb. The check-out girls earn about $5 a day, slightly above the legal minimum. The hotels for Japanese tourists are concentrated near the ladyboy shows.

At the very end of downtown, after a cluster of streets quaintly named 'Pattayaland', and including the self-explanatory 'Boyz Town', is the infamous Walking Street, which pullulates as elsewhere, only more expensively. Travel agents abound, all offering 2,000 baht visa runs by minibus to the Cambodian border, five hours there, five hours back. Small sections are Arab or Russian in flavour. Beyond that, there is the hill, a promontory of increasingly deforested and villafied land, atop which is the temple of the Big Buddha. Horrible pseudo-grand hotels cluster by the shore, all boasting the finest wine list in Asia. Over the hill is the more tranquil beach suburb of Jomtien, with vast concrete hotels for Russian tourists, and full of honking bars like everywhere else. As you turn left up the beach road, there is fruit corner, with gyms and gay bars, called 'Hardbody' and suchlike. Although Pattaya has an estimated half-million people, the tourist area is quite compact, and has everything for the freespending visitor, every type of cuisine, and would-be exotic shopping malls. The scenery in the hinterland is nothing, but Pattaya Bay, glittering with yachts, is spectacular. After dinner, you can stroll around the back streets listening to the girls hoot and holler, if you want to ...

I chatted on the bus (160 km for 70 baht) with an English alleged former racing driver – not again! – who said he lived in Chiang Mai, and came to Pattaya for the sea air. Sure you do, buddy. So I landed in Pattayaland, the downtown strip, in the hotel he recommended, run by another English type called Roland or Rupert. Hotel! Decorated in cloying plush, like a London Odeon cinema of the 1930s, it was more like a cathouse. It was a cathouse, with its own go-go bar thudding downstairs. The bedroom was full of sexual trinkets, all for sale, and the furniture looked suspiciously adaptable to your favourite perversion. The owner helpfully provided an instruction manual about girls, acquisition, enjoyment, and remuneration of, written in fluent Loserese, and I was reminded of that favourite English epithet which begins with W.

Opposite was a geezer bar run by Arthur, from Somerset, which I thought might be the Pattaya equivalent of Henry's, seeing that the mildly spoken Arthur, who had run a bar in Oakland for nine years, had a sign up requesting gays to 'haul their sorry asses elsewhere'. He earnestly admitted that he didn't want any blacks there either as, after nine years in Oakland, he hated them, and said that quite frankly he hated Thais, and all Asians whatsoever. Narrowed things down somewhat. The posh downtown condo where he lived had been taken over by

Bangkok gangsters. They simply marched in with guns, and a list of holiday apartments, and told the office girls that they were the new owners. Just like that. Rather as Thailand had annexed the Muslim south. The girls naturally bowed to force majeure, and changed the names on the title deeds.

Alas, there was no round table of doom, just smug petit-bourgeois English gents of the onanistic class, who'd cashed in and settled here, wobbling their jowls in praise of Mrs Thatcher as they pondered where to go a-prowling. This was a serious question; a young Welshman assured me Pattaya was a fishbowl. He had gone whoring way up in north Pattaya, leaving his missus at home a safe distance away. Arriving home in the morning, after jollies with two hookers in a hotel, he had gone to sleep while his missus went to market. She returned, screaming 'You butterfly, have two ladies last night (etc.)!'

There was one amusing English drunk who had just done eleven years in an Australian jail (presumably for murder; he wanted me to ask, but, unkindly, I didn't), and who, repatriated to the UK after ten sexless years, had promptly flown to Thailand with $500 to his name. I am afraid Pattaya, for all its virtues, lacks the intellectual rigour of Patong, if that is possible. I contented myself with getting my bearings with a quick tour of Walking Street, indistinguishable from anywhere else – bars, girls, shops, restaurants, discos, Boots the Chemist – then found that not far up the road were scores of good, modestly priced hotels, so I decamped to one, at half the price of the Wood Green Erotic Odeon.

The neat hotel room hosted my first romantic event in Pattaya, a handsome bar girl called Nern; at 35, a quiet type, not a razzle-dazzle squawker, with a lovely smooth young girl's skin, a rather homely peasant smile, and fabulous legs. She was nice, not a clingon, and I saw her – I mean had her – often. One of her charms was in the genital department; pretty as a flower, and I was reminded of Om's erotico-horticultural Jersey boyfriend. She took me home to her barracks, which she shared with the usual centurion of girls, including her schoolgirl daughter, who gave me a surly look. I sensed she disapproved. What does a teenage girl, taught to be modest and respectable, think, when her mother is a bar girl? I am afraid I have no answer.

Walking around, I soon found an apartment with a view of trees and a few metres from the sea, in a swanky new four-storey block, where I was the first occupier of a nice modern studio. Soi 2, between the sea road and Second Road, at that time was a quiet street, almost suburban, very leafy, although now it pullulates; across the road was a huge, grotesque hotel for the Japanese, shaped like a ship, and beside that, a Belgian hotel, run by the usual deranged alcoholic, with an afternoon cathouse right on the premises. You would hear whistles blowing as identically suited Japanese were herded across the road by their supervisor for their morning dip. At the top end of the street, beside Second Road and opposite the Big C super-market, clustered dozens of box bars, back to back. On the other side of the road was the Alcazar katoey show, and a few sinister clubs for Japanese only.

I soon got to know a few neighbours: Jerry was a huge black man from Los Angeles, who had been some kind of special agent for the National Security Agency, I think a heavy rather than a spy, with time murkily spent in Nicaragua. Such things were undiscussed and he never went into details, saying it was all secret. I'm happy on the rare occasions when bloodcurdling and dubious wartime tales are left untold. Jerry had no toes, and had to wear special shoes, and go to chiropodists. He wouldn't tell me how he lost his toes, so I assumed it was war-related.

He also couldn't use his hands very well, after a stroke, so I typed letters for him, mostly to his wayward, sulky (etc.) teenage daughters living with their divorced mother back in California. She was Mexican, and Jerry had spent a lot of time in Mexico, so we had that in common. I loved his crisp, evocative English, free of white men's circumlocutions: his wife left him because he was 'messin' some'. Our only points of disagreement were his belief that OJ was innocent, and that syphilis and gonorrhea were the same thing. Soon, he was shacked up with Noi, a third his age, took her to the movies, shopping, and so forth, but was apparently not bouncing her. Jerry was new in Thailand, so asked my advice – my advice! Noi said 'I cannot love you the way you want,' which disturbed him, as it suggested non-bouncing.

'Jerry, she doesn't really know what these words mean. Lots of older guys just want to hold hands and stuff. Remember it's your dime, and you have to tell her what you want. Maybe she wants sex, but fears you just want to be her grandpa. So don't confuse her. Thai girls like to know the ground rules.'

A couple of days later, Jerry arrived in my apartment, whooping and hollering and slapping his thigh.

'You the man! I took your advice and, man, she can't get enough of my big black ass!'

I saw Jerry off and on over the years; he moved to a town nearer Bangkok, his girl left him, then came back, then left him again, I suppose, for I got a melancholy email saying he had gone back to California for good, to avoid bird flu.

Downstairs lived Middle-Class Charles from Wimbledon, always apologising for his 'bourgeois respectability', and for being so middle-class, even though he had been sent to a ghastly state school in Wandsworth by his champagne socialist parents, who were of Scots ancestry, and unwilling to part with the bawbees for a private education. He described, shame-facedly, going queer-bashing on Wimbledon Common with assorted oiks, and got a laugh from my mimicry of the prolo London accent. We would converse in mockney: 'You wanna start? Don't come it, my son, I'm well 'ard' – 'Phwoarr, I bet she goes' – 'Lovely jubbly' and so on. On the passage of some tasty girl, Charles would contort his face in a proletarian grimace and make simian 'Ook! Ook!' noises, while thrusting his hips in copulatory fashion. Of course this was postmodern irony, to satirise people who did such things in earnest. He was almost the only farang who dared mouth the forbidden L-word, 'loser'. On seeing a particularly squalid farang, fist strikes forehead, the 'L' stamp ...

England is the only country I know which has a comedy of accent. In France, Germany or the US, for example, it doesn't matter what accent you have, whereas certain English accents are automatically funny, or criminal, no matter what you say in them. Charles was not long settled in Pattaya, and unforgettably let slip 'Thailand reeks of sexuality'. I would fire this back at him now and then, in his own tremulous middle-class accent, then he would say: 'You want some? Don't come it,' etc. Our American friend Wayne did not quite grasp this British funny-voice humour.

Charles had inherited his parents' thriftiness, and was forever saving pennies, on drink, room, or girls: ironically, since he had recently inherited £180,000 from his deceased mother, half the proceeds of selling the family home, and the other half going to his *Guardian*-reading sister in London, who was 'married to a poof'. Having spent years in Korea as an English teacher, he now felt entitled to live it up, and wasn't even spending all the interest on his capital.

Unfortunately, Charles had one of those tantalising sums, enough to make you feel rich, but not enough to feed you for life. When Wayne, the accountant, told him so, Charles would shrug, and say Byronically, 'I don't expect to live long, anyway.' Charles admitted he had a history of pill-popping; although quite good-looking, he confessed to being shy, embarrassed about not having gone to university, and needing to fortify himself with vodka before the night's girl hunt.

On the prowl, he would, in a diffident middle-class way, classify girls as rock apes, bush pigs, or scragglemuffins, with the familiar sperm-drained, drink-ravaged farang prettily defined as a 'stumble-wreck', something Charles was in danger of becoming. (Of course, not all foreigners are stumble-wrecks. There is also pimply Norman, thirsting for oriental wisdom, and reborn in a saffron robe as Brother Upanishad Bananarama.) By 3 a.m., after an evening of drinking, slobbering over a variety of hapless bar girls, and telling you how horny he was, and simply had to score a scragglemuffin, or even a bush pig, he usually lurched home alone, rubber-legged, or, if accompanied, was unable to perform.

When he did succeed, you got a graphic description of writhings and grapplings and the girl's physiognomy, usually with some minute imperfection, like a mole on her buttock, which gave Charles, terrified of permanence, the excuse to discard her as a possible mate. If all went well, he would say he had enjoyed a 'mammoth blast-off' or two. Charles had a breast fixation, and would bounce anything if it had 'monster jugs'. 'Ohh ... look at that,' he would gasp, whine, or sigh, looking at some perfectly ordinary, indeed respectable girl, top-heavy in the balcony. Once, when he was drunk, I had to pull him off a vast-breasted *Hausfrau* selling fried chicken from a stall.

'Charlie!' I squawked. 'She's not a bar girl, she's a chicken-seller!'

'I must have her,' he drooled, Dracula-like, before I was able to propel him to the nearest barstool.

Once, he confessed to me that he fantasised about being whipped by a black girl, and was incredulous when I told him plenty of guys shared the same dream, or even made it reality. He only had to inspect the 'Miss Whiplash' postcards in all the phone boxes in central London.

'Get away,' he said. 'You're joking.'

'You're a Londoner! Surely you must have noticed?'

'Well, I never had to make a phone call.'

He liked the buxom California girls, but said darkly he couldn't go back to the US because of trouble with the law. It turned out he had skipped a parking fine. Charles actually had a sweet little girl in the Philippines, who was stuck on him, and of course he treated her badly. He used to fly back and forth to the PI, to Angeles, the brothel town that festered round the former Clark USAF base. His honey lived in some idyllic fishing village, and he would grant her a few days of his presence before returning to the stews of Angeles.

The PI sounded awful: crass, noisy, violent, commercial, gum-chewing; but part of its attraction for Charles, unfortunately, was smoking shabu, similar to ya-ba. He sometimes stayed with LA Rob, who lived there off and on with his big-breasted girlfriend, both of them hooked on shabu, and Charles would secretly bounce with Rob's girlfriend when Rob was asleep. Charles was sneaky like that. There was another American doper Charles stayed with, whom I met briefly, called Could've-Should've, because his life was a litany of missed opportunities and wrong choices, and he lived there too, with his wife, in a house he had bought. Eventually Charles and he were arrested for drugs, the cops tipped off by his wife, who wanted, and got, the house for her and her Filipino boyfriend. They escaped, after disbursing a huge bribe, to flee to Thailand. Could've-Should've lost his house and wife, and turned to dealing – another Asia addict, who couldn't put his hands up and go home – and is now doing seven years in the Bangkok Hilton, having been caught with 400 ya-ba pills in his Pattaya hotel after some girl snitched on him, as they always do in Dopeworld. Not good, if you're over fifty and broke.

Bustling to and from airports helped Charles feel busy and important. I pointed out that Pattaya was, by the sound of it, a lot more fun than the PI, the girls cheaper, less clinging, and less homicidal, and that his forking out for air fares made a mockery of his penny-pinching. 'I know, I know,' he would reply mournfully, shaking his head as though powerless to do anything about it. He had cell phone mania, every week a new one, the previous one usually stolen by a girl, and making absurd calls from bars, or glaring at his watch, and claiming he had to 'be somewhere', meaning another bar, or dope purchase. Like many farangs, he said he envied me the fact that I had work to do, i.e. writing things. Aimlessness affects many expats, who find Thailand an alien culture. If you don't read books, you are forced to drink, fornicate or golf yourself to death.

Chris the Cybernaut and Swashbuckling Chester turned up as refugees from Patong, and Chris bought a lot of computers and set up a school to spread the cybergospel to the Thais, employing Thais to do so; naturally, they lost interest, and the thing folded. Then he started a one-man computer consultancy, and that folded too. He didn't need to work, but had to feel busy. Lately, he had a scheme to buy repossessed houses from the bank, and resell them, taking advantage of arcane laws governing bad loans. I don't know the fate of that, but I'm not holding my breath. Chester, meanwhile, bought some wretched farang bar in Bangkok from a guy who was setting up in China instead (I wonder why), only to discover that the clientele, who came to watch American football at 5 a.m. Thai time, didn't buy drinks, as they had to proceed to the office.

Middle-Class Charles played tennis, and at the tennis club he met Wayne from Milwaukee, so I hung out with them both. Wayne was even cheaper than Charles, and each, separately, moaned about the other's being obsessed with money. Wayne admitted after a while that he couldn't help cheapness, having been brought up by strict Seventh-Day-Adventist parents, and 'if you think I'm cheap, you should see them'. He confessed to me – 'but don't tell Charlie' – that, because of religion, he had been a virgin until age 25, and was making up for lost time. His first sexual experience had been in the back of a bus, on some school outing, when some girl gave him a spontaneous toe-job. Perhaps that was why he was obsessed with massage parlours.

Once, he leapt from a *song teo*, the prowling taxi-buses that are converted pick-up trucks – *song teo* meaning 'two benches' – and sprinted across the road, narrowly avoiding death. When I caught up with him, he boasted that he had given the driver only 4 baht and 75 satangs, instead of the customary downtown 5 baht. He had risked his life to save .625 of a cent.

Mind you, some *song teo* drivers can be appallingly rude and extortionate; stopping in the middle of nowhere to demand an absurd sum, as if you were some greenhorn, and as if there wasn't a vehicle every thirty seconds. The trick is get into the vehicle wordlessly, for then it is a bus, standard fare 10 baht. If the unwary ask to go to downtown, he will demand 100 baht, for now he is a taxi, even though he is going there anyway. The drivers are the male equivalent of bar girls, hicks flocking to Pattaya, expecting streets paved with gold, to find it a buyer's market, where every third vehicle is a taxi, as every third shopfront is a bar. No wonder they get ratty.

When we went to the Marine Disco, a sleazy, barn-like pick-up place with wildly overpriced drinks, Wayne would spend most of the time waltzing around trying to avoid the prowling waiters, who would oblige you to buy a drink, instead of just buying a drink straight away and concentrating on the girls. Avoiding spending money, rather than finding a girl, seemed the object of the visit.

He once took his Filipina girlfriend, Marivec, of whom more below, on a fiancée visa, for a tour in his car of the western US, which had to be curtailed when she objected to sleeping in the car. Wayne couldn't see her point, after all, every third night, he treated her to a Motel 6! It didn't help when she announced that she had no use for America, and wanted to come and live there purely to make a lot of money, so that they could retire to the PI as soon as possible, buy a big house, and impress everyone in her village. He dithered, in his kind of Napoleonic game-playing way, with the idea of actually marrying her, and took her to Milwaukee to meet his pious parents, unsure if they realised, or cared, she was a bar girl.

Then I got a fervent phone call from the Philippines, and was invited to their wedding! Yes, it was really on, and Wayne had spent a whole $250 for licences, priests, and liquor. I made my excuses, wisely, for it was cancelled when Wayne was mortified to find that after the $250, he would have to spring for a roast pig as well. Later, he turned up at my place and produced three cans of beer from his backpack. The brand was unfamiliar; he had bought them in Las Vegas, and carried them halfway round the world, rather than waste a few dollars.

Wayne and Charles would each complain the other was obsessed with winning at tennis, which was 'only a game'. If one was smitten by some bar girl, the other had to have her first, or else sneak in for sloppy seconds, then disdainfully proclaim that she 'wasn't bad'. Unlike me, with my gormless insouciance, both refused to use condoms, and lost time, money, and several potential blast-offs by demanding sheathless sex. They also shared their constant affliction by sexually transmitted diseases, notably chlamydia, which was practically Charles's middle name, and I suggested plonkingly that non-rubberised activities might just have something to do with this. Both had a chemist's knowledge of antibiotics, and Zithromax was the current wonder drug, for all drips and itches. I got a laugh once, in a pharmacy, when this hulking Burnt came in, tattoos, chains, scars, piercings, the works. Curious to hear where Conan the Barbarian was from, I heard a reedy New York voice warble: 'Do you have Zithromax?'

30. HOT AND COLD

Soi 6, near my dwelling, was the raunchiest street in Pattaya, not well discovered by the tourist hordes, who tended to hang around expensive Walking Street. The King Kong was the raunchiest bar, always full of beer-swilling, guffawing guenthers, getting oral, or manual, or le plein shag, in public. Pantiless girls would flash and pretend to frig, or maybe not pretend. They would bounce on the bartop. It was great laddish fun. The Swiss owner insisted on honesty: no wheedling, no stealing, no demanding extras, and a short time meant two hours. If a girl came back to the bar before that time, she was reprimanded. Also, his girls were keen on sex, or outright nymphomaniacs, and said that doing what they enjoyed was better than picking rice. I took a few, and they were all astonished when I appreciatively tipped them over the odds. Charles didn't like it there, as it was 'full of guys'. His idea of fun was a deserted bar where, without competition, he could slobber over some poor girl, whining 'Do you really like me?' before panicking, and rejecting her, as her elbows were the wrong shape.

Predictably, the cops started hassling the King Kong, raiding the upstairs rooms, and carting some hapless fornicator down to the station, then throwing the furniture out of the window, as the place didn't have a hotel licence. When the Thais see a farang making money, they want to take it away from him. Eventually the Swiss sold up, and the place is now owned by a senior police officer. Just as predictably, it does hardly any business. Thais fail to grasp that customers prefer somewhere not mafia-owned, just as a rich, gooned-out guenther can't understand that if nine neighbouring box bars lose money, his own new one is likely to lose money as well.

With Wayne and Charles, I did the rounds: roaring bars on Soi 7 and 8, where clingon girls would instantly perch on your knee; cool, expensive go-go bars on Walking Street, like Super-Baby A Gogo, where the dancers were young, adorable, aloof, and wildly expensive; bleary 5 a.m. bars still open on Second Road as dawn crept up. They both had this irritating habit of flirting with girls, without actually taking them. Their line was, I'm working on her, using some mysterious woo-chemistry. I responded that the only wooing she needed was a banknote, but Wayne thought he would charm some girl into doing it for free, and Charles had to be sure she 'liked' him.

I had many girls from the standard noisy bars, often proving clingons – turning up drunk in subsequent small hours, to bang on the door and demand money, the building's 'security' usually being asleep. But I preferred prowling alone, Bogartishly walking the dark, deserted city, round the few bars still open in the back streets. I would find places of wonder, hole-in-the-wall shacks straight out of the Isaan, no words exchanged, no squawking, no 'hello sexy man, where you from', just a crooked finger and a nod, and a happy girl, and the mama-san putting down her knitting to anoint your face with water, and give you a wai salutation. In one bar, on Soi Bukaow, the only thing open near dawn, there were two females, the pretty, brassy mama-san behind the bar, and a teenage girl of utter, willowy gorgeousness. There was also a pissed-up Scotsman, listening to the mama-san, with great giggles, on the phone to her fiancé calling from England.

'You not send me money, you fuck off!' she cackled gleefully, closing the call.

'He call back,' she said.

I propped up the bar while she showed us her photo album of her and this simpleton, until, sure enough, he did call back. You could hear his shrill tones protesting undying love, then she told him to fuck off again. Meanwhile I got draped around the willowy beauty hovering near me, and I politely asked the Scot if she was by any chance taken.

'Ach, no, pal,' he said, 'you have her. I'm with her' – nodding at the mama-san – 'she's the best fucking fuck in Pattaya, that one.'

As the best fucking fuck in Pattaya was telling her fiancé yet again to fuck off, I made my arrangement with Miss Perfection. We walked hand in hand back to my place, past all the closed bars, feeling like *Les Parapluies de Cherbourg* or something, very romantic. Unfortunately Miss Perfection spoke good English, so I got the saga of her recently ex-boyfriend, some ancient small-time face from east London, who beat her, starved her, wouldn't let her go out on her own. She said that, though technically free of him, she couldn't go with men during daylight, or some spy would inform on her and she'd get a beating. Her previous boyfriend, another crim, had been just the same! Men are so rotten, etc. I didn't ask why she picked them.

Anyway, eventually, I shut off the stream, and we had a satis-factory bounce, although she was quite lethargic, but her great beauty made up for that. It was a masturbatory sort of thrill, I suppose, with this centrefold shivering discreetly under my attentions, after I had cruelly excited her with an extra-long bout of cunnilingus. I went back to that bar a few days later, looking for Miss Perfection, but the mama-san – who was again on the phone to England telling him to fuck off – said she had fired her, as she didn't seem to realise she was an employee, obliged to go with customers. A bit of a prima donna. Her photo was still on the wall, and I took Charles and Wayne there, to show them the classy gangster's moll I'd enjoyed.

We sometimes went around with Extreme Bill, who lived on the ground floor. Now, everything I quote him as saying should be taken with an unusually large (even for Thailand) pinch of salt. Bill was Australian, of Greek parents, from Melbourne, the largest Greek city outside Athens. He was powerfully built, chubby, and had learnt kick-boxing in order to fend off anti-Hellenic bullies. Twentyish, he was coy about his money source, but seemed able to pursue his career of venery through Pattaya and Angeles.

Bill was a sex maniac, enduring, or enjoying, the condition of satyriasis, and needing sex at least once a day; back home, in sexless Melbourne ('Australian girls are all lesbians'), he had to take female hormones to dampen his ardour, otherwise he went mad with lust, sporting a permanent erection. He belonged to swingers' clubs, where his stamina and genital enormity – which, happily, I didn't have a chance to verify – were much in demand amongst middle-aged married couples, where the male was fond of the buttered bun. There must be a word for voluntary cuckolds ... bunists?

He had a sly Aussie mate, with whom he used to enjoy spitroasts, one pleasuring a girl's mouth, the other, her rear end: a slightly dubious form of male bonding. Both were adamant that Australian girls of the blonde-surfer-goddess class were frigid prickteasers. Australia was finished, you needed SE Asia for real action. Bill spoke fondly, though, of an Italian girlfriend he had had in Melbourne, who liked it up the rear, so much so that she liked to bounce with two blokes in her anus at once. This not totally unbelievable feat gave Bill great pleasure, but is a form of male bonding I find less than enticing. Bill recounted with great relish his conquest of one prickteaser, whom he punished by bouncing her for two hours, without climaxing, until she was screaming for him to finish.

'That's real fucking, from a real man, you bitch whore slut (etc.),' Bill snarled, and when he had finally finished, and was giving her a lift back to the city, threw her out of his car by a deserted beach, leaving her to walk, or hobble; I prefer to think of this story as vainglory.

Charles and I concluded that Bill was really interested in punishing girls for not being like his saintly Greek mother. However, Bill was funny, strolling up Soi 6 and cheekily asking various girls if they took it in their ear, or their arse, or their armpit. (When I mentioned my penchant for toe-sucking, he exclaimed, 'You're one sick unit!') Of course, to a simple business proposition, he always got a straight answer. My mimicry of his Australian drawl, 'D'yew tike it up the lift nostrull?' drew laughs. He was a passionate believer in Viagra, which does indeed help you to perform stirring deeds, and in Pattaya, everyone of every age takes Vitamin V. It leads to a delightful 'big power' and you feel like a horny teenager again, useful out here, where naked women are no longer the thrilling novelty they once were, and older guys must master the art of faking orgasm.

Bill favoured the packed, glitzy discos such as Frankie's Cool Spot in Walking Street, half-American Frankie being the star of his own show, belting out 'It's Not Unusual' with hairy-chested, medallioned ferocity, although in real life he was married to a katoey. It was almost impossible to move in Frankie's, so if you wanted a girl, you were more or less forced to take the one that chance had squashed you against. I even found a girl there, Charles having (once!) lured me, and sure enough, the crowd was too packed to move, so I took the girl beside me. She was very sweet, and didn't like horrendous discos any more than I did. Charles, needless to say, was mortified, having to leave empty-handed, while I had acquired a companion with no obvious effort.

Wayne and I preferred, amongst others, the more homely, less deafening Hot and Cold A Gogo, to which we sometimes dragged a reluctant Charles: reluctant, until he had found a large pair of mammaries to slobber over. Charles's problem was that he couldn't sit still, always saying 'let's move somewhere else', and leaving a beer half-finished. This got worse as time went on, and I sensed it was something to do with dope ingestion.

I should warn the reader that the Hot and Cold is rather dull these days. At that time it was a joy, another chunk of the Isaan, totally relaxed, with luscious teenage girls wandering round in the nude, perching on a knee at random to pursue a screeching conversation with a girl sticking a Heineken bottle up her behind on stage, then abruptly haring off to sit on another knee and jabber at another girl. It was as if they were in their own back yard, in the village, and we were just handy crates to sit on. They had a complete cor-blimey show – darts, beer bottles, eggs, hot wax, tape or razor blades pulled from pussies, lesbian writhings – and the olafs and guenthers were all agog, but, frankly, once you've seen one, you've seen the lot.

The trick was to cajole a girl into meeting you outside, after her work, so that you could take her without paying the extortionate bar fine; or to ascertain that she was proceeding to the Marine Disco, open till 4 a.m., where you could pick her up, supplement-free. If you were still not satisfied when the Marine closed, you could go to the smaller Marine Disco 2, which closed well after daybreak. Extreme Bill liked to kerb-crawl on his motorbike, picking up unsuccessful scragglemuffins from those venues, and usually they were glad of a lift and a bed to sleep on, after he had punished them for not being like his mother. He planned to go to Uzbekistan, where the sex action really was, as described by a mate of his who lived there; Pattaya was finished.

Still, the Hot and Cold was friendly, and Wayne and I would sit, enjoying free caresses with unabashedly naked teen beauties, while they and we had our separate conversations. There is an etiquette about these things: if you buy a girl a lady drink, and tip her fifty cents, you are entitled to a bit of decorous groping in return, even though it is obvious you are not a long-term bouncing prospect, although I took a girl upstairs once, having negotiated a reasonable fee, which I was forbidden to mention to her comrades. The room was delightful, a junk room stuffed with rural clutter, just as in the village.

One evening, during the show, with my hand on a particularly nice bottom, and Wayne looking bemused, in that innocent midwestern American way, as he explored a pair of breasts, he interrupted his usual lecture on high finance and the meaning of life to exclaim, 'Hell, if we were both millionaires, we'd still be sitting right here.' I could only agree, although, on my solo rambles, I selected a few regular, friendly girls, in the dingy and little-frequented bars. One of them was little Lin, a delicious teen with a divine coffee-coloured body, the very image of Thai pornotopia. I enjoyed her person several times, and she valiantly strove to give the impression she enjoyed mine. Uninhibited cunnilingus helps: food and sex inextricably linked, with a sadistic satisfaction at giving pleasure.

Extreme Bill disappeared, along with his rented motorbike, which he was assumed to have stolen. But he resurfaced, and was nabbed in the street by the rental lady, who extracted 30,000 baht. He had allegedly crashed the bike, another driver to blame, and it was naturally her fault for not having insurance. He was seen with a sinister-looking older Frenchman, and said they were going to Latvia, where the sex action really was. Uzbekistan was finished. I imagine he is still lurking in Pattaya, if not in jail. They always come back.

Wayne and I, and occasionally Charles, frequented a cosy little Swiss bar in Soi 8, staffed by nice friendly girls, where you could have a pub-type conversation. We would talk into the night about world affairs and things, while Charles ogled a buxom, very sweet, matronly girl called Pou, which means 'crab', but whom we called 'Wisconsin', because of the udders, Wisconsin being America's dairy capital. I think he bounced her once, when we weren't there, and he claimed to have bounced a lovely honeypot called Nok, whom both Wayne and I wanted, except that she was usually clutching a Burnt. Wayne had one of his usual disastrous assignations, with the daughter of the mama-san, who met him outside, then ran away up some stairs, so he pursued her, and found her defiantly in the apartment of her Thai boyfriend, to whom she was going to be married in a week. Go figure.

The star of the show was another nice girl dripping with gold, who was stunningly beautiful, Italianate, a young Sophia Loren: long curly hair, firm breasts, straight nose. She was the preserve of the seriously wealthy. We called her 'Kaputt', because once she staggered back from a tryst with a Burnt, rubbing her bottom, and squealed: 'Ooh! *Tote kaputt!*' which means 'arse ruined'. I once had a friendly conversation with Kaputt, in which she showed off her gold, earnestly insisting she had bought it all herself, and was proud of her independence. A few months later, I saw her in there, scarcely recognisable, no longer the goddess, minus gold, with dirty hair and clothes, and a worn, sad face. Dope? Maybe. The goldlessness said it all. After that, she just disappeared, no one knew where. Kaputt was kaputt. T, once again, is T.

31.   A SOCIO-LINGUISTIC DIGRESSION

They do use foreign words a lot, like 'kaputt', 'beautiful', 'broken heart', 'horny' and so on. Thai is a simple language with a small vocabulary. It is tonal, so that a word may mean many different things depending on voice inflection. *Sou-ai* means beautiful, if correctly pronounced, otherwise it means ugly. *Song*, with a lilt, means two, but liltless, an envelope, or packet. So if you want two packs of cigarettes, you ask for '*song song?*' The written language is difficult, with 42 consonants, of which 16 alone represent the letter 't', and, due to tonality, an almost unlimited number of vowels. Thai school-leavers are considered achievers if they have learned to write. What they write doesn't really matter, as long as it is something. There is not much time to study actual subjects: rote-learning is the thing, because you are safe expressing thoughts that wise men have expressed before.

The future tense is normally eschewed in favour of the historic present, because there is no future, and the Thais are only vaguely aware of the past, or 'before long time'. There is no definite or indefinite article; thus 'house' does not distinguish between houses in general or one house in particular. Compare the needless complexity of our own languages. 'I am going to go to Bangkok' becomes 'Go Bangkok.' 'Do you think you'll be having a few beers later on?' is 'You drink beer?' Some foreigners start to think in Thaispeak, and forget their own language. 'I go hotel Nong Kai, room beautiful too much, see river Mekong, water big big, have girl small money,' an amorous traveller will report, at which point you must shake him vigorously.

A German sentence is a railway line, straight and to the point; an Italian sentence, an operetta; a French sentence, an intricate cathedral; an English sentence, a London taxi, meandering a bit, but getting you there in the end. A Thai sentence is a sort of prayer on a fish hook, which, if waggled enough, might get you something. If you repeat 'rice' or 'money', something resembling rice or money might perchance float by. Reasoning is irrelevant.

The Thai world view is binary: yin or yang, black or white. A thing either is, or is not. The lovelorn tourist imagines his beloved is dreaming of him from afar. She is not, because he is not here. There is little fondness for abstract thought. Nonsensual things belong to the spirit world, and hence are bad luck. A Thai lady with a map of Thailand cannot point out her home town. She will complain that the map is in English, then claim her home town is too small to be marked, and sweep her palm vaguely from Burma to Cambodia. If asked to point out Bangkok, she will have a headache. If she cannot show you where she comes from, she can tell you in detail how she gets there: where the buses stop, or the best chicken stalls are. As for neighbouring Malaysia or Burma, she has no more idea where they are than where the Andromeda Nebula is. Why should she have? They are as much use to her as the Andromeda Nebula. What use are maps? She knows what exists, for her practical benefit. After comically stilted conversations about money and food and possessions, it uneasily dawns on even the stupidest lump of eurotrash that they are smarter than we are.

The average westerner has his head stuffed with 'news'. He prides himself on knowing 'what is going on' in the world and must be constantly updated. Thais are not interested in 'news', unless the USS *Kitty Hawk* is in port, or someone they owe money to has been shot dead, or there has been a terrific earthquake somewhere, with piles of corpses.

A farang will try to impress his girl by showing her on the world map how far he has travelled. It means nothing. He might as well have come from Mars, or the neighbouring province of Thailand, of whose whereabouts she is equally insouciant. He is here, not there; so is she. His money is in his pocket: soon this unhappy state of affairs will be put right, and it will be in hers. That is all that matters and all that ever will matter. When he returns to Mars or Minneapolis, another rich alien will replace him, and that is the purpose of aircraft.

Do Thai demi-mondaines enjoy their work? It depends what you mean by 'enjoy', or 'work'. Most people enjoy the result of work. Sex, to a Thai bar girl, is no different from any other job. A girl may like her customer, or not. She may be a nymphomaniac. She may even fall in 'love' with a man, meaning a teenage-type crush, for a few days. Westerners fail to see sex as 'work'. Especially when the lady, asked to name her price, as though she is a restaurant menu, says, with a coy smile, 'Up to you.'

A demi-mondaine accurately calls herself a 'service girl'. She does like some clients, in the same way that hairdressers or taxi drivers like theirs ... as long as the tariff is mounting. The universal 'Up to you' has many meanings, mainly 'Up to me' or 'No'. When Pat's restaurant in Patong was flooded, she asked the repairman where the water came from. 'Up to you,' he answered. Truth, after all, to a Buddhist, is relative, and language in the Orient often serves to conceal rather than convey meaning. Monks, supposed to revere life, do not kill fish, they 'remove them from the water'.

Typical dialogue:

He: How much do you want?

She: Up to you.
He: 1,500?
She (shrugs): Up to you.
He: 2,000?
She (shrugs slightly less disdainfully): Up to you.
He (consumed with passion): 3,000?
She (smiles hugely and embraces)

Actually, it is wrongly imagined that inside every bar girl is a housewife longing to get out. Inside most bar girls is a bar girl longing to get out – get rich enough to have her own beauty salon, massage parlour or bar. Working bar is more agreeable than breaking her back in a rice paddy for starvation wages. And she might strike it rich, with Gold-Plated Guenther!

Bar girls are not slaves, and sex is not an industry, contrary to the prurient tabloid press, although, upcountry, as mentioned, there are girls in whorehouses, chained to their beds, for the Thais. Many, or most of the girls a farang meets in Patong and Pattaya, are motivated by nothing more than greed, indolence, poverty, drug addiction or simple sensuality – many, especially the tattooed ones, simply like to party – and they are actually the cream of the crop, not sold by their parents to settle a debt.

It is a bit like nineteenth-century England where, to judge by Victorian novels, nobody seemed to have sex at all, though the streets were full of 'gay girls'. Of course gents did have sex, but it was with the proles, freelance girls in the music halls or gin palaces, which were similar to Thai bars today. They weren't brothels, you just found a lot of available women. Thus, gentlemen could devote their minds to higher things, like true love, while their gonads were taken care of by the lower classes. Thai bar girls figure they might as well profit from what they do all the time anyway, and enjoy male attention every day, whether they are shrewd or naive, shy or horny, new or battle-scarred, sober or drunk. Some shy little country girls are prim, and want the lights off, and a towel wrapped every-where. Others fling their clothes off, without inhibition.

Sex is on the agenda from smile one. A Thai lady does not fill herself with your food, then say 'I thought we were just good friends.' She finds no nobility in unrequited love, unlike westerners who enjoy suffering, frustration being the basis of our whole culture. If a Thai lady is bored, she simply departs – as farangs, who have taken the marriage plunge and provided her with a new home in Birmingham or Brussels, continue to discover.

She must be kept in a constant state of fun, and in return she provides service with a smile. Thai sexual culture is tolerant, Buddhist, pleasure-oriented – unlike our repressed western culture, crammed with porn mags and lonely hearts ads. Mail-order brides, indeed! There is uninhibited sex in Thailand because Thai ladies are not sexy, and they are not sexy because they are not unattainable. Western females cultivate dress sense – the tease, the peek – but Thai ladies have grace, which becomes them whatever they wear. They are at ease in their skin. You can talk to them without encountering a wall of suspicion: is this some kind of creepy pervert? Sex, at street level, is a product for hire. A bar girl is a free agent who gets her customers where they want to go, comfortably and with a minimum of fuss. Afterwards, the 'For Hire' sign lights up again.

She is neither saint nor harlot – a bit of a goddess, and a bit of a party animal. Her latest boyfriend is no more special than her last, but neither is he less special. You see the girls practising their smiles, with shop windows for mirrors. It is sincere practising. She is not confused. She does not worry what her friends will think, because they think the same as her. She does not wonder what she looks like, because she knows what she looks like. Her body is a sacred temple, only to be displayed for proper reward. In bed, she will perform the most extraordinary gyrations in the way of service; but when her big toe peeps outside the bed, suddenly she must be covered in a towel. She is modesty itself. This is Thai logic. You are either one thing or the other; having sex, eating, or in the bathroom;

with no overlap. Mrs Rolf used to tell (frustrated) Rolf that he should go to Kristin Massage! Massage did not interfere with marriage, and was a good excuse for a pay rise, as she could demand the same tip as the masseuse ...

Neither is there much national jealousy about the millions of sex tourists, which is why farangs basically despise the Thais, and they despise us, as mere animals. What western husband would send his wife out to prostitute herself? If Myrtle Beach or Southend had a million foreign sex tourists every year, convinced that the girls were 'easy', what would the men of South Carolina and Essex have to say? The average Thai income is $2,000 a year. In the northeast, where most bar girls come from, it is much less, and people gladly send their daughters south, to remit money with the fiction that they are hotel receptionists. If a farang is so smitten that he follows her home, he finds himself a meal ticket not just for his beloved, but for a whole village. Everybody needs a new water buffalo.

Thai boyfriends, which girls assure customers they do not have, are delighted to see the money come in from all the infatuated olafs and guenthers. Often katoeys, they are delighted to sit at home watching TV, drinking whiskey and playing cards with fellow-toyboys, while mademoiselle is horizontal. Grief frequently ensues, when a Thai girl pretends she is not a prostitute, and when her besotted farang also pretends she is not a prostitute. That is why marriages with teenage bar girls tend to fail. She thinks he wants her for her snoring, guzzling, TV-addicted self, whereas he is marrying a girly-mag fantasy, all he has ever seen of her. It is wise to follow the old adage and choose a spouse half your age plus five. Satisfaction often results.

32. SISTERS

Then Lek turned up, or rather, Lek and Tou, a two-sister combo, both twentyish. *Lek* means small, and *tou* means cupboard. They were not really sisters: Lek had been adopted by Tou's family, and, though the elder, had to endure Tou's teasing. I met them one evening outside the 7-Eleven down near Walking Street. Lek, the more articulate, did the talking.

'You want two ladies?'

I said I would opt for just one, Tou: conventionally pretty, svelte, big bottom, quite a hottie, while Lek was tough, boyish, thin and bony, with only one eye. The other had gone in some drunken motorcycle accident. She was street smart because she had to be, and both of them proved completely without inhibitions. However, as I later discovered, Lek was much sexier, that is, more imaginative, than the sensual, but dopier Tou. I was persuaded to take them both, and we rode a *song teo* back to my apartment. I faced the choice: which one to enjoy first? Decisions, decisions. I had the bright idea of staging a nude housework contest, to see which one made the most merit. They thought this splendid fun. Tou chose to scrub the bathroom, while Lek swept the floor. In a jiffy, they were naked, giggling and sweating and toiling energetically.

After half an hour, I declared a draw, and said they would both enjoy my favours. Lek drew back, with a resigned look, as she was obviously used to being second string, so I had Tou, on the bed, while Lek sat beside us, watching TV. Then we sat around in the nude, eating and drinking, with no indication of my new friends rushing away. We eventually snuggled up in the bed, and this time Lek demanded my services, so I provided them, while Tou watched curiously, with little scornful giggles from time to time as I humped, and Lek genuinely orgasmed, something Tou had left undone, although she had seemed close when I chewed her nipples. Lek said that Tou lived off and on with a French dude in some condo, while she herself had a septuagenarian guenther, who really was called Guenther, and sent money from Germany occasionally. It seemed that Tou liked it in the anus, while Lek didn't, so in the morning, I obliged her while Lek bustled around making breakfast. This time Tou did orgasm. She had a lovely silky anus, but then it would be, with so much practice. We all took a shower, laughing and slapping bottoms. Tou enjoyed having her bottom slapped.

Money changed hands, not a lot, but enough for gratitude, then Tou scurried off to her Frenchman, while Lek hung around. I had to go out, so she went, too, but turned up again at dusk, in case I wanted a replay. I didn't mind, so the scenario was repeated, with Lek solo. Of course, with her sister ('my best friend') absent, she at once began bad-mouthing her, telling me what a lying, thieving bitch she was, as Thai girls invariably do about their best friends. I have to say Lek was great at athletics, and enthusiastically climactic; her head and body were completely shaven, her King Kong fright wig being in fact a wig. She politely said my penis was just the right size (of course), and comically described some German boyfriend with an enormously long, thin penis, which was uncomfortable, unlike Guenther's, which was minuscule.

She also had a Norwegian boyfriend named Kjel, another fisherman busy with the fockin big prawns, as well as a cop from Dubuque, Iowa, whose photo was a caricature of a redneck cop: little moustache, piggy eyes, and beer belly. He too sent money, but didn't want to have sex with her, his only pleasure being to watch her defecate, or photos thereof. Lek spoke quite good English, and had a sense of humour, meaning she laughed at my jokes, so gradually, her visits stretched longer, until she was more or less a fixture. I learned she had no fixed abode, sometimes dossing with other girls, sometimes sleeping on the beach.

With Lek in place, Tou came round to party. Like many Thai girls, she was not imaginative in coupling activities, content to recline, or crouch, buttocks up, and let it happen, though putting marginally more oomph into the anal side of things, whereas Lek leapt around like a walking *Kama Sutra*. Lek confided that Tou was 'sadic', so I tried spanking her bare behind. Both girls enjoyed the spectacle, Lek perhaps vengefully; Tou soon demanded penetration of her favourite aperture, a cute little brown wrinkle. Fancying myself a connoisseur of such tender flowers, I obliged, sodomising her, while hand-spanking her bottom, with her nonchalantly masturbating; effervescent from the combined operations, she quickly orgasmed.

The sound undoubtedly carried, but the hooker next door was rarely in, while, on the other side, Genial Geoff the car-rental man was a bit pervy himself, judging by the nightly sound effects. From then on, I matched him spank for spank. One of his spiv confederates once knocked on my door and entrusted me with an envelope for him, containing 100,000 baht. 'Thanks, mate, you're a pal,' he said. That would have bought me a first-class ticket to New York.

Though, like a good western liberal, I dutifully denuded the rubber plantations for erotic events, Lek and Tou found my apparent condom obsession rather exotic, even perverse: why, for the price of a pack of Mr Durex's finest, you could get two plates of duck soup! All the same, I clung to my wimpish obsession, though Wayne sneered I was a 'rubber hound', to which I retorted he was the one always dripping. Wayne and Charles practically lived on Zithromax, one of their few interests in common. I always felt a bit left out as they swapped stories of drips, pus, warts and antibiotics.

Once, when both Tou and Lek were present, and after I had bounced Tou, Wayne came round, and we adjourned to a bar, excellent fun, until Wayne admitted he really, desperately needed a girl, and it was getting late. I said, why not take Tou? So in due course he did. This added to my mystique as a wondrous European-type sophisticate, but, though I was happy to oblige her with a sophisticated European-type bare spanking, I didn't enter Tou's person again for a while, until I reckoned the coast was clear. I wasn't that carefree.

I got very fond of Lek, and amused by Tou, despite her stormy temper: she would spitefully remind Lek that she was not her blood sister, just an orphan, thus last in the pecking order. Each was on guard lest the other steal from her, which they did whenever they had the chance, as is normal amongst Thai siblings.

'She has babies, but she's a baby!' Lek would exclaim in disgust.

Tou had some Portuguese boyfriend, and brought me the usual letters to decipher, which I could do, though I couldn't write back. If she wasn't sleeping at her Frenchman's place, she was in somebody else's hotel room, smoking ya-ba. This I discovered when both girls brought their fixings, grinding up pills into powder, then melting it using an arrangement of tinfoil and tobacco, and lit up on my balcony. At the time, I made no protest, never having encountered this before, and innocently imagining it was like smoking a joint, although I don't myself. This ya-ba was just another amusing feature of those zany, wacky etc. Thai girls. Trouble is, it's not zany or wacky, it's evil, and expensive. Lek didn't mind sleeping on the beach, for she was out of her gourd.

Like her sister, Lek was a keen nudist, always ready for sex, multi-orgasmic, and eager for me to match her, blast-off for blast-off. She was joyfully raunchy. I was once in a bar on Soi 6, with Middle-Class Charles, me as straight man to his idiotic fumblings, and I told girl #2 that I already had a girl at home, so wasn't playing. Asked her name, I rashly told the truth, and said 'Lek'. She promptly asked if Lek was thin, head-shaved, and one-eyed. There are thousands of girls called Lek; I had never even visited that bar before.

There was only one suicide during my time at that apartment, an English fellow who was found on his bed, having OD'd on whiskey and pills. There was a curious odour around the place for a few days, which I thought was just Thai cooking smells, but it turned out to be a corpse. Apparently he had plenty of money, so it wasn't that. Maybe his girlfriend left him. Or he'd just had enough of paradise. It was an easy misunderstanding, because the noxious smell of frying chillis pervades, like tear gas, and most Southeast Asian cuisines rely heavily on sauce made of fermented fish. For Thai fish sauce, you leave a barrel of fish and chillies in the sun for a month, now and then collecting the liquid dribbling from a spigot. Yet stinking Southeast Asian fermented fish is the basis of our ubiquitous brown sauces, thanks to Messrs Lea and Perrin, who brought it from Malaya back to Worcester.

You see? That last paragraph, I started about suicide, and got on to food, just like a Thai. Suicide is humdrum, food constantly fascinating.

Guenther arrived in town, at which Lek was all excited, and took two weeks' leave, only to return with the melancholy news that Guenther was shacked up with, or had even actually married, another, more voluptuous girl. Then it was Kjel's turn to arrive, after phoning frequently – I pretended to be Tou's boyfriend – and Lek was to stay in his hotel. We had a farewell bounce before she departed, but she returned two hours later with Kjel, though she knew I wanted to avoid meeting any of her paramours, especially Kjel, who sounded like a nice guy, however stupid. He wanted a man-to-man chat about Lek's dope habit, and I managed to get through the session without revealing that my bed was still damp from his beloved's bodily fluids. Did she have other boyfriends? Certainly not! It's a bit grim having to tell a Thai girl's lies for her.

But the sisters' ya-ba habit got worse, and the last time I saw Tou, her head was covered in a scarf as her hair was falling out. Lek ripped off the scarf (causing a shouting match), to show me, and it was awful. She had hardly any tresses left. Lek of course shaved her head, so you wouldn't know. Then Tou got arrested, and beat the drug rap, as is normal, by becoming an informant; thereafter, setting people up and snitching on them seemed to occupy most of her time. This Frenchman of hers, I learned, was a real 'monger, he did katoeys and boys and pretty much anything that moved.

Lek's behaviour got more and more erratic, with constant mood swings. She was smart enough not to do her dope in my apartment, but would rant and scream at the slightest thing, say, if I wanted the air-con or TV adjusted, then become weepily apologetic. Exasperated, I gave her some money to go and find a room for herself; of course, she spent it all on ya-ba. At last, when she was out scoring dope, I dumped her bags at the door, with instructions that she was not to be allowed up the stairs. When she returned, there wasn't the expected scene, she was just glumly resigned, wondering why I hadn't kicked her out sooner, 'like all the others'. I gave her some more money, and off she went to sleep on the beach, leaving me feeling rotten.

A week later, she turned up drunk and manic, and forced her way in. I couldn't wrestle her out the door! She was shrieking about killing herself, and locked herself in the bathroom, which contained nothing more lethal than a jar of brewer's yeast tablets. She eventually came out, with brown goo dribbling down her chin, a devilish leer of triumph, and a pungent aroma of B vitamins. She had swallowed the lot.

'Now you see what I do!' she cried, waving a brown finger. 'I love you, but you not love me! I die in your room!'

Adopting a sofly-softly approach, I furnished her with the requested paper and pencil, so that she could write me a suicide note. Now that the deed was done, and she was existentially engagée on her course for the beyond, she was quite calm and melancholy, a sort of Mary Queen of Scots. She wrote a whole page of script, with tears and brown goo dribbling all over the paper, and I had never felt so sorry for anyone in my life. Her strength seemed to wilt, and she crumpled up, so I gently forced her on to the bed, and told her to go to sleep. She held my hand as she drifted off, and when she was snoring heartily, and emitting whiskey fumes, I went to sleep beside her.

In the morning, she woke up bright and breezy, delighted that it was not her time to go. She had tested the spirit world, and it had backed off. I didn't have the heart to tell her that she had swallowed nothing more poisonous than vitamins. Off she tripped, serene, with a new lease of life, and a banknote in her hand. The room stank of brewer's yeast for days afterwards.

I saw Lek once again, long afterwards, at the Royal Garden shopping mall. She looked good, had put on weight, said she was off the dope (probably a lie), and had a wonderful new potential boyfriend, another Burnt. I gave her some money and said I was sorry things hadn't worked out, or similar western claptrap. She said it was OK because she was 'too strong' for me, with which I fervently agreed. After that, she disappeared, although I think of her often, with great fondness and sadness, hoping against hope that some Burnt has indeed carted her off to the fjords.

But I doubt it. Chester once said, rather despairingly, 'I'd just like to do something good, something meaningful, for one of these girls, send her to college, or something.' But you can't. Whatever you give them, money or marriage or opportunity, they blow it, and sink back into the Thai swamp: grasping family, prostitution, debt, dope. That may sound like the rationale of somebody too cheap to slip a few coins to a beggar, 'because he'll only spend it on drink', but it's true.

33. SLEEP

The Thai lady loves and needs to sleep, but hates to sleep alone. Preferably, she should have a male person beside her, who will later reward her for sleeping. 'You sleep alone' is a gross insult. Thais do not like to be alone, and cannot understand the farang's occasional need for solitude. Many Thai dwellings have no front wall, insulation being uncessary in the constant heat, and the living-room opens directly on to the street, with only a canvas to pull down when it rains. The rest of the time, the doings of an entire family are open to public scrutiny, as in a doll's house. When it is very hot, they will sleep in the street.

On the rare occasions when the Thai lady finds herself alone, she seeks a female friend to sleep with. I have slept chastely with three girls in one huge bed, all curled up, sucking their thumbs. My own girlfriend separated my person from theirs, so I came into the 'papa' (over thirty) category. In Patong, a Swedish drunk, called 'Salala' for some reason, and who was a popular, free-spending stud, had rammed his motorcycle and brains into a taxi at noon, while blitzed out of his skull. Our guests were frightened that his lecherous ghost would come and haunt them; more precisely, they did not relish the idea of being bounced from beyond the grave. It would be cold!

The clinging habit gives some farangs the illusion that they are wanted for their personality or bouncing powers, but often one is simply a kind of giant teddy bear. There are worse fates.

In the rut hour, the streets are plied by vendors of soft cuddly toys, all enormous, which perch like Everests of fluff on their carts. A girl will squall and giggle; a few notes will leave the pocket of a lust-sodden farang, and the two will proceed to their trysting place, with the lady clutching her lovely new keepsake to add to her collection. This love of giant cuddly toys is not just because Thai girls are sentimental. They have a practical, auto-erotic purpose.

Connoisseurs of French provincial hotels may recall that, instead of a pillow, there is often a bolster about four feet long, like a giant granite salami, presumably prescribed by some osteopathic savant. It puzzled me that Thai hotels offer both proper pillows and the granite salami as well, until I discovered that a Thai lady asleep will grasp the bolster to her and cuddle it between her breasts and thighs, like a giant phallus, perhaps more satisfying than a teddy bear. In fact, the farang might well wonder, from her beatific smile as her thighs cuddle the bolster, if his western phallus is needed at all.

The Thai sleep is connected to the Thai smile. The most strung-out bar girl can flash her dazzling smile at you, and all your worries about the meaning of life will simply evaporate, along, in due course, with your bankroll. But Thais do not really smile out of friendship or happiness or allure – although they are friendly, happy, and alluring. They are shy, too. It is as though you have seen them naked, or counting large money, or some other preposterous and unnatural state. They smile in embarrassment. You have caught them awake.

Three teens of my acquaintance announced they were going to the cinema. On their return, none of them could remember the name of the film, or who starred, or what it was about. On sitting down, they had promptly fallen asleep, and slept through the entire film. All agreed they had enjoyed a happy afternoon.

Ask a western woman if she is 'happy', and she may frown. What do we mean by happy? Happy in life generally, or happy at this moment? Ask a Thai lady the same question and she will assure you that she is happy because she has just been bought a new tube of lipstick. And she means it! She radiates happiness! Then, when the tube of lipstick runs out, she will be unhappy. But there is usually a generous farang to replace it, and that will make her happy all over again! And nothing guarantees happiness more than sleep. Watching a Thai lady sleep is a beautiful experience, because she is beauty itself. Her serene, finely chiselled face, and her feline body, contain centuries of mystery, and all the tumult, slaughter, superstition and inter-breeding of an entire continent. All that madness somehow seems worthwhile, for it has produced her. Whatever is going on in her brains or her genes, you will never know. She opens her eyes, smiles, stretches and yawns, and announces to her world (at the moment, you):

'I want sleep, I not can sleep. I want bouncing.'

She needs a little helper – you! – to get to sleep. What could be more practical? Of course you love her insanely!

34. RUNNERS

Like Charles, Wayne used to jet back and forth to the
Philippines, where he had a steady long-term girlfriend
called Miranda whose teenage daughter Jenny imagined Wayne
was her father. In fact, she was the result of a long-ago drunken
rape, one reason why Wayne was certain of Miranda's fidelity,
as she claimed to hate Filipino men. They used to hump under
a bedsheet, with the girl supposedly asleep beside them; I
figured this slightly suspect exhibitionism meant Wayne really
had the hots for Jenny, and was biding his time till she was old
enough.

He would return to the US, make some more money as a
freelance accountant, fly to the PI, perhaps meet Charles,
then proceed to Pattaya. In this complicated skein of travel
plans, everybody would go somewhere, like men arranging to
rendezvous in a distant pub in order to do the same thing they
did in the last one. Wayne's travelling was dictated by how
many free air miles or discounts he had. He went to Europe,

which he disliked, simply to take advantage of budget air fares.

He freeloaded to Peru with LA Rob, and told funny stories about Rob's strenuous enjoyment of a fifteen-year-old Peruvian hottie, while he, Wayne, as usual suffered a comic series of erotic setbacks. One girl, in Lima, wasn't allowed in his hotel; another, invited on a trek up into the highlands, fell ill with altitude sickness; another finally joined Wayne in bed, but with her infant parked aggressively between them, to ensure chastity. Meanwhile Rob came to a kind of grief, because his girlfriend's American father, who kept a hotel in Iquitos, found out about them (his little angel had been on the game since the age of thirteen), and demanded at gunpoint that Rob marry her.

Rob did a runner, something he perhaps learned from Wayne, who boasted of his prowess at dumping unwanted females. He would leave them at airports; in trains, by getting off alone at an unexpected stop; at bus stations; or in hotel rooms, where he would do a midnight flit, frequently via the window, leaving the unsuspecting girl snoring in his bed. Funnily enough, if he ran into the same girl a year later, she would welcome him with open arms, as if nothing untoward had ever happened. Leaving Miranda all the time didn't count as a runner, as she said, 'I will wait for you forever.' Besides, he sent her money, although he pretended it was just a logical accounting procedure. 'Every mammoth blast-off (we had both caught Charles's jargon) costs me on average 2 dollars and 47 cents,' he would say.

Once, he insanely brought her to Pattaya, which of course she hated, sniffing that Thai TV lacked romance and passion (i.e. it was all about money), and especially as he dragged her round the go-go bars, thinking she would share his interest in lesbian shows. He declared that all women were secret lesbians, and once gave me a stack of photocopied junk from various biblical websites, proving that God intended men to be polygamous. That was when he had taken up with his other Filipina, Marivec, who sounded to me like a brand of French mineral water. I said patiently that you could be as polygamous as you liked, as long as you had the money to pay for it. It reminded me of the stumble-wrecks boasting about how many Thai girlfriends they had. 'I have five girlfriends,' some Burnt would smugly belch, which is rather like boasting you have five shirts. Of course you have, if you can afford them! I said he could have five hundred girlfriends, if he had five hundred banknotes.

Marivec was the opposite of placid, maternal Miranda, a jealous little firebrand, who had sold her cherry to a Japanese for $400, although Wayne insisted she wasn't 'hard core'. We had earnest debates about just when a demi-mondaine 'crossed the line' which separated an amateur good-time girl from a serious brass. He kept doing runners from Marivec, and from his stories of her jealous tantrums and sulks, coupled with physical violence, I could understand why, but not why he kept going back to her; I suppose it was the lure of those $2.47 blast-offs.

He preferred Filipinas to Thais because with all their Catholic passion, they were more 'romantic', meaning they could be induced to fall in love with him and thus provide cheap or even free blast-offs. 'Women are just commodities' was his accountant's eye view of things. He brought Marivec to Pattaya, too, for the round of hot wax and lesbian shows, which she hated, and once, when I arranged to meet him for a quiet drink near his hotel, in the early evening, he arrived with his hand bleeding. Hearing that he was about to go out, however innocently, without her, she had broken a tooth glass in their room and socked him with it.

I told Wayne, try and get something for nothing and you get nothing for something, but in vain. He was constantly in the soup. On one occasion, he was in the bathroom when his girlfriend of three days called the cops, as he hadn't given her any money. In the presence of law and order, he coughed a thousand baht, promising to have the rest the next day, upon which girl and cops departed, and so, quick as a flash, did Wayne. One stiffed girl pursued him up the street, waving a beer bottle. (Charles once chased a girl halfway down Soi Bukao, him clad only in his underpants, because he wrongly suspected her of stealing a banknote.) His excuse was always that she didn't actually ask him for money. I said he should know better – nothing's free, and if a girl uses the 'no want money, love you too much' ploy, you pay her anyway. Then you don't owe her anything, for the 'no want money' ploy is a preamble to demanding the price of a water buffalo later. Extreme Bill's ladmanship of the left was to accept a girl's invitation, but offer no money. 'Have too many ladies already.' Usually, they agreed! But in the morning, he would wisely donate a purple persuader – 500 baht – 'for breakfast'.

I continued my brief liaisons over the months. It is actually difficult to remember any names, or even faces, although Joy sticks out, and that's probably a Freudian slip. She was a lovely little girl, trim, compact, well-muscled under a smooth skin, and possessed of extraordinary breasts. They were more than massive, like two zeppelins which had crash-landed on her chest, and during coitus they would flop around as if trying to escape. Neither of us knew quite what to do with them. I saw Joy quite a few times, for on her first visit no sooner was she in the door than she grabbed a broom and started sweeping, which she said was her second nature and part of the service. The broomstick test is always proof of good heart. Once, she said she couldn't go with me as it was her time of the month, and I said that didn't matter and we had a good and (for her) illuminating, if squelchy time.

I described her mammary charms to Charles, to tease him, saying vaguely that I had picked her up in a bar on Second Road, but couldn't remember which one; I rather wanted to protect Joy from Charles's fumblings. He spent a whole night visiting every single bar on that road, desperately seeking this udder extravaganza. It was, I think, girl one-upmanship, which is quite common, and rather ridiculous. Macho lads like to remark, about their friend's beloved, 'oh yeah, I had her'. Hey, she's, like, for rent, you know? Anybody can have her. Yet there lingers the competitive idea of 'my' girlfriend, as if money hasn't entirely replaced the rigmarole of courtship.

I had a brief live-in experience with another Porn, whom I took from a bar at the end of Soi 2. She was 32, I think, very beautiful, with a firm body and full figure, truly voluptuous. Plus which, she was another nudist, anal-friendly, and uninhibited. She had a fourteen-year-old son, apparently gay, but luckily he wasn't often around, once it was established we weren't going to copulate for him to watch. We would be at it most of the night, doing just about everything, the high point being long, slow doggy fashion, with her buttocks jerking (I wanted to eat them), as I visited her rather tight anus, evidently not as practised as Tou's. By day, the seemingly sleepless Porn would work bar, getting off at 8 p.m., and coming down the street to join me. She promptly called me 'my husband', which I didn't much like, and brought her friends round, quite fun, but distinctly rough trade. In no time, I was involved in yet another gossip network.

I explained to Porn that I was going to give her 200 baht a day, as an honorarium, but meanwhile she could carry on chatting up the guenthers, and letting them enjoy and reward her ample charms. After a few weeks, she had a tantrum, and wept that she had no money, and I was neglecting her. It turned out she had been paying the bar 200 baht every day, as her bar fine, because they knew she was living with me. But, I said, she was still working! So what she did off-duty was her own business. She insisted that because of her vast love for me, she was emotionally unable to go with customers. Lies, greed and theft you can put up with, nay expect, from demi-mondaines, but idiocy is a no-no, so Porn had to go, in rather surly fashion. A pity, because with lovely caramel skin, Charliesque breasts and a superbly rounded bottom, she did have a memorable body. I wasn't with her long enough to get beyond physical euphoria and investigate the soul part.

Every now and then, there was another tale of woe, of some lunatic who had gone the whole nine yards, and married his

Thai beloved, to whisk her back to the inappropriate splen-
dours of Duisburg or Wolverhampton, from which she invariably escaped. This happened to a Cornish acquaintance of
mine who became enamoured of a go-go dancer, a very nice
girl, and well-preserved, but over thirty ('old lady'), seriously
hardcore, and encumbered with a surly brat of a ten-year-
old son. Her address book was a veritable EU of guenthers,
olafs, and huberts. They were both cell phone nuts, and he
would phone her even when she was within eyesight, about to
cross the road – a depressing variant of the 'I'm on the train'
routine.

They were always squabbling, usually something to do with
phone calls, or lack of them, why she had turned her phone
off, or why was she not where she said she would be. The
Thaiette's passion for secrecy is a frequent cause of bust-ups,
even where the secret is entirely innocent, like going shopping,
or to the movies, or disappearing for a few days to visit family.
'Why didn't you tell me?' wails farang. 'I don't mind, as long
as you tell me.' But farangs are so prone to mysterious mood
swings and temper tantrums that she is frightened to tell him
lest he get upset. So of course she does upset him, by trying
not to.

Between visits to Pattaya, he would spend hours on the
phone from England, moaning about her, with me as a highly
unqualified agony aunt: one minute it was off, the next minute
on, until finally she caved in and married him.

He took her off to his obscure village near Bodmin Moor,
which I happened to know, and treated her like a slave, not
letting her go out unescorted, or drive the car, or even go to
the pub, which was the village's sole entertainment. Not only
had he imposed culture shock on her, but he had taken her to
a place which to most British girls would be culture shock;
on top of that, they lived with his parents, in the bourgeois
dwelling where he had spent his entire life, and intended to
spend the rest of it.

He would explain all this in still-anguished phone calls, as if her unhappiness was quite unreasonable, while he was being entirely reasonable, in fact doing her an enormous favour. Worst of all, he forbade her a cell phone, as she would be calling her old flames. A Thai bar girl without a phone is like beer without a head, it quickly goes off. I said you can't expect a marriage to last if you treat her as a holiday souvenir, and it didn't. Once she had her British passport, hence EU access, she did a runner, leaving behind her new baby, and brattish son.

'What a same story!' is our Thai refrain; after a while, the endless cycle of folly and disillusion does your head in, as they say in certain quarters of London. The phenomenon of Thai trophy brides, and the ensuing grief, deserves learned socio-logical study. Like, why are men so stupid? If you go down to the dirty sauna for a surreptitious jolly, or park your car off Hollywood Boulevard for some oral fun, you don't usually tell your temporary companion, with high mileage and not a lot of rubber left on the treads, that you want to marry her, and look after her and her entire family forever and ever. Do you? Well, in Thailand you do.

35. HAPPY ENDING

Having said all that, having said all that ... the events in this book stretch over six years, or maybe it's seven. Hell, this is Thailand. Now, at the risk of serious party-pooping, I have to confess all that stuff has been behind me for a couple of years. Look, if you don't like happy endings, leave now. There is the missus in the frame, you see – these things happen, man! – and I'm not going to say too much about her, for she absolutely is the missus, and although she doesn't read English, she'd look at these pages and *know*. They always do. I admit I'm a shocking hypocrite, ligger and scrunter, and you have every right to gnash molars, but that, as is so often the case in Thailand, is the way things are. No more kaleidoscope of brown honeypots! Nobody, not even devil-may-care (who else would?) me is immune to domestic bliss, and that.

It happened this way. After a year or so of gadding about Pattaya, fancying myself a true stumble-wreck and boulevardier, I was downtown with Wayne, who picked up his usual teenage bar scragglemuffin (who promptly gave him a dose of the clap), and then we went to a restaurant, where I saw this fine woman exuberantly frying garlic and chillies, and through the tears and sneezing and coughing I made an on-the spot decision of the life-changing class. Well, what more can a fellow want? Not a bar girl, go-go dancer or streetwalker, and can cook! Happily she was prepared to cook things that did not involve tear gas, pepper spray and other traditional Thai delicacies. Manao, which means lemon, is not the traditional moon-face glamour girl, though she does have lustrous long black hair. She is straight-faced, aristocratic, why, a princess! Even her first language isn't Thai, but, adding to the mystery, Khmer, for her home is near the Cambodian border. She's different! And – I admit sheepishly – she was the woman in my recurring dream ... like, uh, after my dutiful service as a Pattaya boulevardier, she was the one for me. All right, I didn't have a face to go by, but she was slim, and had long hair. That narrows it down, surely? Anyway, one thing and another, she moved in with me, and didn't move out again. Bonjour bonheur. I know what I've written about my fellow-stumblers, and she's-differentism. *I know*. Give me a break here.

We moved out to Jomtien Beach and rented a house by the sea, with a garden and mango and papaya trees, which her lovely daughter shins up to gather breakfast, a basket of free mangos, when trendy clowns in London or New York pay three bucks just for one. I've watched this girl grow from a skinny waif, when she came down from the village to live with us, into a strapping teen who eats a mountain of my food every day, and wants to be an army officer so that she can *a* defend the king, and *b* shoot farangs on big noisy motorbikes. My virtuous glow of satisfaction at having done some good for somebody may be paternalistic imperialism, but I ain't giving it up.

Meanwhile I am the ruler of my modest empire. Socks are washed, floors swept, toenails clipped, oranges squeezed, and belly filled, without my having to raise a finger. If I murmur to no one in particular that I like roast duck, then, in a couple of hours, a roast duck appears on the table, and will continue to appear every day, until I murmur that perhaps it is time for prawns. Of course, telepathy works both ways. When I observe the females enthusing over a bicycle catalogue, I become vaguely aware that a new bicycle is required, without anything so vulgar as an actual request. And when I present banknotes, with my novel suggestion – of buying a new bicycle! – no praise is lavish enough for my limitless, all-seeing wisdom. Were I, unthinkably, an unreconstructed male chauvinist, this lifestyle would be enough to make furious feminists eat their wooden earrings. Thank goodness I'm not.

Manao got a great laugh out of the story of my hapless Bodmin Moor chum and his fleeing temptress. 'Take off clothes a go-go!' she cried, miming bra removal, in hilarious distaste: immodesty leads to doom. The thing stumble-wrecks and indeed feminists rarely grasp is, though this town seethes with luscious, available bodies, fun does not really make you content. Contentment makes you content. My Turkish peasant outlook comes in handy: why waste time lusting after chicks when you already have one? On the other hand, time spent in the Whorror does give you a certain realism: here as elsewhere, contentment is enhanced by a well-nourished bankroll, and foodstuffs deriving therefrom.

A cousin of Manao's lives next door, and the extended family of charming kids play or stay. My bar-hopping functions have been taken over by a surrogate, my English neighbour Paul, a lad of lads, who has a computer business that he runs from home, for the internet permits you to be anywhere in the world. (Just do it!) He still has a different girl more or less every night, except when they stay for months, until his confirmed bachelorhood becomes apparent. I witness all this, still a sort of armchair stumble-wreck. There are furious rows, curses, throwing things and so on, but when these girls come across the road to eat, or play with the kids, they are the soul of gentility.

Cute little moon-faced Noi, a large-breasted stripper and serious clingon, stayed for nine months before she got too frustrated at lack of water buffalo money, and went back to being a teenage go-go dancer. She turned up once, with flame-dyed hair, and looking really hardcore, no longer the nice little village girl who used to sit in our garden chomping on mangos, for an unsuccessful bid to steal Paul's motorbike. Last heard of, she had married a US Marine sergeant and was living in Okinawa.

Nong, a nineteen-year-old pin-up hottie, lasted a few months before getting the elbow. That occurred when she and Paul were in a bar and she was hiding in the loo, making assignations on her cell phone with the Italian slob sitting next to them! She had a serious crystal meth problem, and once went through a quarter-million baht in a month, with her friends. The money had come from some guenther, for her to set up a beauty salon. Nong would buy friendship, like all Thai girls, terrified of loneliness; she gave away two motorbikes, one to an ex-boyfriend, the other to a junkie. She went off with an Englishman, to Uckfield, Sussex, taunting Paul with text messages about how happy she was, until the messages predictably turned to wails, how dull Uckfield was, and how she wanted Paul to take her back.

Twenty-five-year-old Ming was the most interesting and intelligent. Her mother was doing twelve years in the monkey house for peddling ya-ba, then trying to have the informant assassinated. Ming was seriously sexy ('I evil girl!'), with piercings of tongue, eyelids, clitoris, tattoos everywhere, saying 'number one sex machine' etc. She had a shoulder tattoo of the name of her previous swain, an ex-foreign legionnaire who lived with his mum in Ipswich, but loyally had this removed, and replaced by 'Paul'. She danced and did lesbian shows and hot wax and everything, and when Paul took her for a night's bar-hopping, she would rip off her clothes and dance onstage, for fun. Every now and then she disappeared for a few days with some Burnt. Eventually, she left definitively, not without breakages, although she still phoned, trying to wheedle her way back to the suburban comforts rashly abandoned, with cries of 'I go fuck ten men, not you, ha ha!' Spurned Thaiettes imagine this is some bloodcurdling threat. Paul answered 'Up to you. Have fun.' So not much has changed, except that I have become spectator rather than activist. Ming is now a biker's moll in Scunthorpe.

Middle-class Charles dropped in from time to time – past tense – to stash his TV set or motorbike or suitcase prior to a runner to the PI. He was hanging with his off-on girlfriend Moo ('pig'), who was heavily into ya-ba, and had sex with her katoey boyfriends in Charles's apartment. This was his English middle-class suffering bit, which tied in with his fantasy about a black dominatrix. When he was away, Moo would slouch round, demanding possession of the TV or motorcycle, and we had to lie that we hadn't seen Charles at all. He looked increasingly awful, losing weight, for ya-ba keeps you awake without eating, and his hair was falling out.

Paul's lad-about-town cronies hover around. One of the nicest guys you could meet is Canadian Chris, jovial, marijuana-growing, maple-leaf-tattooed, and 'proud to be trailer trash'. He distinguished himself one afternoon, when Paul had stepped out to buy smokes, by leaping into the bedroom to penetrate the girl Paul had just vacated. Bemused, I sat there while he humped, and in less time than it took me to finish one cigarette, he was finished. Not even four-and-a-half minutes. 'That must have been the shortest shag on record,' I said helpfully. Of course, when Paul returned, he was too much the English gentleman to complain, although he did raise an eyebrow when Chris borrowed a thousand baht to pay her.

Charles left his TV and bags with me, and was away in the PI for longer than usual. Then after my solicitous email, he phoned to say he would be round in his rent car to collect his things. He had been back in Pattaya for some time but had throat cancer, and was so emaciated and ugly he was ashamed to show his face. Sure enough, he was like a scarecrow, scarcely recognisable, but still quite chipper, taking supposed wonder drugs, and talking about some miracle doctor in the Philippines. He gave me a ride downtown and insisted on taking me into a go-go bar, where he was still the same old Charles, groping some unfortunate chick, asking her if she liked him, trying to get her to kiss him. I later heard he was in hospital, no one knew where, having radiation treatment. A few months after that, Wayne called from Milwaukee (for free, naturally, having hijacked some office phone) and said Charles was dead. He had heard it from LA Rob, met by chance in the Manila airport, and had no details. I felt pretty sad, though Charles was no saint.

Some time after that, I went down to one of the back street bars, in search of little teenage Lin, curious to chat, for old times' sake, but she, too, was dead, a kidney infection which made her swell up hideously. Such doctors as she could afford were powerless, and she went back to the village to die. Which is what they do. That made me feel bad, too, for she was ripe to snare some rich guenther who would transport her off to a life of luxury, and make an honest *Hausfrau* of her. Way it is.

Anyway, life goes on, Pattaya-style: my Parisian neighbour, dapper, alcoholic, well-heeled Jean, bought a house in her village for his paramour of eight years, so that they could live in rural bliss. I watched them load her brother's pick-up truck with all his expensive furniture and machines. As I said goodbye, Jean said he was just nipping round the corner for some cigarettes, for the long journey. I then watched the pick-up truck disappear in a cloud of dust. Jean had been nieder-mayered. I learned that he had flown back to Paris, to lick wounds and drown sorrows, but, months later, was now back in Thailand, in the village, happily funding his beloved, who had discovered (as many do) that running a house costs money. Jean believed in l'amour fou. Or, after so many years here, his brains had turned to French mushy peas.

The news media inform us of Thai essentials. The suicide page of the local paper is crammed; there are gangland slayings in north Pattaya, part of cable TV turf wars. An increasing number of foreign girls are raped and murdered on the idyllic beach of their dreams. The government has expressed concern, because it 'hurts Thailand's image', like the European tourists who were murdered, robbed, and dumped in the river by rogue airport taxi drivers. The police excused their inaction because the publicity would be bad for the tourist business. Three Thai drug suspects in a village up north were found dead in their cell, hanged neatly in a row, by their own surprisingly long shoelaces. The police were naturally exonerated of extra-judicial killing. The youths must have killed themselves out of simultaneous shame. The fourth cellmate said he had slept through it all, and the guard said he had been afraid to inves-tigate, for fear of ghosts. Just another day in paradise.

Oh, yes, I mentioned the golfer, Kenny, who lived round the corner. He was another American Nam vet, secret agent and all the rest of it, a serious alcoholic, with sores and wounds all over his body, because his constant drinking rendered antibiotics powerless. He ran golf tours and, in the absence of customers, liked to go out on the links in the rain, when it was all muddy, with a Thai honeypot as caddy. She would strip off and roll in the mud while he took exciting pictures, and then (he claimed) swived her in the mud. He died too, just a while back. Poor old Kenny. Poor old all of us.

One day, Manao's sister came down from the village, proudly pregnant. Then our opposite neighbour called in to apologise for the sounds of copious vomiting from her daughter, who had just got married, and whose husband was working 50 km away. The vomiting was from whiskey and pills, to cause an abortion, because they couldn't afford a baby. The husband mustn't know, for he would be angry. This was all said as casually as if discussing the weather. Then, Moo, paramour of Middle-Class Charles, called, asking where he was. We said he had died. He had left her with a year-old baby boy, about which he had told nobody. Now she wanted to find out where his sister was in England, so that she could extract money from 'family'. But none of us has any information about Charles except that he's dead.

Such is the bizarre Thai lattice of sex, death, greed, secrecy and fertility. However, stay under the radar, pay your way, enjoy the sunshine, try not to be too stupid, and you've a chance of survival. There are few things nicer than pottering around the garden, seeking shade from the blazing afternoon sun, on our blissfully quiet street, far from the din and bustle, while the missus mashes a mountain of pineapples from the family farm upcountry, and the kids play badminton in the road, plant things, or climb trees to fetch mangos, and the primordial Thai sounds permeate the air – that is, the rhythmic swish-swish of a bamboo broom, the mortar and pestle going pok-pok to crush vegetables and chillies, and make what is not unreasonably called pok-pok. Sometimes a truckload of her country relatives drive six hours to enjoy an overnight by the seaside. There is a point in life when you find what you have been looking for, even if you didn't know you were looking for it. Wayne and I were having one of our interminable late night student-type conversations, and got on to love, what is it, how much should it cost, etc. Wayne asked me if I loved Manao, and I said I supposed I did, never having thought much about it.

'I mean, would you die for her?' he asked melodramatically.

I was genuinely taken aback at the question.

'Is that all? Of course I would,' I said. 'That's the least of things. This is Thailand.'

Canadian Chris met her, and roared: 'Man, that is a treasure! That is for life!'

I imagine he's right. Nothing surprises you in this place.

THE END